WAR, GENOCIDE,
AND JUSTICE

War, Genocide, and Justice

. . . .

Cambodian American Memory Work

Cathy J. Schlund-Vials

University of Minnesota Press
Minneapolis
London

Portions of the Introduction were previously published in "Cambodian American Memory Work: Justice and the 'Cambodian Syndrome,'" *positions* 20 (Summer 2012). Similar material to chapter 4 was published in different form in "A Transnational Hip Hop Nation: praCh, Cambodia, and Memorialising the Killing Fields," *Life Writing* 5, no. 1 (2008): 11–27.

Lyrics from the songs "Child of the Killing Fields" and "Resurrec" are reproduced in the Introduction and chapter 4; written and produced by praCh Ly, *Dalama: The End'n Is Just the Beginnin'*, Mujestic Records (Long Beach, California), 2000. Lyrics from the song "Hidden Truth, Open Lies" are reproduced in chapter 4; written and produced by praCh Ly, *Dalama: Memoirs of an Invisible War,* Mujestic Records (Long Beach, California), 2010. Lyrics from the songs "STORIES" and "Art of FaCt" are reproduced in chapter 4; written and produced by praCh Ly, *Dalama: The Lost Chapter,* Mujestic Records (Long Beach, California), 2002.

Poetry from "Visiting Loss" by Anida Yoeu Ali, reproduced in the Epilogue, was originally published in *Shout Out: Women of Color Respond to Violence* (Seal Press, 2007).

Published by the University of Minnesota Press
111 Third Avenue South, Suite 290
Minneapolis, MN 55401-2520
http://www.upress.umn.edu

Library of Congress Cataloging-in-Publication Data

Schlund-Vials, Cathy J.
War, genocide, and justice : Cambodian American memory work / Cathy J. Schlund-Vials.
Includes bibliographical references and index.
ISBN 978-0-8166-7096-3 (hbk. : alk. paper) — ISBN 978-0-8166-7097-0 (pbk. : alk. paper)
1. Cambodian Americans—Ethnic identity. 2. Collective memory. 3. Genocide—Cambodia—
History—20th century. 4. Political atrocities—Cambodia—History—20th century.
5. Cambodia—History—1975–1979—Atrocities. 6. Historical museums—Cambodia.
7. *Killing Fields* (motion picture). 8. Hip-hop—California—Long Beach. 9. Political refugees—
Cambodia—Biography. 10. Political refugees—United States—Biography.
11. Cambodian Americans—Biography. I. Title.
E184.K45S35 2012
959.604'2—dc23
2012029386

To my parents, Charles and Ginko Schlund,
and my twin brother, Charles

Contents

Battling the "Cambodian Syndrome"

The wheel of history is inexorably turning: he who cannot keep pace with it shall be crushed.

—Khmer Rouge slogan, *Pol Pot's Little Red Book: The Sayings of Angkar*

Dear Friends:
Thank you very much for your letter of June 14. I'm sorry to be so late in answering but for some reason your letter has just only reached my desk. I'm happy you have found friends and freedom here in our land. I hope with all my heart that your homeland will one day be free from the cruel conquerors who have brought so much suffering to Cambodia. Many of us are doing our best to see that Cambodia is not forgotten....
Sincerely, Ronald Reagan

—Letter to Ty Him Hel and Eng Sun Hel, August 27, 1982

THE KHMER ROUGE REIGN OF TERROR began at approximately 7:30 a.m. on April 17, 1975, when black-uniformed soldiers marched into the nation's capital (Phnom Penh) during the Cambodian New Year.[1] Emboldened by American foreign-policy disasters and an unpopular Lon Nol dictatorship, the Khmer Rouge found little resistance from Cambodians wary of illegal bombings, chaotic civil war, and ceaseless military violence.[2] Grounded in untenable agricultural revolution and determined to eradicate Western influence by any means necessary, the Khmer Rouge regime systematically evacuated Cambodia's cities and forcibly relocated residents to countryside labor camps. Single-minded in this so-called "year zero" focus—which, given the regime's anti-Western stance, ironically hearkened back to analogous "year one" frames at work in France's 1793–1805 "Revolutionary Calendar"—the Khmer Rouge renamed the former French colony Democratic Kampuchea, tortured countless numbers of Cambodian citizens, and executed thousands of alleged "enemies of the people."[3]

Suggestive of inchoate place and subtractive time, the tabula rasa nature of year zero was most plain vis-à-vis the wheel of history, a state-produced metaphor configured along a paradoxical, ahistorical axis of "progress." This dehistoricized, state-authorized dictate was not limited to governmental slogans. The Khmer Rouge's wheel of history fulfilled its promise, crushing virtually all facets of prerevolutionary Cambodian society.[4] The Khmer Rouge prohibited religion, outlawed education, disallowed currency, proscribed private property, and forbade the use of affective family names (for siblings, mothers, and fathers). As Ben Kiernan maintains, Democratic Kampuchea's "slogan became *kchat kchay os roling* ('scatter them to the last')." Correspondingly, the Khmer Rouge "scattered libraries, burned books, closed schools, and murdered schoolteachers."[5] Within this compulsorily forgetful milieu, Cambodia's National Library—the country's chief cultural repository—was emptied and converted into a pigsty.[6] In the months after Democratic Kampuchea's dissolution, journalist John Pilger reported that the Khmer Rouge banned the word "sleep," privileging instead less permanent allusions to "rest," a lexical move congruous with an overriding emphasis on extreme labor.[7]

Demanding that its citizens "give up all [their] personal belongings" and "renounce their father, their mother, all their family," the Pol Pot–led Khmer Rouge (aka Angka, or "the organization") dismantled by way of totalitarian repudiation the principal pillars of Cambodian society: centuries-old tradition, prerevolutionary socioeconomic infrastructures, and Khmer familial affiliation.[8] Democratic Kampuchea's wheel of history had little need for those who could not keep pace, including the sick, the starving, the weak, and the elderly. Nor did Angka have use for teachers, lawyers, judges, civil servants, doctors, artists, returning Cambodian expatriates (who were fellow leftists), Cambodian Muslims (principally the Cham), Khmer Khrom (Cambodians living in South Vietnam), and ethnic Vietnamese Cambodians, who were specifically targeted, tortured, and executed. Between 1975 and 1979, over the course of three years, eight months, and twenty days, the Khmer Rouge was responsible for the deaths of an estimated 1.7 million Cambodians (21–25 percent of the extant population) due to execution, torture, starvation, overwork, and disease.

Unquestionably, this period—known as the era of the Killing Fields to those outside Cambodia and "Pol Pot time" for those within—would have profound consequences long after the dissolution of the regime. Following Democratic Kampuchea's demise, approximately 65 percent of the population was female, highlighting the disproportionate number of Cambodian men killed during the regime. The majority of Cambodia's teachers (three-quarters) died or fled the country.[9] Equally catastrophic, by the time the Vietnamese ostensibly liberated Phnom Penh on January 7, 1979, 90 percent of Khmer court musicians and dancers were dead, nine judges were left in the country, and out of an estimated 550 doctors, only forty-eight survived.[10] Faced with famine, lack of medicine, no infrastructure, and persistent political uncertainty, approximately 510,000 Cambodians fled to neighboring Thailand; 100,000 sought refuge in close-by Vietnam.[11] Between 1980 and 1985, almost 150,000 Cambodians came to the United States, facilitated by the congressional passage of the 1980 Refugee Act, though others would eventually find asylum in France and Australia (among other countries).[12] To date, more than 237,000 individuals of Khmer descent live in the United States, making it home to the largest population of Cambodians living outside Southeast Asia in the world.[13]

The dramatic movement of these Cambodian/American bodies across borders, camps, and asylum states—the consequence of in-country authoritarianism, genocide, and cold war refugee legislation—presages the textual emphases, theoretical stakes, and juridical inquiries that undergird *War, Genocide, and Justice: Cambodian American Memory Work*. Focused on both collected and collective memorialization, this project begins with James Young's evocative examination of Holocaust memorials and remembrance. As Young maintains, these sites, which reflect a potent mode of "memory work," are places wherein multiple significations fuel critical debates over Shoah history, survivor memory, and juridical politics.[14] Such readings of remembrance foreground this book's interdisciplinary investigation into how Cambodian American cultural producers analogously (yet divergently) labor to rearticulate and reimagine the Killing Fields era vis-à-vis three distinct and unfixed modes of negation: dominant-held erasures, refugee-oriented ruptures, and juridical open-endedness.

Concentrated on 1.5-generation Cambodian Americans (defined as those who were children during the Killing Fields era or individuals born after the dissolution of the Khmer Rouge regime), *War, Genocide, and Justice* engages the collected memory of the Killing Fields era and the legacy of Democratic Kampuchean authoritarianism for in-country Khmers and diasporic Cambodians. This exploration of Cambodian American cultural production juxtaposes past/present state-sanctioned directives to forget with resistive moves to remember familial stories of survival, narratives of forced exodus, and memories of contested resettlement. Concurrently, as *War, Genocide, and Justice*'s multivalent readings of Khmer American film, literature, and rap make clear, the interdisciplinary routes taken for genocide remembrance correspond to a *collective* debate invested in a re-negotiation of history through survivor memory. Expressly, artists such as Socheata Poeuv (filmmaker), Loung Ung (writer), Chanrithy Him (author), Prach Ly (aka praCh, hip-hop artist), and Anida Yoeu Ali (performance artist/slam poet/dramatist) confront historical amnesias in origin sites such as Cambodia or a nearby refugee camp. Simultaneously, these artists undermine frames of forgetting in their country of settlement (the United States) and—perhaps most important—engender in their respective productions alternative modes for and practices of justice.

By traversing national borders, geographic distances, and sociopolitical schema, Cambodian American writers and artists generate culturally specific forms of genocidal remembrance from identifiable rubrics of diasporic dislocation and transnational reimagination. Indeed, these producers adhere to what Kandice Chuh defines as the geopolitical function of "transnational": a "cognitive analytic that traces the incapacity of the nation-state to contain and represent fully the subjectivities and ways of life that circulate within the nation-space."[15] As a brief evaluation of present-day memory politics both abroad and at home underscores, this "cognitive analytic" traces the "incapacity" of a post–Khmer Rouge Cambodia and a present-day United States to "represent fully the subjectivities" that circulate within a diasporic refugee nation-space. The unbounded histories and experiences that determine the Cambodian American refugee subject bespeak an involuntary movement of bodies in conflict with exceptionalist national narratives of reconciliation. Within the context of a displaced Cambodian American subject, this incapacity is evident in the relative (non)pursuit of justice following the 1979 dissolution of the Khmer Rouge regime.

To illustrate, on January 7, 2009, an estimated fifty thousand Cambodians packed into the Phnom Penh National Olympic Stadium to commemorate the day Vietnamese forces entered the capital city and ousted the Khmer Rouge from power.[16] Known in-country as Victory over Genocide Day (or Nation Day), the celebration featured a parade, political speeches, and a keynote address by Chea Sim, the current Cambodian

People's Party (CPP) chairman and longtime politician. The setting for such festivities assumes an uncanny register given the stadium's past Khmer Rouge purpose. Designed by renowned Cambodian architect Vann Molyvann and completed in 1964, the sports complex was an execution center for former Lon Nol officials in the early days, weeks, and months of the Democratic Kampuchean regime.[17] Alternatively, the stadium's twenty-first-century function—as a temporary space for genocidal remembrance—prefigures a vexed matrix constitutive of national accounts about and collective remembrances of the Killing Fields era. Notwithstanding Sim's commemorative speech, which in its focus on the Khmer Rouge past articulates a saved nationhood by way of human loss, the absented presence of genocide justice within the contemporary geopolitical imaginary underscores—to varying degrees—a particular contestation between history and memory.

The struggle between history (as a dominant a priori linear narrative) and memory (as a radial recollection and processing of the past) foregrounds Sim's keynote address, which opens with the hopeful Buddhist wish that "all the millions of people who died during the Pol Pot regime will be reborn in paradise."[18] Sim then quickly reminds, "We are gathered here today in order to remember the people who sacrificed their lives to save the nation from the genocide."[19] Subsequently concentrated on a synchronous, two-sited conquest (over the Khmer Rouge and state-sanctioned mass loss), Sim's speech strategically acknowledges the Democratic Kampuchean past via triumphant memories of sacrifice, perseverance, and liberation. Set against a backdrop of Victory over Genocide (a countrywide holiday), Sim accesses a set of genocidal memory politics that converge at the level of nation. Accordingly, Sim's address—predicated on conquered authoritarianism—codifies a legible (albeit revisionary) postgenocide nationalism. As Jenny Edkins reminds, "as long as memories are organised in a framework of nations and states there will always be attempts to recount even genocides and famines as triumphs and their victims as having sacrificed their lives for future generations."[20] As per occasion (a national holiday) and venue (the Olympic Stadium), the celebration of genocidal defeat constructs the nation-state as the primary locus for triumphant remembrance.

Concomitantly, Sim's ensuing narrative of incontrovertible sacrifice and seemingly inevitable liberation gives way to a state-sanctioned story of forfeiture and triumphalism. Conforming to such politicized frames, this post-genocide account was delivered to an audience of regime survivors, those born after the Khmer Rouge era, Prime Minister Hun Sen, and other leaders in the Cambodian government. Such luminaries were—like Sim himself—once affiliated with the Khmer Rouge. All the same, the former CPP chairman declared:

> The victory of [the] 7th [of] January saved the fatherland and the people of Cambodia from the harsh regime of genocide in a timely manner. . . . Although in the past three decades Cambodia has made great progress, difficulties . . . left by war and genocide have been far reaching and are yet to be completely removed.[21]

Sim's admission that "difficulties . . . left by war and genocide . . . are yet to be completely removed" dramatically brings into focus what continues to face survivors of the authoritarian Khmer Rouge regime. The "far reaching" and unresolved legacy of war and genocide—inclusive of trauma, poverty, and political instability—is partially attributable to the very history of Democratic Kampuchea. As places like the Olympic Stadium, Phnom Penh's Tuol Sleng Prison (S-21), Choeung Ek killing field, and countless reeducation camp sites bring to light, the Khmer Rouge specifically targeted those associated with the previous Prince Norodom Sihanouk administration and Lon Nol dictatorship, tragically concretizing the following Khmer Rouge axiom: "to destroy you is no loss, to preserve you is no gain."[22]

The 1978–79 Vietnamese invasion of the country—the final product of long-standing border disputes and a continuation of Hanoi's more expansive anti-Chinese policy—signaled the seeming demise of Democratic Kampuchea. Unquestionably, these end points, which bracket the genocide by way of Khmer Rouge coup and Vietnamese liberation, form the foundation for the Victory over Genocide annual commemoration. In the face of teleological celebration, however, the tactical forgetting of catastrophic upheaval perseveres in twenty-first-century Cambodia. Despite Sim's public acknowledgment about the genocide, there is still no nationally sanctioned memorial for victims of the regime, even with Prime Minister Sen's 2001 promise to construct one.[23] Furthermore, the far-reaching consequences of the regime are evident in Cambodia's current state of affairs. The nation remains the second poorest nation in

Southeast Asia, and 33 percent of its population lives on fifty cents a day. More than 60 percent of the population was born after the end of the Democratic Kampuchea regime, a demographic fact that contributes to a pervasive disbelief that such state-sanctioned violence actually occurred.[24] Compounding this widespread amnesia is that, notwithstanding increased efforts, genocide education continues to face politicized impediments at the level of municipality, province, and nation.[25]

Whereas the terms through which victory is configured (and, more significantly, remembered) are unstable at best, likewise vexed is the un-resolved question of genocide justice. Even with the passage of more than thirty years since Democratic Kampuchea's dissolution, only *one* Khmer Rouge official has been tried and convicted for war crimes and crimes against humanity in an international court of law. Moreover, the destruc-tive policies of the Khmer Rouge—which did not exclusively target one ethnic, racial, religious, or national group—have caused some in the in-ternational community to problematically question its classification as a genocide as per the 1948 United Nations Convention on the Prevention and Punishment of the Crime of Genocide. In particular, Article II of the Convention states,

> In the present Convention, genocide means any of the follow-ing acts committed with intent to destroy, in whole or in part, a national, ethnical, racial or religious group, as such: (a) Killing members of the group; (b) Causing serious bodily or mental harm to members of the group; (c) Deliberately inflicting on the group conditions of life calculated to bring about its physical destruction in whole or in part; (d) Imposing measures intended to prevent births within the group; and (e) Forcibly transferring children of the group to another group.[26]

Consequently labeled by scholars and historians as an autogenocide, the prosecution of state-sanctioned violence was from the beginning obfus-cated by an inadequate, non–legally binding label. Though eyewitness accounts and regime documents suggest that Muslim Cambodians (the Cham) and Vietnamese Cambodians were specifically targeted by the Khmer Rouge, it was not until 1991 that the United Nations began to refer to the period of Democratic Kampuchea as one marked by genocidal policies.[27] After a seemingly endless back-and-forth between Prime Minister Sen and the United Nations, the hybrid UN/Cambodian War Crimes Tribunal heard opening arguments on February 17, 2009.[28]

Such belatedness—which encompasses a profound after-the-fact (non)reaction—largely frames contemporary juridical discussions in Cambodia. Not surprisingly, this belatedness presages a temporal unease about whether those facing the tribunal will indeed survive the process. As Youk Chhang (director of the Documentation Center of Cambodia, or DC-Cam) contends, "If one of the leaders dies before the trial takes place, the public will judge the tribunal a failure."[29] In an obituary written for Cambodian journalist and activist Dith Pran (who passed away in May 2008), Senator John Kerry analogously reminds, "Day by day, survivors die without seeing any accountability for the horrors that were committed and without lending their voices to the record of history," dramatically underscoring the advanced age of both defendants and witnesses.[30] At least two of the regime's principle actors—Pol Pot (Brother Number One) and Ta Mok (the Khmer Rouge's military commander, aka The Butcher) died from natural causes in 1998 and 2006, respectively. Recently, hospitalizations involving UN/Cambodian War Crimes Tribunal defendants (chief ideologue Nuon Chea [Brother Number Two] and former Prime Minister Khieu Samphan) fuel growing apprehensions that justice will, in the end, remain elusive.

Complicating the already problematical terrain of genocide justice is that former Khmer Rouge members still occupy multilevel positions of governmental power (including Sim and Prime Minister Sen). These connections make visible the ubiquitous nature of the Khmer Rouge regime, which regulated (via biopolitics and necropolitics) the lives of every single Cambodian during the Democratic Kampuchean era.[31] Even so, current leadership in Cambodia is undeniably responsible for impeding wholesale in-country reconciliation. Soon after his 1997 coup, Prime Minister Sen orchestrated a series of pardons and amnesties for former Khmer Rouge leaders in exchange for political truces. In December 1998, the self-installed leader urged his fellow Cambodians to forgive the Khmer Rouge and "bury the past."[32] It remains uncertain whether these amnesties will hinder the prosecution of pardon recipients Chea, Samphan, and Ieng Sary. In addition, there is the qualified question of Sen's sustained cooperation with the tribunal. The prime minister has repeatedly argued against further indictments; when faced with such a possibility in March 2010, Sen asserted that he "would pray for this court to run out of money and for the foreign judges and prosecutors to walk out."[33]

Hence, regardless of Sim's declaration that "we have always remembered those who have sacrificed their lives to save us from genocide," genocidal commemoration and concomitant juridical practice in Cambodia is marked not by coherence and standardized public recognition but rather by contestation, disruption, and (most troublingly) silence. Such nonadmissions and omissions are apparent in Sim's address, which makes no mention of the UN/Cambodian War Crimes Tribunal. Nor did the CPP chairman verbally indicate that four other Khmer Rouge leaders were concurrently in custody for allegations of war crimes and charges of crimes against humanity.[34] Last, but certainly not least, Sim fails to address the incontrovertible perception held by a "significant minority of Cambodians" that Victory over Genocide Day marked "the start of a 10-year occupation."[35] On the whole, Sim inadvertently renders palpable a challenging set of memory politics that continues to haunt the contours of Cambodian genocide remembrance.

While Sim inadequately remembers victory over genocide, the current tribunal, and oppositional readings of the Vietnamese liberation, Secretary of State Hillary Rodham Clinton analogously forgets the problematical bond between past U.S. foreign policy and Cambodia's present. In a November 1, 2010 visit to Cambodia, Clinton announced:

> Earlier today, my staff and I toured the genocide Museum in the old Tuol Sleng school. It's a very disturbing experience. And the pictures—both the pictures of the young Cambodians who were killed and the young Cambodians who were doing the killing were so painful. But I also came away very impressed, because a country that is able to confront its past [is] a country that can overcome it.[36]

Clinton's declaration that the Southeast Asian nation has been "able to confront its past"—made almost three months after the UN/Cambodian War Crimes Tribunal rendered its first verdict—prematurely celebrates a neoliberal accomplishment over genocide via the prosecution of low-ranking former Khmer Rouge Kaing Guek Eav. Indeed, Clinton's statement of confronting the past—fixed to present-day U.S. diplomacy—obscures a complex relationship between the United States and Cambodia that hearkens back to cold war realpolitik and accesses twenty-first-century debt.

Despite the financial fact that it was largely amassed under the American-backed Lon Nol regime (1970–75), such debt remains a factor in postconflict Cambodia, which struggles to fund domestic programs and is largely reliant on humanitarian nongovernmental organizations.

Clinton's misreading of the Cambodian case fits—admittedly to different degrees—a consistent and strategic misinterpretation of the Democratic Kampuchean era accessed by other executive-level U.S. state actors. From Gerald Ford to Ronald Reagan, from George H. W. Bush to George W. Bush, from Bill Clinton to Barack Obama, and from the cold war to the war on terror, Cambodia's Killing Fields past occupies a thorny place in late twentieth- and early twenty-first-century U.S. foreign policy. Expressly, the Khmer Rouge era has become an oft-used justification for militarization and occupation abroad. Contrary to Reagan's epigraphical assertion that "Many of us are doing our best to see that Cambodia is not forgotten," the convoluted relationship between the United States, prerevolutionary Cambodia, and the Khmer Rouge era is distressingly disremembered.

As a close reading of President Bush's speech at the annual Veterans of Foreign Wars convention underscores, the politicized memory of U.S. culpability in the tragedy of Cambodia's Killing Fields assumes the registers of a preventative humanitarianism. On August 22, 2007, far from the chaos in Iraq and Afghanistan, President George W. Bush reiterated his administration's commitment to the contemporary war on terror at the Veterans of Foreign Wars national convention in Kansas City, Missouri. In a speech punctuated by veteran applause, Bush highlighted purported U.S. foreign-policy successes over the course of the twentieth century: the overthrow of fascism in Japan, the establishment of democratic rule in South Korea, and lessons gleaned during cold war campaigns in Southeast Asia. Connecting U.S. foreign policies in the Far East to the continued occupation of the Middle East, Bush repeated past and present conservative arguments about "winning hearts and minds," the intoxicating nature of "democracy," and the naiveté of antiwar activists. Chiefly guided by what presidential predecessor Ronald Reagan labeled "the Vietnam Syndrome" in the 1980s to explain U.S. foreign-policy failures due to a lack of domestic support, Bush asserted at length that

The tragedy of Vietnam is too large to be contained in one speech. So I'm going to limit myself to one argument that has particular

significance today. Then as now, people argued the real problem
was America's presence and that if we would just withdraw, the
killing would end. . . . The world would learn just how costly these
misimpressions would be. In Cambodia, the Khmer Rouge began
a murderous rule in which hundreds of thousands of Cambodians
died by starvation and torture and execution. . . . Three decades
later, there is a legitimate debate about how we got into the
Vietnam War and how we left. There's no debate in my mind that
the veterans from Vietnam deserve the high praise of the United
States of America. (Applause) Whatever your position is on that
debate, one unmistakable legacy of Vietnam is that the price of
America's withdrawal was paid by millions of innocent citizens
whose agonies would add to our vocabulary new terms like "boat
people," "re-education camps," and "killing fields."[37]

While Bush acknowledges the war's expansive Southeast Asian reach, he
nevertheless relies on an aftermath reading that commences with U.S.
withdrawal and includes the Cambodian genocide. Stressing that such
withdrawal led to "hundreds of thousands" (not 1.7 million) Cambodian
deaths, Bush revises the Vietnam War script and the Khmer Rouge era to
fit a humanitarian, not militaristic, end.

Correspondingly, Bush strategically overlooks the extent to which military intervention—prior to the formation of Democratic Kampuchea—
was a contributing factor in later humanitarian crises. Incontrovertibly,
the 1969 to 1973 Operation Menu bombings that targeted alleged North
Vietnamese communist sites in the Cambodian countryside had a contradictory impact that far surpassed their original realpolitik intent.[38]
In particular, the consequential destabilization of Cambodian governmental power, coupled with the subsequent installation of the Lon
Nol government in the early 1970s, facilitated the eventual rise of the
Khmer Rouge, who promised peace and stability to the war-torn nation.
Moreover, in stark contrast to Bush's "villainous" characterization, the
United States was an unquestionable Khmer Rouge ally following the
1979 deposal of the regime by the Vietnamese. Such support was evident
in U.S.-backed UN aid to Khmer Rouge leaders who fled to Thailand
and reflected a vehemently anti-Vietnamese cold war policy that per-
sisted until 1989, when the Vietnamese occupation of the country came
to an abrupt end.[39]

This contested relationship between the countries continues in the twenty-first century as Cambodia attempts to try former Khmer Rouge leaders for war crimes and crimes against humanity on the international stage with limited U.S. support. Specifically, the contentious history that undergirds the current UN/Cambodian War Crimes Tribunal—most manifest in debates over funding—makes visible the tenuous nature of U.S.-Cambodian relations following the removal of the Khmer Rouge from power.[40] Even with the passage of the Cambodian Justice Act in 1994 by the U.S. Congress, which established the Office of Cambodian Genocide Investigations (an entity officially charged with "investigating the atrocities of the Khmer Rouge period"), it was not until 2006 that the United States formally agreed to finance the tribunal.[41]

In the face of contemporary diplomatic turns and regime changes (from the Bush presidency to the Obama administration), U.S. funding for the tribunal remains precarious due to a combination of cold war politics, aforementioned issues involving debt relief, a still-combative relationship with Prime Minister Sen, and ever-present charges of corruption and human rights abuses in Cambodia.[42] As significant are an enduring set of war on terror frames that promulgate the deliberate conflation between Cambodia and Iraq evident in Bush's speech. These collapses are echoed in a contemporary debate involving U.S. funding of the UN/Cambodian War Crimes Tribunal. As *Washington Post* reporter Nathaniel Myers argued in a 2005 op-ed piece on the Foreign Operations Appropriations Act (which engaged the question of Southeast Asian aid), central to such discussions was a decidedly opportunistic reading of the Khmer Rouge and present-day Cambodia. According to Myers,

> Speaking to a Senate subcommittee two years ago, Senator Mitch McConnell (Republican—Kentucky) said that, given the level of "lawlessness and impunity" in the country under discussion, it made "no sense" to even consider convening a human rights tribunal to conduct trials on the heinous crimes of the ousted regime. The country he was referring to was not Iraq . . . but Cambodia, where the United Nations had finished negotiations with the government to establish a joint tribunal to prosecute surviving leaders of the Khmer Rouge.[43]

Juxtaposing the $75 million commitment to fund a tribunal in Iraq with the congressional resistance given to the Cambodian tribunal, Myers uncovers one of many contradictions between cold war legacies and recent war on terror initiatives.[44] As the *Washington Post* journalist surmises, tribunals in Cambodia are deemed nonsensical in light of allegedly inherent "lawlessness and impunity" with no concomitant acknowledgment of U.S. culpability and accountability.

Alternatively, the well-funded Iraq tribunal, which represents an idealized juridical restoration of order, symbolically conceals the profound problems of and resistance to U.S. imperialism in the region. In an even more imagined vein, American nonintervention during the Khmer Rouge era operates as a useable past for euphemistic assertions of U.S. democratic virtue, engendering a what-if narrative predicated on potential—and unfulfilled—humanitarianism. To be sure, this useable past, when set against the continued occupation of Iraq, instantiates a revised narrative of interventionism replete with justified aggressive humanitarianism (i.e., increased troop deployment and greater U.S. militarization). An embedded state actor, the United States unquestionably invests in an Iraqi tribunal to strengthen invasionist claims of human rights activism and virtuous liberation. Situated adjacent to Cambodian memory politics, these strategic deployments, paradoxical conflations, and syncretic collapses of two distinct U.S. foreign-policy moments constitute what I term the Cambodian Syndrome, a transnational set of amnesiac politics revealed through hegemonic modes of public policy and memory.

Built on the deliberately incomplete acknowledgment that the genocide was somehow linked to the Vietnam Conflict, the Cambodian Syndrome in part encompasses the paradoxical nonadmission of U.S. culpability before, during, and after the Democratic Kampuchean era. Cognizant of the Killing Fields as genocide event yet tactically forgetful of the U.S. role in the making of the Khmer Rouge, the Cambodian Syndrome encapsulates President Bush's recent characterization of the contemporary war in Iraq and Senator McConnell's relegation of Cambodia as (to draw from William Shawcross's infamous characterization) perpetual "sideshow."[45] From speeches that accentuate the preventability of the Khmer Rouge through U.S. militarization to legislative practices and foreign-policy initiatives that relegate the genocide to the margins, the Cambodian Syndrome contains politicized and selective processes of remembering the genocidal past.

This Cambodian Syndrome—which marries incomplete frames of forgetting to schemes of strategic remembering—is articulated through politicized back-and-forths in the United States and Cambodia. Drawing on what nineteenth-century political theorist Ernst Renan characterized as integral to nation-building—a profound sense of "shared grief"—such affective declarations necessarily obscure a less-than-noble governmentality redolent in state regulation, violent intervention, and militarized imperialism in both the United States and Cambodia.[46] Correspondingly, the Cambodian Syndrome rhetorically shields from view the multivalent governmental apparatuses that brought not only the Khmer Rouge but also the regime's victims into being. Whereas CPP chairman Sim maintains that Cambodia has achieved a victory over genocide, Secretary of State Hillary Clinton declares an equally celebratory reconciliation. Even though these triumphant frames are countered by President Bush's use of the Killing Fields era as a tragic lesson of nonintervention, all three state actors access an incomplete national narrative.[47] What is more, if Reagan—via the Vietnam Syndrome—asserts that the Vietnam War was lost because of a lack of public support and legislative commitment, then Bush redirects this interior reading outward by providing a further justification for U.S. intervention via amnesia and omission.

Within a post-9/11 milieu, such pathological justifications and amnesiac articulations carry dramatic consequences for Southeast Asian refugees living in the United States. Domestically, these forgetful frames are embedded in the increased enforcement of the 1996 Immigration Reform Acts, which carried a strict deportation clause for noncitizens who committed "aggravated felonies."[48] Soon after the September 11 attacks, the United States orchestrated—in the face of previous claims of asylum as per the 1980 Refugee Act—a repatriation treaty with Cambodia, which carried no human rights guarantees. Tragically, these agreements have had an undeniable impact on Cambodian American communities from Long Beach, California, to Lowell, Massachusetts. Between 2001 and 2002, almost 1,500 Cambodian American refugees (who were not naturalized U.S. citizens) have been (or are waiting to be) deported to Cambodia.[49] Making matters worse, those slated for deportation have on average spent twenty years in the United States, have no working knowledge of Khmer, and are wholly unprepared for life in Cambodia.[50]

Taken together, the codification and practice of contemporary U.S. empire in a post-9/11 age—troublingly embodied in Bush's address, evident in contested tribunal funding, and manifest in punitive deportation—collapses cold war logics and war on terror politics vis-à-vis the selective, opportunistic recapitulation of Southeast Asian history.[51] Returning to the Cambodian case, Sim's Victory over Genocide Day speech and Sen's neglectful appeal bring to light an in-country war on memory that ironically (although not mimetically) echoes past Khmer Rouge directives to forget. If, as cultural critic Marita Sturken compellingly asserts, "the way a nation remembers a war and constructs its history is directly related to how that nation further propagates war," then the Cambodian Syndrome functions as a transnational analytic through which to evaluate a distinct relationship between history, memory, and—most significantly—trauma.[52]

Defined by Cathy Caruth as "the response to an unexpected or overwhelming violent event or events that are not fully grasped as they occur, but return later in repeated flashbacks, nightmares, and other repetitive phenomena,"[53] trauma encapsulates ruptured national narratives about the Killing Fields era. Moreover, these traumatic rubrics address the multiple returns to this genocidal past by politicians and policy makers within and outside Cambodia. The ability of the nation-state to negotiate such trauma—and its capacity to mediate dramatic episodes of state-authorized violence—is perhaps most recognizable by way of international tribunals. After all, such multilateral formations are, since the 1945–46 Nuremberg Trials, quixotically envisioned. To that end, in the international tribunal, clearly delineated victims and self-evident perpetrators emerge as primary players in a flattened, tripartite melodrama: human rights violations are adequately acknowledged; crimes of genocide unrelentingly prosecuted; and state-authorized violence gives way to internationally orchestrated peace.

Even so, as is the case with all such tribunals, the calculated decision to try a handful of defendants for unimaginable crimes against humanity is necessarily incomplete. Furthermore, in moving from perpetrator to victim, the enormity of such crimes tragically limits the number of survivors afforded an opportunity to have their proverbial day in court. In other words, the selection of both defendants and witnesses is from the outset political, reliant on a set of deliberations intended to swiftly bring about national—not individual—reconciliation. Correspondingly, as Edkins maintains, the privileging of particular witness accounts more often than not problematically coheres with the dominant desires of an international community invested in a strategic rehabilitation and conservative maintenance of the nation-state.[54] Within this politicized and complicated juridical milieu, the hybrid UN/Cambodian War Crimes Tribunal is faced with an arguably impossible multilateral charge: to render comprehensible a contested genocide past, to make feasible a reconciled present, and to provide justice for not only 1.7 million dead but for the almost five million survivors of the regime.

Set against these tremendous odds, the UN/Cambodian War Crimes Tribunal is distinctly delimited by the aforementioned belatedness, previously discussed transnational politics, and a heretofore unexpressed mandate to limit the prosecution to crimes committed during the three years, eight months, and twenty days of the Khmer Rouge. As Michael Karnavas (the cocounsel for former Khmer Rouge official Ieng Sary) reminds,

> As [in] any tribunal of this nature, the enormity of the task at hand can be overwhelming. The events took place some thirty to thirty-five years ago, so the gathering of evidence for both the prosecution and the defence will be challenging. There is also the issue of the quality of justice that can be provided by an institution that is also political in nature, with the U.N. and the local government, as well as the donor countries not necessarily sharing the same goals. ... My opinion is that [reconciliation cannot be] accomplished by having a trial or two where the events and jurisdiction of the court is limited to just the KR period (75–79). These trials may be able to establish historical facts but can never establish the historical truth.[55]

If, as Karnavas suggests, reconciliation hinges on establishing "historical fact" from "historical truth," then the question remains as to how one engages the former and promulgates the latter. These historical negotiations—between facts and truths, betwixt events and experiences—are at the forefront of *War, Genocide, and Justice,* which on one level locates Khmer American cultural production within frames of remembrance and state-sanctioned forgetting.

Accordingly, Cambodian American artists and writers militate against the amnesiac registers of the Cambodian Syndrome by concentrating on the facts of U.S. intervention and Khmer Rouge authoritarianism. At the same time, such producers articulate a collected historical truth through narratives involving familial stories of war, genocide, and relocation. Situated within a transnational context of incomplete memorials and unfinished tribunal politics, what thematically connects Socheata Poeuv's *New Year Baby,* Loung Ung's *First They Killed My Father,* Chanrithy Him's *When Broken Glass Floats,* Prach Ly's *Dalama* rap trilogy, and Anida Yoeu Ali's performance/installation pieces to one other is a collected rescripting and restaging of the forgotten conditions, circumstances, and consequences of Pol Pot time. Committed to legacies of trauma and articulations of resistance, Cambodian American memory workers reimagine (via cinema, literature, hip-hop, and performance) alternative sites for justice, healing, and reclamation.

As Edkins productively observes, at stake in such memory work is not *what* is represented but *who* is represented—the very bodies who "get to mourn, in what way, and with what political outcomes."[56] Imbued with the enormous charge of genocidal remembrance, further complicated by the politics and actualities of location, Cambodian American filmmakers, writers, and artists labor to make whole (by way of multiperson testimonials, individualized narratives, and familial genealogies) a historical truth that moves beyond the amnesiac registers and politicized reaches of the Cambodian Syndrome. For Cambodian Americans who, according to Khatharya Um, have "one body, but two lives," remembering becomes "the ultimate resistance."[57] Set within this bifurcated, memory-driven milieu, Poeuv, Ung, Him, Ly, and Ali (like other Cambodian American writers and artists who engage the genocide in their work) are remembrance activists who actively re-collect and archive an intimate story of life before, during, and after the Khmer Rouge regime. What is more, in linking public memory to political power, Um's characterization of resistance by way of the contested terrain of memory highlights the political objective that undergirds contemporary Cambodian American memory work: the fight against state-authorized erasure through individual and communal articulations about the Killing Fields era.

Foundational to Cambodian American cultural production is its engagement with survivor testimonials, which make visible—by virtue of a refugee orientation—juridical formations that exist outside the traditional confines of the contemporary nation-state. In turn, this extrastatal location carries the simultaneous potential to destabilize essentializing narratives of refugee victimhood and engender an alternative mode of politicized selfhood. These Janus-faced negotiations of both past and present correspond to Dori Laub's claim that testimony

> is a dialogical process of exploration and reconciliation of two worlds—the one that was brutally destroyed and the one that is different and will always remain so. The testimony is inherently a process of facing loss—of going through the pain of the act of witnessing, and of the end of the act of witnessing—which entails yet another repetition of the experience of separation and loss. It reenacts the passage through difference in such a way, however, that it allows perhaps a certain repossession of it.[58]

The politics and practices that obstruct genocidal remembrance, along with the resistive capacity of testimonial forms outside traditional nation-state borders, are significant sites of inquiry in *War, Genocide, and Justice*. Concentrated on the ways in which memory politics in Cambodia and amnesiac policies in the United States shape the work of Cambodian American writers and artists, *War, Genocide, and Justice* likewise characterizes such production as unique in its engagement of genocidal remembrance as per a transnational, justice-oriented project.

The cultural relocation of justice from public sphere to private imaginary accretes further meaning when juxtaposed with the juridical expectations at play in the contemporary UN/Cambodian War Crimes Tribunal. Illustratively, in a 2007 *Time Magazine* issue devoted to "100 Heroes and Pioneers," previously mentioned DC-Cam director Youk Chhang notes, "Cambodia is like broken glass. . . . Without justice, we cannot put the pieces together."[59] Analogous to UN Secretary-General Ban Ki-Moon's April 15, 2008 call to "deliver long-overdue justice for the people [of Cambodia]" because of the "urgent importance of bringing to closure one of history's darkest chapters," Chhang's metaphor of "broken glass" underscores the imagined role of justice in "putting to rest" (i.e., reconciling) Cambodia's genocide history.[60] Even so, as dominant memory politics make clear, Cambodia's Killing Fields past will most likely remain a contested source of a profound unsettledness notwithstanding the passage of time and amid the uncertain trajectory of the UN/Cambodian War Crimes Tribunal.

Chhang's "fragmented" metaphor unintentionally (yet aptly) characterizes the Cambodian American refugee experience, which analogously commences with and converges on disjointed, ruptured, and unreconciled sensibilities. Alternatively, as *War, Genocide, and Justice* makes clear, this "broken glass" anticipates a *refractionary* set of memory politics. In particular, such refractions—suggestive of bends in perception and shifts in interpretation—foreground an inward/outward assessment of contradictory orientations and seemingly disparate cartographies part and parcel of Khmer American selfhood.[61] From Cambodia's Killing Fields to Thai refugee camps, from Phnom Penh to Long Beach, from Seattle, Washington, to Lowell, Massachusetts, Cambodian American history is incontestably drawn according to the coordinates of U.S. empire. Alternatively, the directional registers associated with geographic coordinates figuratively underscore refugee movements (from south to north, from east to west) and, to a less obvious degree, stateless temporalities. Metaphorically, like longitudes and latitudes that are measured in degrees, minutes, and seconds, Cambodian American memory work concentrated on the Killing Fields era is evocatively gauged by way of magnitude (1.7 million), decades (more than thirty years), and generations (the first and 1.5 generation).

As importantly, these refracted positionalities—wherein Cambodian American cultural producers *transnationally* reimagine and critique the past via Khmer and U.S. cultural practices—correspond to what Michel Foucault highlights as a difference between utopias and heterotopias. According to Foucault,

> Utopias afford consolation: although they have no real locality there is nevertheless a fantastic, untroubled region in which they are able to unfold: they open up cities with vast avenues, superbly planted gardens, countries where life is easy, even though the road to them is chimerical. Heterotopias are disturbing, probably because they shatter or tangle common names, because they destroy "syntax" in advance, and not only that less apparent syntax which causes words and things (next to and also opposite one another) to "hold together."[62]

Stressing "consolation" and "no real locality," Foucault's reading of utopias fits the "fantastic, untroubled" contours of the Cambodian Syndrome. From Sim's triumphant "Victory over Genocide" address to Hillary Clinton's celebratory characterization of facile reconciliation, from Prime

Minister Sen's "forgetful" directive to President George W. Bush's amnesiac humanitarianism, these utopic articulations of both Cambodian and U.S. exceptionalism emerge as central oppositional sites (utopias) for Cambodian American cultural production. Accordingly, these distinctly heterotopic formations indubitably disturb, shatter, and destroy the utopic syntax at work in the Cambodian Syndrome, which in the end attempts to make falsely whole what is fragmented and unreconciled.

If (as Foucault contends) these countersites bespeak an "epoch of simultaneity" forged via "juxtaposition," the "near and far," and the "dispersed," then Cambodian American memory work, rooted in a legible transnational orientation, is expressly heterotopic in its critical articulation of non-state-authorized "other spaces" for genocide remembrance and justice.[63] Often "linked to slices in time," such heterotopic formulations and formations encapsulate the before, during, and after story of the Killing Fields that forms the foundation for Cambodian American cultural production. In response and by contrast, by bringing together the "simultaneously mythic and real contestation of the space in which we live," Cambodian American cultural producers reimagine *alternative* nonhegemonic sites for justice by way of heterotopic negotiations in film, literature, hip-hop, and visual culture.[64]

In turn, these heterotopic readings foreground a revised notion of what Lisa Lowe productively characterizes as an identifiable "Asian American critique." Such a "critique," which Lowe reasons "begins in the moment of negation that is the refusal to be the 'margin' that speaks itself in the dominant forms of political, historical, or literary representation," captures the political labor performed by Cambodian American artists and writers who engage genocide remembrance and thus disavow past/present directives to forget.[65] Born out of both cold war realpolitik and Khmer Rouge authoritarianism, circumscribed by contemporary U.S. racial logics, and faced with multivalent amnesias, Cambodian American artists such as Poeuv, Ung, Him, Ly, and Ali (among others) defiantly refuse to occupy the proverbial and political margins. Notwithstanding resistive registers, Cambodian American critique is incontestably haunted by the absent presence of the Killing Fields, which, to draw from Lowe, carries an immanent function for Cambodian American cultural producers.

Correspondingly, as Cambodian American rapper Sambeth Hy (a former member of Seasia, a Lowell-based hip-hop crew) surmises:

My first year visiting Cambodia in 2001 with Seasia, I wrote the lyrics to "Trashland Kids" after walking through the mass grave museum and listening to master instrumentalists tell their stories. Suddenly I was an artist turned walking zombie. I was seeing and hearing all these terrible acts about my homeland. I was numb. I was just a recorder. I remember writing the lyrics in my journal on the bumpy van ride back to our fancy hotel. . . . I rap about what I know from my experiences, how I feel and what I see in my mind. The era of the Killing Fields are part of my history. There's no escaping it.[66]

Hy's admission that the Killing Fields era is an inescapable "part of my history" evocatively establishes the past/present contours of Cambodian American cultural production. Moreover, Hy's account—which brings together fatalistic "mass grave museums" (e.g., Tuol Sleng Genocide Museum and Choeung Ek Center for Genocide Crimes) and more hopeful "master instrumentalists"—instantiates a particular paradox that, as *War, Genocide, and Justice* examines, shapes, influences, and characterizes contemporary Cambodian American cultural production. Fixed to and situated within the interstices of genocide, war, and relocation, 1.5.-generation Cambodian American artists and writers like Hy nevertheless produce art that isometrically reflects their history, inclusive of survivor stories, forced exoduses, and the legacy of the Killing Fields. At the same time, Hy's contention that his songs are a "true representation of who I am" underscores an artistic investment in articulating—by way of individual experiences—a complex Cambodian American selfhood.

Whereas Hy emphasizes his Cambodian roots, fellow Khmer American rapper Ly accentuates a bifurcated, transnational subject position. As Ly avers in a track titled, "Resurrec":

I love my land to death
a child of the Killing Fields.
Northstar Resurrec,
Generation X what's next?
It's time for us to heal
We've been suffering for decades,
decades of genocide

Annihilation of generations
a demonstration on Khmer
Now why do we do what we do?
like Hitler to the Jews,
Whites to the Blacks,
they act like we slaves
I rather be back where I was born
than here confused and dazed
I love America . . . but anyways.[67]

Drawing on Ly's assertion that he is both "a child of the Killing Fields" and a member of "Generation X," *War, Genocide, and Justice* concurrently explores how Cambodian Americans repeatedly negotiate "over there" histories (the Khmer Rouge) and "over here" domestic politics (racialized characterizations and racial formations). From the Holocaust to American slavery, from the Killing Fields to Long Beach's "Cambodia Town," Ly's "Resurrec" accesses multiple histories of genocide and oppression and advocates for reconciliation ("it's time for us to heal"). Inadvertently, the title of Ly's track (which emerges from his affiliation with the West Coast hip-hop group Northstar Resurrec) coheres with the undead characterization of Hy's artist turned zombie. Likewise vexed, Ly's opening and closing assertion—that he "loves" both his "land to death" and "America"—intersects with an "anyways" ambivalence that he would rather be back to "where [he] was born" than over "here confused and dazed." These interior contradictions render intelligible the transnational registers of a particular Cambodian American critique, signifying in the process the book's concomitant examination of how Khmer American cultural producers—through genocide remembrance, juridical activism, and refugee experience—simultaneously imagine both the country of origin and the country of settlement.

To summarize, *War, Genocide, and Justice* opens with a concentrated assessment of in-country remembrance and post–Democratic Kampuchean politics by way of built memorials. Responding to the UN/Cambodian War Crimes Tribunal's recent Case 001 rulings, wherein (to reiterate) former S-21 head warden Kaing Guek Eav was sentenced in tandem with the court's verdict on reparations (inclusive of morally driven apologies and collectively articulated memorials), chapter 1 begins with a close reading of Cambodia's Tuol Sleng Genocide Museum and the Choeung

Ek Center for Genocide Crimes. Rehabilitated and curated during the early years of the Vietnamese-ruled People's Republic of Kampuchea (1979–89), both sites continue to engage a memory politics that obscures and makes unfeasible collective commemoration and diasporic reconciliation. Maintaining that both Tuol Sleng and Choeung Ek reproduce a master narrative of Vietnamese liberation, chapter 1 moves to a brief examination of both the People's Revolutionary Tribunal (1979) and concurrent articulations of state power at work in two national holidays (including Victory over Genocide Day). Chapter 1 then shifts to the present -day problem of atrocity tourism, in which former Khmer Rouge sites have recently become popular destination points for a profitable, foreign-driven economy. Such dark tourist frames presage a return to the United States vis-à-vis a contradistinguished reading of the Cambodian American Heritage Museum and Killing Fields Memorial in Chicago, Illinois.

These master narratives and contested remembrances prefigure chapter 2's investigation of cinematic memory work, which initially focuses its analytical attention on Sydney Schanberg's "The Death and Life of Dith Pran" (1980), the source text for the most well-known production about the Democratic Kampuchean era, Roland Joffé's Academy Award–winning film, *The Killing Fields* (1984). Acknowledging each text's overt critique of cold war realpolitik, chapter 2 nonetheless maintains that both article and film instantiate a master narrative of the Killing Fields era wherein U.S. culpability is eschewed in favor of a stateless humanitarianism. This humanitarian narrative intersects with the premise that *The Killing Fields* proffers an apolitical apologetics in its emphasis on individualized—and not state-sanctioned—reconciliation.

Invested in a narrative of pathological criminality, affective remorse, and eventual absolution, *The Killing Fields* draws on a now-familiar Vietnam War trope of American saviors and Southeast Asian victims. Chapter 2 juxtaposes this master narrative of redemption and liberation with Cambodian American Socheata Poeuv's *New Year Baby* (2006), an intergenerational story premised on the Khmer Rouge's policy of forced marriage. Incorporating Marianne Hirsch's concept of "postmemory" as a means to explore the impact of parental trauma on the children of survivors, chapter 2 evaluates the decidedly less-successful role apology plays in reconciling the genocidal past. Additionally, Poeuv's particular emphasis on Democratic Kampuchean biopower foregrounds a deeper consideration of biopolitics and necropolitics.

Chapter 3 shifts from cinematic narrative to literary memoir in its evaluation of Loung Ung's *First They Killed My Father* (2000) and Chanrithy Him's *When Broken Glass Floats* (2000). Commencing with a reading of autobiography as a distinct genre of self-mapping, chapter 3 analyzes each memoir's historic and contemporary function vis-à-vis two stories about growing up under the Khmer Rouge. Such bildungsroman frames— born out of a profound crisis at the level of individual and nation— necessarily incorporate a series of familial narratives that foregrounds an at times nostalgic contemplation of prerevolutionary gender roles. As significantly, both Ung and Him utilize daughterly metaphors that bring to light profound distinctions between pre–Democratic Kampuchean and Khmer Rouge forms of selfhood. These competing modes of selfhood assume an indubitable juridical register, and chapter 3 maintains that *First They Killed My Father* and *When Broken Glass Floats* makes visible Cambodian American–specific testimonial form replete with familial, transnational, and intergenerational frameworks. Notwithstanding the popularity of both narratives within the U.S. public imaginary (as best-selling memoirs), chapter 3 concludes with an evaluation of two controversies involving reliability and authorship, which paradoxically confirm the stakes of Cambodian American life writing and make less stable claims of authenticity.

Connecting the previous chapter's discussion of Cambodian American memoir to the musical imaginary of hip-hop, chapter 4 focuses its evaluative attention on previously mentioned Khmer American rapper Prach Ly, who was identified by both *AsiaWeek* and *Newsweek* as Cambodia's "first MC." Reading hip-hop as a practice and a movement, chapter 4 on one level asserts that the genre, born out of civil rights and people of color movements, affords Cambodian American artists such as Ly an established, persuasive vocabulary of resistance and revision. On another level, chapter 4 returns to the issue of Cambodian American critique, which encompasses both in-country and country of asylum politics. What is more, as a close reading of Ly's *Dalama* trilogy (2000–2010) underscores, at stake in such hip-hop memoirs—which incorporate traditional Khmer pin peat, 1960s Cambodian psychedelic rock, American R&B, and contemporary rap—is an interdisciplinary negotiation of the past by way of lyric, beat, and sample. Chapter 4 investigates the progressive politics and unadulterated critiques at work in Ly's final *Dalama: Memoirs of an Invisible War*, which the rapper himself asserts is his most overtly political album to date.

This evaluative focus on performance and politics presages *War, Genocide, and Justice*'s epilogue, focused on self-described "Cambodian American Muslim transnational" writer/poet/performer Anida Yoeu Ali's epic poem "Visiting Loss" and installation piece "Palimpsest for Generation 1.5," which similarly reproduce a transnational refugee subjectivity forged in the interstices of U.S. foreign policy, Cambodian genocide, Cambodian American remembrance, and juridical activism.

As *War, Genocide, and Justice* consistently maintains, Cambodian American cultural production makes salient a justice-oriented agenda that emerges from a commemorative desire to articulate the experiences of those lost during the Khmer Rouge era. Typified by testimonial accounts of the genocide and its aftermath, based on familial stories of survival, and fixed to a disenfranchised, socially conscious 1.5 generation, Cambodian American memory work forms the foundation for a multivalent archive constitutive of Cambodian history, Khmer/American culture, and U.S. racial politics. From memoir to documentary film, from hip-hop to staged performance, Cambodian American cultural producers strategically access legible forms of testimony within the United States—hearkening back to modes found in nineteenth-century slave narratives and American autobiography—to generate both a literal and an imagined space of justice in Cambodia while living in the United States.

Last, but certainly not least, to be Cambodian American postgenocide necessarily embodies a tripartite identity formed by way of catastrophic collisions with U.S. cold war foreign policy, traumatically shaped by Khmer Rouge totalitarianism, and problematically fixed to post–Vietnam War humanitarianism. Read within and outside euphemistic narratives of refuge and asylum, Cambodian American selfhood lays politically bare the troubling course of U.S. empire and globalization at the turn of the twenty-first century. Within Asian American studies, what arguably makes Cambodian American critique distinct is its direct and tireless engagement with genocide, human rights, and civil rights. To that end, Cambodian American memory work begins with and converges on the realities of large-scale human loss, forced relocation, and involuntary resettlement. These ruptured modalities cohere with Khatharya Um's evocative question: "As the bodies move, where does the memory lie?"[68] In concise yet productive fashion, Um's emphases on movement, bodies, and memory dramatically underscore the transnational, political, and commemorative stakes of *War, Genocide, and Justice: Cambodian American Memory Work*.

CHAPTER 1

Atrocity Tourism

Politicized Remembrance and Reparative Memorialization

Set incongruously in a lovely residential neighborhood, the genocide museum brings you up short almost immediately with a sign warning that any loud talking or laughter is strictly forbidden. That warning seems all but superfluous as you enter the first-floor galleries and see walls covered with black-and-white face shots of the Khmer Rouge's many victims.

—Stuart Emmrich, "Next Stop: In Phnom Penh, Hopefulness Replaces Despair," *New York Times,* February 11, 2007

The purpose of the compound was unclear . . . although the single-story building, littered with papers and office equipment, had obviously been used for some sort of administration. In rooms on the ground floor of the southernmost building, the two Vietnamese came across the corpses of several recently murdered men. Some of the bodies were chained to iron beds. The prisoners' throats had been cut. The blood on the floors was still wet.

—David Chandler, *Voices from S-21: Terror and History in Pol Pot's Secret Prison*

LOCATED AT 113 Boeng Keng Kang 3 in the Tuol Svay Prey subdistrict of southern Phnom Penh, Tuol Sleng Genocide Museum is strikingly nondescript, despite its present-day international reputation as a former epicenter of Khmer Rouge atrocities. Contrary to travel writer Stuart Emmrich's characterization of a "lovely residential neighborhood," very few Cambodians actually live in the area, which is currently home to international nongovernmental organizations, a small number of local businesses, and a few restaurants.[1] All the same, the incongruous location of Tuol Sleng Genocide Museum is reinforced by way of a plain corrugated metal fence, which initially obscures the site from street view. The museum's unexceptional facade is, as Emmrich relates, interrupted by a pictorial sign at the gate that forbids loud talking or laughter. Such strict imperatives aptly foreshadow the draconian registers of Tuol Sleng Genocide Museum, which remakes—by way of exhibits comprised of blood-stained floors, rusted implements of torture, and haunting prisoner photographs—the building's panoptic function under the Angka.[2]

Months after the April 17 takeover of Phnom Penh, in August 1975, the Khmer Rouge established Tuol Sleng Prison, which was previously Chao Ponhea Yat High School.[3] Known by Angka leaders as Security Prison 21 or S-21, the jail featured a slogan that epitomized Tuol Sleng's overriding mission: "Fortify the spirit of the revolution! Be on your guard against the strategy and tactics of the enemy so as to defend the country, the people, and the Party."[4] S-21's primary objective involved "guard[ing] against the strategy and tactics of the enemy," and those detained were alleged traitors to "the country, the people, and the Party." As prisoner photographs, hundred-page confessions, and a paucity of survivor accounts reveal, S-21 was not only a detention center for so-called enemies of the people. It was also a torture facility, repository complex, and execution site. Under the exacting management of former math teacher Kaing Guek Eav (aka Comrade Duch), S-21 would infamously be branded by workers outside the prison as *konlaenhchoul min daelcheng,* "the place where people go in but never come out."[5]

Though the overwhelming majority of inmates were Cambodian, administrative records indicate detainees hailed from across the region and globe, including Vietnam, Laos, Thailand, India, Pakistan, England, the United States, Canada, New Zealand, and Australia.[6] From Khmer Rouge cadres to foreign prisoners of war, from returning expatriate intellectuals to prerevolutionary diplomats, from teachers to students, and from engineers to farmers, Tuol Sleng's population was diverse, underscoring by way of geography and profession a far-reaching regime paranoia. As David Chandler maintains, a central S-21 objective was the extraction of confessions, which grew out of an increasingly expansive Khmer Rouge policy to pursue and eradicate supposed "networks of traitors" or *khsae kbot.*[7] Focused on eliminating threats from within, or enemies of the people, this ruthless nationalist agenda included the detention, torture, and execution of entire families, making visceral the Khmer Rouge saying that "To dig up grass, one must also dig up the roots."[8]

Despite the disciplinary single-mindedness of Tuol Sleng's administrative agenda, those brought to S-21 were, at first, not charged with specific crimes. Instead, detainees were accused of engaging in general prerevolutionary behavior. As Im Chan, a sculptor and former Tuol Sleng prisoner, relates, "When they arrest you there are no charges, they just say 'You have known a modern life. You used to go to the cinema, the restaurants, the bars. If we leave you, then you will tell the youth stories and they will want some.'"[9] In turn, these past lives were used in allegations of treason and were mostly comprised of accusations involving anti–Khmer Rouge political memberships. After hours, days, and months of torture (including waterboarding, electrocution, starvation, and beatings), prisoners would admit to covert activities involving the American Central Intelligence Agency (CIA) and the Soviet Komitet Gosudarstvennoy Bezopasnosti (KGB), which conveniently coincided with the regime's antagonist politics in relation to the United States (the embodiment of Western imperialism) and Vietnam (whose principal ally was the USSR).

Ironically, within a political imaginary marked by state-authorized assaults against national archives and historical memory, Tuol Sleng Prison would become a disturbingly invaluable and tragically impressive regime storehouse. Extensive records were kept on-site, including internal memos, correspondences with senior Khmer Rouge leaders, regime publications, inmate dossiers, photographic prints, prisoner portrait negatives, and thousands of written confessions.[10] Such archival work intersected with Tuol Sleng's final administrative agenda, concentrated on the eradication of enemies of the people. And, as confessions were processed, so too were S-21's detainees. Drawing on Khmer Rouge parlance, those who confessed would—largely without exception—be "smashed."[11]

The prison's reputation as a killing machine is evident in its staggering prisoner/execution ratio.[12] Of the approximately twelve thousand to fourteen thousand detained at S-21, less than twenty survived their imprisonment, and only seven are still thought to be alive.[13] Most of Tuol Sleng's inmates were detained between 1977 and 1978, as tensions between Vietnam and Democratic Kampuchea rose and fighting between the two countries intensified. For those particular prisoners, Choeung Ek (located approximately 14.5 kilometers south of Phnom Penh) would serve as execution site and final resting place. According to eyewitness accounts and S-21 records, up to three hundred detainees were taken each night to the former Chinese graveyard and unceremoniously executed.[14]

After an eleven-month military campaign, the Vietnamese army triumphantly entered Phnom Penh on January 7, 1979, signaling the end of both the Cambodian-Vietnamese War and the Democratic Kampuchean era. The next day, on January 8, two Vietnamese photojournalists found Tuol Sleng Prison, purportedly after following the odor of rotting corpses to the recently abandoned site.[15] Armed with the initial intent to photograph the Vietnamese liberation of Cambodia, the two came across fourteen recently killed prisoners and five still-living children (including two infants). No prison personnel were present, and the jail was in disarray.[16] Indeed, twenty years would pass until the prison's head warden was identified, arrested, and placed in Cambodian custody. Furthermore, thirty-one years would elapse before Kaing Guek Eav—the first Khmer Rouge official to face the UN/Cambodian War Crimes Tribunal—was found guilty of war crimes and crimes against humanity.[17]

As the opening epigraph by Chandler illustrates, the photographers who located S-21 were originally unaware of its use. Notwithstanding preliminary uncertainty, what quickly became apparent—first to the photographers and subsequently to the occupying military force—was the presence of various evidences (in the form of aforementioned forced confessions, prisoner photographs, and human remains). Almost a year later, the Vietnamese and their in-country allies discovered Choeung Ek killing field, which carried even more gruesome proof of Khmer Rouge mass violence. As investigators labored to document, archive, and categorize forensic evidence, they systematically unearthed 129 mass graves filled with bleached bone, tattered clothing, and fractured skulls. Taken together, Choeung Ek killing field at present contains the remains of an estimated 8,985 regime victims.[18]

Incontrovertibly, Tuol Sleng Prison and Choeung Ek killing field were and remain potent sites for remembrance that, on one level, make visible the unimaginable bounds of Khmer Rouge atrocity. On another level, the story of how each site was rehabilitated—by way of politicized recovery work—underscores a more complex project fixed to Vietnamese occupation and regime change. In particular, during the Vietnamese-ruled People's Republic of Kampuchea (PRK) era (1979–89), Tuol Sleng and

Choeung Ek figured keenly in post–Democratic Kampuchean nation-building efforts, which depended on vilifying the former regime through allegations of genocide and depictions of war crimes. Admittedly, the Viet Cong had, prior to the formation of Democratic Kampuchea, been allies of the Khmer Rouge. In the aftermath of Angka authoritarianism, the PRK had to substantially distance and differentiate—via the public sphere—Khmer Rouge totalitarianism from Vietnamese communism.

Therefore, amid politicized shift and political reorganization, to remember the Killing Fields era was from the outset determined by domestic nation-building efforts. And, as a brief history of the PRK brings to light, the still-forming state of in-country remembrance intersected with a post–Vietnam Conflict politics forged within the context of a vexed cold war relationship with the United States and the United Nations. Domestically, even with the January 7, 1979 Vietnamese takeover of Phnom Penh, the Khmer Rouge still held strongholds in the country's northwest provinces and continued to wage skirmishes against the occupying army. Internationally, the newly installed PRK was under attack from the former regime's high officials who, until 1989, were recognized as the nation's rightful rulers. Recently ousted Khmer Rouge leaders including Pol Pot (Solath Sar), former Prime Minister Khieu Samphan, Foreign Minister Ieng Sary, and Social Minister Ieng Thirith claimed that they and their countrymen were victims of a "war of aggression against Democratic Kampuchea." Central to such accusations of "aggression" was the increasingly disputed claim of genocide.[19]

As Peter Maguire recounts, Samphan (who, like Sary, Chea, and Thirith, is now in UN custody for crimes of genocide) vociferously (and ironically) declared that during the eleven-month war between the Khmer Rouge and the Vietnamese, "more than 500,000 Kampucheans have been massacred and more than 500,000 others have died from starvation."[20] To buttress in-state authority and assert international sovereignty, the PRK directly engaged the genocide question and initiated trial proceedings against former Khmer Rouge leaders. In August 1979 (eight months after the Vietnamese takeover and four years after the establishment of S-21) the People's Revolutionary Tribunal tried Pol Pot and Ieng Sary in absentia for crimes of genocide, which began with the allegation that three million Cambodians perished during the Khmer Rouge era. Further, the People's Revolutionary Tribunal utilized evidence found at Tuol Sleng Prison and gathered 995 pages of survivor testimony that confirmed acts of torture and orders of execution authorized by the authoritarian Democratic Kampuchean regime.[21]

On August 19, 1979, Pol Pot and Ieng Sary were expeditiously found guilty by a ten-person jury and sentenced to death. As Maguire contends, notwithstanding "a great deal of legitimate evidence, such as the testimony of S-21 survivors Ung Pech [the first director for Tuol Sleng Genocide Museum] and [the previously mentioned] Im Chan," the "indictment's strange categories of criminality, the short duration of the trial, and the absurd defense combined to create the impression of primitive political justice."[22] Such "strange categories" included accusations of state-authorized cannibalism and spectacular charges of executions involving pools of water filled with crocodiles.[23] Moreover, attorneys assigned to Pol Pot and Ieng Sary categorically refused to represent their clients on the grounds that they were—in light of genocidal crimes—morally indefensible.[24] Responding to such unorthodox legalities, the United Nations subsequently delegitimized the People's Revolutionary Tribunal because it did not adhere to the standards of international law.

Notwithstanding the People's Revolutionary Tribunal's "strange categories" and eccentric jurisprudence, the genocide case against the Khmer Rouge was undermined more profoundly by post–Vietnam War realpolitik. In the immediate aftermath of the American War in Vietnam, the United States maintained a strict anti-Vietnamese policy, composed of embargos, epitomized by trade restrictions, and marked by antithetical alliances with the Khmer Rouge. Given its indubitable anti-Vietnamese politics, the Chinese-supported Khmer Rouge—regardless of anticommunist agendas—became a cold war ally of the United States. Between 1980 and 1986, the United States funneled $85 million in aid to the Khmer Rouge through the euphemistically named Kampuchea Emergency Group, countering Soviet-backed Vietnamese humanitarian efforts in the region.[25] Such nonmilitary support was matched by the United Nations, which (under the Security Council sway of the United States and China) refused to recognize the authority of the PRK on the grounds that the Vietnamese were an occupying—not liberating—force.

Within this politicized cold war milieu, the national and international acceptability of the PRK, as Rachel Hughes argues, "hinged on the exposure of the violent excesses of Pol Pot exemplified by S-21 and the continued production of coherent memory of the past . . . of liberation and reconstruction at the hands of a benevolent fraternal state."[26] On one level, fundamental to PRK legitimizing agendas was the strategic restaging of Khmer Rouge atrocity, which was emblematically configured through the Tuol Sleng Genocide Museum and the Choeung Ek Center for Genocide Crimes. On another level, the repurposing of Tuol Sleng Prison and Choeung Ek killing field from Democratic Kampuchean torture center and Angka execution locale into built Khmer Rouge atrocity memorials signaled a particular memory war waged on the terrain of Cambodian genocidal remembrance. Tellingly, amid a context of a nascent governmentality (wherein the production of loyal subjects was integral to state stability) and international back-and-forth, the PRK appointed Vietnamese colonel and war crimes expert Mai Lam to oversee the rehabilitation of the Khmer Rouge jail and killing field.

Prior to this morbid assignment, Lam had curated Ho Chi Minh City's American Atrocities Museum (formerly the Exhibition House of Aggression War Crimes), which was intended to bolster anti-American support for a newly reunited Vietnam. Under Lam's supervision, Tuol Sleng Genocide Museum and the Choeung Ek Center for Genocide Crimes were quickly opened to the public in 1980.[27] Until 1993, most of its visitors included Cambodians and tourists from other communist countries (Vietnam, the Soviet Union, Hungary, Laos, and Poland). The tourist demographic dramatically shifted after the country ceased to be under communist rule. Most present-day museum visitors and memorial sightseers hail from Japan, France, Germany, South Korea, the United States, and Taiwan.[28] Despite changing visitor profiles and the passage of more than three decades since both sites were made public, what persists is the degree to which each location replays—through *body corpus* exhibits (for example, prisoner photographs, inmate remains, and detainee confessions)—the horrific dimensions of the Khmer Rouge *body politic*.

As a close reading makes clear, both places continue to embody Colonel Lam's original curatorial program, which was principally concentrated on a state-sanctioned prosecutorial agenda against the previous Democratic Kampuchean regime. At the same time, Tuol Sleng Genocide Museum and the Choeung Ek Center for Genocide Crimes remain significant in light of contentious politics, regime changes, and contemporary Cambodian genocide remembrance. Such prosecutorial presentations— originally connected to the PRK and People's Revolutionary Tribunal but relevant to the workings of the present-day UN/Cambodian War Crimes

Tribunal—underscore a juridical mode of collected memory fixed to Vietnamese-oriented statecraft and contemporaneous understandings of human rights. As Hughes argues, "the presentation of physical evidence" at both Tuol Sleng Genocide Museum and the Choeung Ek Center for Genocide Crimes evoked (and continues to bring to mind) a "*legal* functioning of evidence; evidence of a *genocide* (universally-defined) [that] necessarily motions to universal (international) laws."[29] Correspondingly, Lam's curatorial focus on war crimes, made plain in graphic depictions of atrocity and the prevalence of perpetrator-driven exhibits, foments a distinct narrative wherein the Vietnamese are cast as liberators, human rights activists, and antigenocide redeemers.[30]

Despite allegedly universal agendas, Tuol Sleng and Choeung Ek are unique in that they exclusively involve the experiences of political prisoners, who constituted a relatively small percentage (less than 1 percent) of the total deaths during the Democratic Kampuchean era. Thus, though they function as *emblems* of the Killing Fields era, they are not *representative* of the hundreds of thousands who died as a result of starvation, forced labor, and disease. Moreover, though local killing fields memorials have been built, Tuol Sleng and Choeung Ek persist as the two principle sites for in-country remembrance, a fact made even more striking given that no nationally sanctioned memorials acknowledging victims (for instance, via name, monument, or cenotaph) exist. Such modes of remembrance are made even less stable when placed within the sociocultural context of the nation's built memorial landscape, which—due to express religious oversights—fail to provide Cambodians with viable spaces for commemoration.

Curating Justice: Tuol Sleng Prison and the Choeung Ek Killing Fields

Upon entering Tuol Sleng Genocide Museum's front gate, one sees an open-air ticket office that processes a $2 admission fee and provides a xeroxed trifold. The brochure, written in English, French, and Khmer, maintains that Tuol Sleng Genocide Museum is "a reminder not only of Cambodia's recent history, but of the inhumanity that sometimes overwhelms ordinary human beings."[31] In stressing everydayness and commonality, the innocuous booklet temporarily strays from the hyperbolic parameters of Colonel Lam's original atrocity-centric script, assuming instead the more quotidian registers of a "banality of evil" character-ization. Concurrently, the mention of "inhumanity" and "human be-ings" addresses the site's direct engagement with human rights violation and genocide, undeniably legible in the aftermath of the Holocaust, the Nuremberg Trials, and the 1948 Universal Declaration of Human Rights. Such memory work occurs within the context of remembrance, and Tuol Sleng Genocide Museum becomes—through its curatorial emphases and found-exhibit format—a multivalent reminder of large-scale human loss and draconian Khmer Rouge policies.

Regarding the site's history, the pamphlet includes a narrative time line that succinctly recapitulates the site's prerevolutionary incarnation as a high school, its 1975–79 utilization as a Khmer Rouge detention/tor-ture center, and its post–Democratic Kampuchean conversion into geno-cide museum soon after the 1979 Vietnamese takeover of Phnom Penh. Consequently, the brochure—explicitly focused on Tuol Sleng's past uses—transforms the site into a de facto screen upon which to project "Cambodia's recent history," inclusive of the time before, during, and after the Killing Fields era.[32] Nonetheless, these chronological delineations—indicative of a forward progression through time and space—are less distinct as one physically moves through Tuol Sleng Genocide Museum, which remembers Democratic Kampuchean history by perpetually re-staging Khmer Rouge atrocity. Such frames echo Susan Sontag's observa-tions about the widely circulated S-21 prisoner photographs, which depict individuals "forever looking at death, forever about to be murdered, and forever wronged."[33]

Correspondingly concentrated on forever death and Khmer Rouge wrongdoing, the museum's exhibits are drawn from the Democratic Kampuchean period (1975–79), reflect the days after the dissolution of the regime (after January 7, 1979), and replay (by way of a visual signifiers) Angka war crimes and crimes against humanity. In the process, Tuol Sleng Genocide Museum foments an uncanny, three-part characterization of the Killing Fields era comprised of identifiable victims (S-21's detainees), clearly defined liberators (Vietnamese photographers and military per-sonnel), and intelligible perpetrators (Tuol Sleng personnel and Khmer Rouge leaders). Such disruptive site effects are initially achieved by way of a stark juxtaposition between the unremarkable and unimaginable. To that end, the ordinariness expressed in the brochure is seemingly matched by the commonplace nature of S-21's exterior landscape and facade.

In particular, Tuol Sleng Genocide Museum consists of four inter-connected buildings that form a U-shaped pattern. The multiplex structure faces a central courtyard framed by stone benches, uneven pull-up bars, a manicured lawn, neatly pruned trees, and ordered walkways. Architecturally, Tuol Sleng is by and large commonplace—the three-story multibuilding structure bears the marks of a typical Cambodian administrative building from the 1960s, manifest in poured concrete walls, a rigidly square edifice, and minimal adornment. All the same, the every-dayness of a typical Phnom Penh schoolyard is disrupted by barred windows and a barbed wire fence, which signal the location's more ominous use as a Khmer Rouge detention/torture center. Furthermore, the routine impression generated by Tuol Sleng's run-of-the-mill facade and outdoor grounds is destabilized by the appearance of a large white sign with black lettering, a stained wooden scaffold, and fourteen rectangular graves situated to the left of the museum's front office.

The sign, the scaffold, and the sepulchers configure a familiar before, during, and after narrative that—like the above-mentioned time line of site usage—corresponds to the processing, detention, and extermination of Tuol Sleng's prisoners. For example, the sign, titled "The Security of Regulation," ostensibly replicates the initial processing of prisoners, issuing the following directives and warnings (rendered in Khmer, French, and English):

1. you must answer accordingly my questions—Don't turn them away.
2. Don't try to hide the facts by making pretexts this and that You are strictly prohibited to contest me.
3. Don't be fool for you are a chap who dare to thwart the revolution.
4. you must immediately answer my questions without wasting time to reflect.
5. Don't tell me either about your immoralities or the essence of the revolution.
6. While getting lashes or electrification you must not cry at all
7. Do nothing, sit still and wait for my orders. If there is no order, keep quiet. when I ask you to do something, you must do it right away without protesting.
8. Don't make pretext about Kampuchea Krom in order to hide your secret or traitor.

Exterior facade and courtyard, Tuol Sleng Genocide Museum. Despite its notorious Khmer Rouge function as a detention and torture center, Tuol Sleng still bears the mark of its original purpose as a secondary high school.

Exterior, Tuol Sleng Genocide Museum. Bars on the windows signal the site's penitentiary use.

9. If you don't follow all the above rules, you shall get many lashes of electric wire.

10. If you disobey any point of my regulations you shall get either ten lashes or five shocks of electric charge.[34]

Notwithstanding grammatical and syntactical errors of an inexact English translation, "The Security of Regulation" reconfirms Tuol Sleng's panoptic function during the Khmer Rouge regime. Moreover, couched in a series of second-person imperative declarations, "The Security of Regulation" temporarily situates the viewer in the subject position of detainee. Although the sign replicates—through iteration and codification—S-21's rigid parameters, its inclusion represents an approximation of what was found on-site. Specifically, such regulations originally appeared on the chalkboards in prisoner cells, and were—because of medium—ephemeral productions. Thus, on one level, "The Security of Regulation" as reconstructed Tuol Sleng Genocide Museum artifact evidences a post-1979, rehabilitative repurposing of S-21 from jail to museum.

On another level, "The Security of Regulation" is a *leading* exhibit that serves as a tour starting point, even if this origin point is initially unclear to the unguided viewer due to the absence of directional markers that usually accompany an open-access museum plan. This unconstrained visitor movement reproduces a nonprisoner perspective analogous to the experiences of Vietnamese military personnel and prison workers. To be sure, "The Security of Regulation" marks the only point in which the museum visitor is placed in the position of S-21 prisoner. Such victim subjectivity is concomitantly undermined by the equally plausible perspective of a Tuol Sleng prison guard charged with issuing regulations to new arrivals and enforcing their tenets for established inmates. This perpetrator personhood coheres with the museum's overall mission, which is first and foremost concerned with "memorializ[ing] the genocidal crimes of the Khmer Rouge regime."[35]

This focus on remembering "genocidal crimes" by restaging and reimagining Khmer Rouge atrocities is emblematized by the aforementioned scaffold, upon which prisoners were presumably hung and (to draw from the "Regulations") given "many lashes of electric wire." In spite of a distinct spatial relationship between sign and scaffold (wherein the former is placed to the left of the latter), the wooden structure stands on its own, with no explanatory placard, leaving the viewer to conjecture about

Second-story view, onsite graves, Tuol Sleng Genocide Museum. Added to the site during the PRK period, the graves contain the remains of the fourteen bodies found by the Vietnamese army on January 7, 1979.

"The Security of Regulation," Tuol Sleng Genocide Museum, instructions for those detained at Tuol Sleng.

its use during the Democratic Kampuchean era. The scaffold's functional ambiguity operates in direct contrast to the articulated context for the fourteen graves, which—as brochure and a concrete marker reveal—contain the bodies of recently executed prisoners discovered by Vietnamese photographers and military personnel on January 8, 1979. Altogether, if "The Security of Regulation" explicitly speaks to the initial processing of prisoners, then the scaffold implicitly attests to the torturous treatment of S-21 inmates. Consequently, sign and scaffold converge to form a particular victim/perpetrator narrative. In a different vein, the fourteen sepulchers foreground an alternative liberator/victim/culprit story in which Khmer Rouge crimes are discovered by a Vietnamese army who lays to rest the regime's victims and begins the juridical process of prosecuting those responsible.

This liberator/victim/culprit agenda is supported by museum placards that detail how each building was used and to what end. For example, a sign located in front of Building A relates:

> It contains three stories divided into 20 cells: the first one has 10 cells—used for jailing, interrogating, and torturing the prisoners who had been the high officials. The second and third ones have 5 big cells each—used for the same purpose as on the first story. Nowadays there are a lot of evidences remaining in all the cells which prove the atrocities of Pol Pot Clique.[36]

The sign establishes an ordered spatiality that incompletely crystallizes how the Khmer Rouge used Tuol Sleng as a place of imprisonment, surveillance, and punishment ("jailing, interrogating, and torturing"). Likewise relevant is the presence of "a lot of evidences remaining in all the cells," which promises criminal corroboration through material proof.

The notice and what it signifies (the various cells) are reminiscent of an untouched crime scene, though the inclusion of Pol Pot's name and the attribution of "atrocities" to his "Clique" establishes—in narrow deductive terms—the primary culprit. What is more, these "evidences"—which assume material form in iron shackles, rusted chains, witness paintings, prisoner mug shots, and posthumous images of bloated, almost unrecognizable corpses—are (to reference Sontag) *forever* tied to the "atrocities of [the] Pol Pot Clique." In viewing such evidence of atrocities, the tourist ceases to be innocent sightseer and is involuntarily brought into a criminal proceeding: first as an investigator, then as a prosecutor, and finally as a jury member. This tripartite transformation is promulgated by the Building A placard, which commences with factual details (related to number of cells and site usage), moves to "evidences" (which suggest that a crime has been committed), and then concludes with the declaration of proof and the identification of guilt (embodied by Pol Pot and his "Clique").

Accordingly, the types of exhibits contained in Tuol Sleng Genocide Museum's remaining three buildings reiterate Building A's memorialization of Khmer Rouge atrocity by way of visual representations of both victims and perpetrator acts. Whereas Building A is comprised of large cells in which Tuol Sleng's fourteen recently slain prisoners were discovered, Building B is analogously focused on detainees and holds galleries of prisoner photographs. These photographs (the previously mentioned S-21 prisoner mug shots) are perhaps the most well-known artifacts from Tuol Sleng Prison, having circulated by way of traveling exhibits in the United States, Europe, and Australia. Indeed, as Rachel Hughes characterizes, these images have, due to their global dissemination, become "the undisciplined envoys of Cambodia's traumatic past."[37] In the face of unbounded global registers, the S-21 photographs carry a particular local function within the space of Tuol Sleng as museum. The images are organized in indistinct rows, wherein women, men, and children are interspersed and carry (with a few exceptions) the same resigned stare. The gaze of detainees is directly met by the viewer, who is subsequently placed in the uncomfortable position of a Khmer Rouge guard (or even more specifically, S-21 photographer Nhem En).

Tellingly, no names or explanations are provided save for brief profession details (e.g., "high officials"), foregrounding an anonymous victimhood that operates in harsh opposition to the explicit naming of Khmer Rouge perpetrators (principally Pol Pot). Moreover, since prisoners were photographed upon detention, the S-21 photographs likewise return the sightseer to a beginning point in the Tuol Sleng imprisonment narrative. Such beginnings are quickly eschewed in favor of a during narrative redolent in the remaining two buildings.

Following suit, Buildings C and D contain exhibits focused on the day-to-day conditions of S-21 imprisonment. Building C holds smaller, individual cell chambers; in Building D, Khmer Rouge torture techniques (including a waterboarding display) are prominently featured. Until recently,

Building D also featured the Tuol Sleng Genocide Museum's most infamous exhibit: a map of Cambodia composed of three hundred skulls and bones, allegedly constructed from victim remains found in each of the five Khmer Rouge provinces.[38] Dismantled in 2002, the map's skeletal components are still housed on site. Indeed, such human remnants are presently displayed, in eerily ordered fashion, on a glass-plated museum shelf. Like the S-21 photographs, these human remains are exhibited sans names, reiterating a *general* and *generalized* characterization of Cambodian victimhood under the Democratic Kampuchean regime.

As one peers in and out of classrooms turned torture cells, what emerges time and again is a particular juxtaposition between the sheer abjectness of Tuol Sleng prison inmates and the unbounded agency of Khmer Rouge perpetrators (S-21 guards). This distinction is principally configured along an identifiable spectrum of movement and mobility practice, wherein tourist—and, by proxy, the imagined Tuol Sleng prison guard—walks freely through the exterior and interior spaces of the former Khmer Rouge jail. The open access afforded the tourist to peruse prison "evidences" and conditions unfettered concretizes the forced immobility of the S-21 detainee, which is metonymically transmitted in the rigidity of

Interior, typical detainee cell and shackles, Tuol Sleng Genocide Museum.

rusted metal bed frames, the inertness of ammunition boxes (which were used as toilets and water containers), and the unyielding nature of iron shackles. Put alternatively, Tuol Sleng detainees—economically represented by prisoner portraits, rendered still by torture artifacts, and claustrophobically set in closed spaces—are hauntingly static.

This perpetrator perspective persists in previously discussed graphic images of bloated bodies and in former Tuol Sleng prisoner Vann Nath's tormented paintings, which depict waterboarding and electrocution and feature an anguished tableau depicting a crying mother about to be separated from her children. Largely uncaptioned, such objects of torture and images of suffering are left in self-evident fashion to "speak for themselves."[39] In so doing, the visitor is simultaneously placed in the position of the Vietnamese photographers who unknowingly discovered Tuol Sleng. In addition, the tourist is also witness to an occupying government's agenda predicated on prosecuting and vilifying the previous regime. The ability to take site photographs sans impediment instantiates an analogous reading between liberating Vietnamese photographer, PRK prosecutor, and present-day tourist. With little to no museum barriers (e.g., ropes that demarcate allowable viewing distances, signs that lead tourists from building to building, and staff who direct sightseers and answer questions), Tuol Sleng Genocide Museum is distinctly open although its primary narrative—focused on perpetrator-driven atrocity—is decidedly not left open-ended.

As placards, exhibits, and Colonel Lam's initial agenda make plain, Tuol Sleng Genocide Museum is chiefly invested in representing atrocity through Khmer Rouge authoritarian traces, epitomized by blood-stained floors, torture artifacts, photographs, and fragmented bodies. Because of its overriding emphasis on regime culpability, the site by and large fulfills what the brochure avers is the central mission of Tuol Sleng Genocide Museum: to memorialize (or remember) Democratic Kampuchean criminality. Even so, the object of such commemoration—the "genocidal crimes of the Khmer Rouge regime"—brings to light an antithetical engagement with memorialization. Indeed, if to memorialize is to participate (via the built environment) in a collective memory act focused on loss, then Tuol Sleng Genocide Museum's collected memorial to state-sanctioned violence privileges a contradictory commemorative mode concentrated *not* on those executed but on the Khmer Rouge leaders, cadres, and soldiers responsible for their victimhood.

Tuol Sleng survivor Vann Nath's painting of Khmer Rouge torture, including waterboarding, Tuol Sleng Genocide Museum.

Vann Nath's depiction of forced familial separation and torture, Tuol Sleng Genocide Museum.

These prosecutorial foci are even more evident at the Choeung Ek Center for Genocide Crimes, which is similarly committed to memorializing the genocidal crimes of the Democratic Kampuchean regime. This agenda becomes strikingly clear by way of a sign announcing "THE CHEMICAL SUBSTANCES STORAGE ROOM":

Here, was the place where chemical substances such as D.D.T. . . . etc. was kept. Executioners scattered these substances over dead bodies of the victims at once after execution. This action had two purposes: firstly to eliminate the stench from the dead bodies which could potentially raise suspicion among people working near by the killing fields and secondly was to kill off victims who were buried alive.[40]

As the above passage underscores, at stake at Choeung Ek is the revelation of Khmer Rouge atrocity forged within a legible perpetrator/victim narrative. Accordingly, perpetrators take the form of executioners who mask their crimes with chemicals; correspondingly, victims are not only summarily executed but posthumously desecrated. Some graves are protected by a four-beam roofed shelter, although other burial mounds lack cover. Small glass stupas (Buddhist shrines for the dead) containing stacked skeletal remains are scattered throughout the site. Distressingly nondescript, Choeung Ek's mass graves are shallow, grassy indentions marked by inauspicious wooden signs. These placards flatly relate (in Khmer and English) what was excavated (e.g., "mass grave of 166 victims with out heads"), a point starkly reinforced in the bone fragments and pieces of torn clothing that literally litter Choeung Ek's sunken burial grounds.

As is the case with Tuol Sleng, Choeung Ek incorporates a found exhibition format wherein tourists are placed in the simultaneous and mutually constitutive role of prosecutor and perpetrator. Although sightseers are told to not "walk through mass grave[s]," few barriers exist to separate viewer from mass graves, echoing the open-access format of Tuol Sleng Genocide Museum. Nevertheless, whereas Tuol Sleng is invested in highlighting acts of torture under the Khmer Rouge regime, Choeung Ek— understandable given its function as a Khmer Rouge execution site—is decidedly more morbid in its profane emphasis on the postmortem treatment of bodies. Even more ghastly, Tuol Sleng's previously mentioned skull map is surpassed tenfold by the dramatic display of Choeung Ek's 8,985 internees, epitomized by the overt restaging and visible reordering of skeletal remains for public view. Thus, if Tuol Sleng Genocide Museum is focused on criminality, then the Choeung Ek Center for Genocide Crimes extends this agenda by way of a macabre corporeality that viscerally replays the dark outcome of Khmer Rouge policies. And such restaging is linked to a politicized curatorial agenda. To that end, the stress on skeletal remains at both Tuol Sleng Genocide Museum and the Choeung Ek Center for Genocide Crimes connects to Colonel Lam's evidence-driven assertion that these displays were in the aftermath of Democratic Kampuchea's dissolution "very important for the Cambodian people—it's the proof."[41]

Despite curatorial coherences, the Choeung Ek Center for Genocide Crimes reflects—unlike Tuol Sleng Genocide Museum—a longer and more gradual rehabilitative history. For example, Choeung Ek as killing field memorial originally featured a long, open-aired wooden pavilion that housed chemically treated skeletal remains. However, the wooden pavilion was anomalous with regard to site rehabilitation, and Choeung Ek continued to be underdeveloped until the mid-1980s, when (as Rachel Hughes notes) "a new memorial, further chemical treatment of the remains, new fencing and an additional brick building for exhibition" were proposed.[42] Such plans precipitated the 1988 construction of a seventeen-story stupa curated by Colonel Lam and designed by architect Lim Ourk. Since then, the majority of Choeung Ek's victim remains were relocated and placed in the glass-encased cenotaph, which currently allows visitors open-view access to ordered rows of skulls and bones. The towering structure, marked by a tiered roof structure and tall walls, drew its architectural inspiration from Buddhist temple pavilions (including those at the Cambodian Royal Palace) and reflects the dominant religion of Cambodia (Hinhayana Buddhism).[43]

Even with such specific religious affects, Choeung Ek was and continues to be a contested site with regard to Cambodian-centric remembrance. Expressly, stupas usually contain the cremated remains of loved ones, and the still-intact bones displayed en masse at Choeung Ek underscore a potential spiritual rupture. According to Hughes, within a Buddhist context violent deaths like the ones experienced by Khmer Rouge victims are considered "highly inauspicious deaths."[44] Although Hinhayana Buddhism does not require cremation as a funeral rite, the practice is nonetheless viewed as a process that "eases the deceased's transition to rebirth." Thus, cremation is important to reincarnation, or movement into the next life.[45] Moreover, if such funerary dictates are violated in cases of violent death, the ghosts of the dead remain bound to the site and may "harm the living by causing great sickness and misfortune."[46]

Consequently, many Cambodians consider Choeung Ek and Tuol Sleng to be "highly dangerous place[s]," and the display of skeletal remains

Mass grave, Choeung Ek Center for Genocide Crimes.

Wide field shot at Choeung Ek Center for Genocide Crimes.

Central stupa containing victim remains, Choeung Ek Center for Genocide Crimes.

Grave stupa containing victim remains, Choeung Ek Center for Genocide Crimes.

represents a "great offence . . . tantamount to a second violence" against victims.[47] What is more, the nameless nature of these victims, and the conditions under which they were exhumed, renders necessarily complex collective acts of commemoration. Indeed, although the bones have been catalogued by way of physiology (e.g., skulls, ulnas, and femurs), the victims have yet to be identified. Within a Cambodian cultural context, cremation is a practice performed by family members, and the sheer number of unnamed bodies undermines the intimate registers of this rite. Therefore, when situated adjacent to this vexed spiritual context, while Choeung Ek and Tuol Sleng memorialize Khmer Rouge atrocities, they do so at the expense of victims, who remain fragmented, incomplete, and anonymous.

Transitional Justice: Revolutionary Trials and Hybrid Tribunals

The fragmented registers of Tuol Sleng Genocide Museum and the Choeung Ek Center for Genocide Crimes prove apt frames through which to consider the incomplete dimensions of Cambodian memory work in the aftermath of war, state-authorized violence, and genocide. At the same time, such unfinished memory work is obscured by an essentializing, seemingly complete narrative of national reconciliation following the arrival of the Vietnamese on January 7, 1979. As Judy Ledgerwood notes, each site's focus on atrocity—in spite of Colonel Lam's assertion that such work was for the Cambodian people—labored to produce a clear yet opaque "master narrative of the successor state" grounded in the story of "a glorious revolution stolen and perverted by a handful of sadistic, genocidal traitors who deliberately exterminated three million of their countrymen."[48] Hence, the memorialization of Khmer Rouge atrocities was part and parcel of a nascent PRK nation-building effort, rendering impossible—from the beginning—a nuanced, complex mode for Cambodian commemoration. Within this express political milieu, Tuol Sleng Genocide Museum and the Choeung Ek Center for Genocide Crimes were repurposed to highlight Khmer Rouge criminality in order to produce loyal PRK citizens by fomenting anti–Khmer Rouge sentiment.

Accordingly, the issue of Cambodian genocide remembrance, manifest in monumentalizing Khmer Rouge atrocities by way of Killing Fields memorialization, encompasses competing spatial narratives of liberation, human rights, and justice. Such spatial parameters, which perpetually reiterate the ruination of the nation under the Khmer Rouge, are temporally restaged in two national holidays: January 7 (Victory over Genocide Day or Nation Day) and May 20 (Day of Tying Anger or *T'veer Chong Kamhaeng*, in 2001 renamed Day of Remembrance). As the name Victory over Genocide Day suggests, January 7—which marked the arrival of Vietnamese troops in Phnom Penh—is remembered not as a day of occupation but instead a time of liberation. Moreover, given the next-day discovery of Tuol Sleng Prison on January 8, 1979, Victory over Genocide Day is geographically connected to the built remembrance of both the Killing Fields era and Vietnamese occupation.

As a date-based memorial, January 7 on the one hand historically acknowledges the dissolution of Democratic Kampuchea. On the other hand, with triumphal connotations and successive registers, January 7 obscures a complex political history, consistent with past border contestations (between Cambodia and Vietnam), troubling alliances (e.g., pre-revolutionary coalitions involving the North Vietnamese and the Khmer Rouge), and international antagonisms (against China, who was the primary ally of Democratic Kampuchea). As the ongoing nature of the UN/Cambodian War Crimes Tribunal makes clear, Cambodia's genocidal past has yet to be juridically reconciled, destabilizing further success-oriented claims in relation to large-scale loss and state-sanctioned violence.

If Victory over Genocide Day is temporally connected to the history of S-21 and Tuol Sleng Genocide Museum, it is also thematically similar to Cambodia's formerly named Day of Tying Anger or Day of Maintaining Anger, which takes place on May 20. Inaugurated in 1984 during the Vietnamese-ruled PRK era, the Day of Tying Anger directly accessed Democratic Kampuchean history. According to a contemporaneous government press release, May 20, 1975 was the "day the Pol Pot gang began to implement its systemic, overt and savage genocidal policy against the Kampuchean people throughout the country."[49] Ostensibly commemorative, May 20 celebrations took (in the 1980s and 1990s) the form of incendiary speeches, reenactments of torture, and the burning of Pol Pot effigies.[50] However, as the holiday's full name suggests, at stake was a specific and politicized mobilization against the still-fighting Khmer Rouge and their supporters.

Specifically, the Day of Tying Anger included criticisms of "American imperialists" (who, after 1979, funded the Khmer Rouge), "Chinese expansionists" (who, from the outset, politically supported the regime), and anti-Vietnamese parties (e.g., the "Sihanouk-Son Sann Reactionary

Groups").[51] Couched as a "day of hatred" or a time of "maintaining anger,"
May 20 was principally concerned with perpetuating—initially to pro-
Vietnamese ends—anti–Khmer Rouge sentiment. As a direct consequence, national reconciliation during the PRK era took vengeful form.
Such state-authorized holidays operated in tandem with the built memorial landscape. Whereas the setting for Victory over Genocide Day included the discovery of Tuol Sleng Prison, Day of Tying Anger was chiefly
fixed to Choeung Ek killing field, the central site for May 20 activities. In
2001, three years after Pol Pot's death, the holiday was renamed (under
Prime Minister Hun Sen's administration) the more charitable-sounding
Day of Remembrance. Even with the more meditative label, May 20 is still
used to achieve less-than-contemplative political ends. Expressly, Sen's
Cambodian People's Party (CPP) time and again accesses the vindictive
registers associated with the Day of Remembrance holiday to opportu-
nistically (and disingenuously) link opposition party candidates to the
Khmer Rouge era.[52]

With regard to post–Democratic Kampuchean statecraft, the PRK's
co-optation of Cambodian memory is not only evident in the repurposing of former Khmer Rouge sites; it is further replayed, restaged, and remembered in the tactical creation of national holidays. Even so, contestations over national memory continued (albeit to differing ends) after
the 1989 dissolution of the PRK. Whereas the PRK was overtly invested
in strategic remembering, subsequent Cambodian governments were
directly engaged in tactical forgetting vis-à-vis genocide justice. Such
amnesias arguably commenced with the October 23, 1991 signing of the
"Agreements on the Comprehensive Political Settlement of the Cambodia
Conflict," which established the United Nations Transitional Authority in
Cambodia (UNTAC).[53] Intended to implement, institutionalize, and en-
force treaty agreements, UNTAC carried a "mandate [that] included aspects relating to human rights, the organization and conduct of elections,
military arrangements, civil administration, maintenance of law and order,
repatriation and resettlement of refugees and displaced persons, and [the]
rehabilitation of Cambodian infrastructure."[54]

Notwithstanding its "human rights" focus and "law and order" imperative, UNTAC by and large avoided confronting Cambodia's genocidal
past, opting instead to include Khmer Rouge leaders in the transitional
process, which concluded in 1993 with the election of two prime minis-
ters (Prince Norodom Ranariddh and Hun Sen). Likewise controversial

was UNTAC's decision to disarm local militias and not the Khmer Rouge, which contributed to in-country instability and postelection political violence.[55] The continued presence of the Khmer Rouge, coupled with a tenuous split-party leadership, precipitated a 1997 coup wherein the aforementioned CPP leader Sen overthrew his fellow prime minister and FUNCINPEC party leader Prince Ranariddh. By 1998, Sen assumed sole control of the now reestablished Kingdom of Cambodia.[56] Shortly thereafter, the newly installed prime minister orchestrated various truces and pardons for former Khmer Rouge officials.

Accompanying the subsequent surrender of Khieu Samphan, Nuon Chea, and Ieng Sary to the Cambodian government in December 1998, Sen (a former Khmer Rouge foot soldier who had been installed by the Vietnamese government following the 1979 invasion) publicly stated that such leaders should be welcomed "with bouquets of flowers, not with prison and handcuffs."[57] The prime minister notoriously concluded, "We should dig a hole and bury the past and look ahead to the 21st century with a clean slate."[58] On the one hand, Sen's directive unintentionally calls to mind innumerable graves dug and untold bodies buried during Pol Pot time. On the other hand, such state-authorized disremembering signals the current terrain of Cambodian genocide remembrance, which from the outset has been subject to what Lisa Yoneyama evocatively terms a "dialectics of remembering." Suggestive of debate, dialogue, and opposition, such "dialectics of remembering" necessarily entail particular amnesias, or what Yoneyama subsequently labels "the forgetting of forgetfulness."[59]

From Vietnamese liberation narratives to Cambodian clean slates, from state-sanctioned recollections to politically sanctioned amnesias, the strategic remembrance and tactical forgetting of Cambodia's Killing Fields history remains a *dialectical* foundation for post–Democratic Kampuchean statecraft and contemporary Cambodian genocide remembrance. As a close reading of Tuol Sleng Genocide Museum and the Choeung Ek Center for Genocide Crimes brings to light, these dialectics continue to operate in Cambodia's most visited commemorative sites, substantiating a politicized examination of both spaces via juridically entangled frames. Cambodian memory work—which necessarily commences with unimaginable human loss and encompasses contested practices of remembrance—represents a specific archive shaped by and revised according to co-opted narratives, politicized juridical agendas, and controversial nation formation.

Congruently, integral to Killing Fields remembrance is an expressly vexed relationship between history, memory, and politics. If, as Marita Sturken observes, the rescripting of past trauma highlights a relationship in which "memories and histories are often entangled, conflictual, and co-constitutive," what emerges in contemporary Cambodian remembrance is an oppositional, *nonconstitutive* narrative marked by a hypervisibility of Khmer Rouge perpetrators rooted in divergent tensions between evidence and commemoration. As significant, such a narrative is even further complicated by the still absented presence of genocide justice.[60] This issue of genocide justice—apparent in the belated paucity of successful trials against former Khmer Rouge leaders more than thirty years after the Killing Fields era—figures keenly in present-day discussions about what to do with the most visceral remnants of the regime: the skeletal remains on display at both Tuol Sleng Genocide Museum and the Choeung Ek Center for Genocide Crimes.

Certainly, these juridical machinations complicate King Norodom Sihanouk's oft-issued call for cremation as a means to national reconciliation.[61] For example, the Cambodian monarch maintained (in a 1991 news conference) that, with regard to Tuol Sleng's (now dismantled) skull map, "We have to liberate the souls and send them to a world of justice and peace. The dead will then give us their blessing so here will be peace. . . . To be in peace in the world they need cremation."[62] Similarly, on the twenty-ninth anniversary of the Khmer Rouge takeover of Phnom Penh, Sihanouk challenged the ostentatious display of bones at Choeung Ek, asserting that "we are Buddhists whose belief and customs since ancient times have always been to cremate the corpses and then bring the remains to be placed in the *stupa* at the pagoda."[63] Predicated on reconciliation by way of spiritual observance, Sihanouk's repeated insistence to cremate remains prompted Prime Minister Sen to announce plans for a public referendum on the issue, with the caveat that it would take place after the completion of a tribunal that at the time had yet to be formed.

Since the UN/Cambodian War Crimes Tribunal only recently issued its first ruling (in 2010) and amid predictions that the case involving the four remaining Khmer Rouge leaders will drag on until 2014, the issue of what to do with the skeletal remains that have become iconic shorthand for the Killing Fields era continues to be unresolved.[64] Even so, the Sen administration did issue the following governmental instruction in 2001:

In order to preserve the remains as evidence of these historic crimes and as the basis for remembrance and education by the Cambodian people as a whole, especially future generations, of the painful and terrible history brought about by the Democratic Kampuchea regime . . . the government issues the following directive: . . . All local authorities at the province and municipal level shall cooperate with relevant expert institutions in their areas to examine, restore and maintain all existing memorials, and to examine and research other remaining grave sites, so that all such places may be transformed into memorials.[65]

In so doing, the Cambodian government's call for preservation coincided with a majority Cambodian view that the remains must be preserved because they bear witness to an unreconciled genocidal past.[66] As Wynne Cougill of the Documentation Center of Cambodia asserts, to date no public outcry has occurred in response to the directive, and the nation's Buddhist clergy by and large support preservation.[67]

This is not to suggest an answer to the question of Cambodian memorialization, which is inflected by the realities of a still-to-be-determined juridical imaginary. Unquestionably, the nonreconciled registers that characterize Cambodia's built memorial landscape are evident in the previously mentioned first verdict issued in the UN/Cambodian War Crimes Tribunal. Fittingly, in light of Tuol Sleng Genocide Museum's emphases on evidence of Khmer Rouge atrocity, this historic case involved former S-21 head warden Kaing Guek Eav. Highlighting the prosecutorial belatedness characteristic of Cambodia's Killing Fields era, on July 26, 2010—almost three years after the trial's November 2007 start date, "thirty-five years, three months, and nine days after the Khmer Rouge entered Phnom Penh," and "thirty-one years, six months, and nineteen days after they were drive[n] out by Vietnamese forces"—"Comrade Duch" became the first Khmer Rouge to be tried and sentenced in an international court of law.[68]

If Tuol Sleng Genocide Museum and the Choeung Ek Center for Genocide Crimes are committed to making experiential (through extreme exhibit and pointed curation) the criminality of the former Khmer Rouge regime at the expense of contemplative commemoration, then Kaing Guek Eav's case highlights an analogous limitation at the level of state-authorized, internationally sanctioned justice. As a total consideration of the verdict brings to the fore, integral to the tribunal's first case was a collective juridical process, inclusive of court officials and Cambodian victims, intended to foment national reconciliation through the rule of law. However, what emerges in a concise reading of trial and verdict is the extent to which perpetrator culpability—complicated by the defendant's declarations of repentance—overshadowed reparative justice for victims. Though understandable in light of the criminal nature of the tribunal, the court nevertheless chose to provide same-day rulings on defendant guilt and civil party claims (reparation cases filed by victims and surviving family members). Indeed, the court juridically collapsed (via simultaneous verdicts) perpetrator guilt and victim redress.

From the beginning, Kaing Guek Eav expressed remorse for his involvement with S-21 prison, although he consistently denied direct wrongdoing. Indeed, the ex–prison warden maintained, in a now-familiar genocide script, that he was tragically and involuntarily a "cog in the machine" and was just "following orders."[69] Concomitantly, the defendant (who in the 1990s had converted to Christianity) accessed affective apologetics as a primary defense. Such apology-driven rhetoric was made plain in Kaing Guek Eav's opening statement to the court on March 31, 2009. In an eighteen-minute speech, Kaing Guek Eav stated, "I would like to express my regret and heartfelt sorrow. . . . My current plea is that I would like you to please leave an open window for me to seek forgiveness."[70] Such frames of "regret" and "sorrow" were foreshadowed in dramatic fashion before the trial began. Apropos the express agenda of each site—to showcase evidence of atrocity committed by "the Pol Pot Clique"—Kaing Guek Eav, along with three S-21 survivors, was transported to Tuol Sleng Genocide Museum and the Choeung Ek Center for Genocide Crimes on February 27, 2008 as per a court-ordered reenactment. According to reporter Ker Munthit, as the defendant traversed prison grounds and killing field, he was "moved to tears" and was "especially moved when he stood before a tree with a sign describing how executioners disposed of their child victims by bashing their heads against its trunk."[71]

Such affective displays were largely absent two years later, as the former prison warden, dressed in a light blue shirt and pressed khaki pants, was led into a packed courtroom for verdict and sentencing. Strikingly, Kaing Guek Eav expressed no emotion as the president of the Trial Chamber, Judge Nil Nonn, read the decision synopsis.[72] In exacting legal detail, the summary (which began promptly at 10 o'clock in the morning, Phnom Penh time) included a brief overview of Tuol Sleng's function, an evaluation of its connection to Choeung Ek, and a rundown of Kaing Guek Eav's relationship to prison and execution site. The actual judgment encompassed charges of crimes against humanity, war crimes (e.g., breaches of the Geneva conventions), and violations of the 1956 Cambodian Penal Code.[73] Over the next hour and a half, Judge Nonn asserted that Kaing Guek Eav was guilty on all counts save for those that fell under the rubric of domestic law. These particular crimes, which involved murder and assault, were deemed outside the jurisdiction of the court due to a lack of direct evidence.

In the end, the former S-21 warden, who was repeatedly characterized as "meticulous," "exacting," and "pitiless," was convicted of "crimes against humanity of persecution on political grounds, extermination, enslavement, imprisonment, torture, one instance of rape, and other inhumane acts."[74] Kaing Guek Eav was also found guilty of war crimes, which involved "willful killing [and] torture, causing great suffering and injury, depriving civilians and prisoners of war of the right to a fair trial, and the unlawful confinement of civilians."[75] Nevertheless, Kaing Guek Eav's judgment was only one aspect of the tribunal's first-ever ruling. In drawing to a close, Judge Nonn issued two distinct sentences. The first involved the above-mentioned civil parties, who had filed for what the court termed "moral and collective reparations." When the hybrid tribunal was formed in 2007, the court stressed it was unable to provide victims with financial reparations and opted instead to issue symbolic redress, inclusive of "orders to publish the court's judgment in the mass media at the expense of the convicted person; orders to fund non-profit services or other activities that aim to benefit Victims; or the creation of a memorial."[76]

Out of ninety civil parties who filed for "moral and collective reparations" in Case 001, the court recognized sixty-six and did so by way of reading the names of the victims on the day of Kaing Guek Eav's verdict.[77] The remaining twenty-four civil parties discovered—at the time of the judgment—that their cases had (notwithstanding their participation in the multiyear court process) been deemed inadmissible. Adding insult to injury, the court rejected civil party requests for a national day of victim remembrance, the commemorative repurposing of a Buddhist pagoda, and the construction of a national memorial, ruling instead to maintain prison sites like S-21 and to publish the verdict, along with recognized civil party names, online.[78] As civil party lawyers stressed in the ruling's chaotic aftermath, the majority of Cambodians have limited to no Internet access, rendering this reparative solution unfeasible and literally inaccessible. Even more controversial was Kaing Guek Eav's final court punishment. Noting that the defendant had been in custody since 1999 and stressing his willingness to cooperate with the court, the chamber sentenced Kaing Guek Eav to thirty-five years in prison, which, with time served, translates into a nineteen-year term.[79] Soon after the ruling, Kaing Guek Eav filed an appeal on the grounds that he had been wrongfully tried as a Khmer Rouge leader.[80]

All in all, the historic ruling in Case 001—which encompassed punishment and reparation—was for many Cambodians (in light of the defendant's sentence and civil party dismissals) wrought with disappointment, frustration, and dissatisfaction. As Theary C. Seng, a Cambodian American activist and the founding director of CIVICUS (the Center for Cambodian Civic Education), potently surmised,

> many Cambodian survivors, including myself, viewed the sentencing to be too lenient and incomprehensible in light of the enormity of his crimes. After the Extraordinary Chambers deducted 5 years for his cooperation and 11 years for the illegal pre–Extraordinary Chambers detention in a military prison from the 35 years, the victims are left with Comrade Duch effectively receiving 11 hours of imprisonment for each life he brutally murdered.[81]

Rooted in a profound sense of incomprehensibility, Seng's response to the verdict reinforces a reading of Cambodia's juridical imaginary as a vexed space for survivors, who, in seeking reconciliation, must negotiate and contend with the limits of state-authorized justice. Prior to the tribunal, Seng—currently a civil party in Case 002—advocated for the construction of other memorials because Tuol Sleng and Choeung Ek "did not commemorate what the victims wanted to remember."[82] Indeed, what is remembered at sites like Tuol Sleng and Choeung Ek in terms of Khmer Rouge atrocity informs the controversial ruling of the UN/Cambodian War Crimes Tribunal, which—via lenient sentencing and denial— privileged perpetrator over victim and criminality over reparation. If, as Ariela Gross argues, the "quintessential *lieu de mémoire*" in modern times is "the courtroom or truth commission hearing room," then the UN/ Cambodian War Crimes Tribunal, as juridical memorial, encapsulates and promulgates the nonreparative dimensions of past and present-day

Cambodian genocide remembrance.[83] As the Kaing Guek Eav verdict underscores, still unanswered is a survivor-driven call for the construction of genocide education sites and national memorials that adequately address (in culturally relevant fashion) the histories, stories, and experiences of the 1.7 million who perished during the Democratic Kampuchean era.[84]

Hence, practices of and sites for in-country remembrance time and again intersect with complicated and complex questions of justice. Correspondingly, the politicized narratives of the Killing Fields era manifest in spaces like Tuol Sleng and Choeung Ek perpetually circulate within an unreconciled Cambodian sociocultural imaginary. In the shadow of no state-sanctioned memorial, Tuol Sleng Genocide Museum (which has a varied political history) and Choeung Ek Center for Genocide Crimes (which is likewise politically inflected) emerge as unstable and troubled memorial sites. As Cambodia's memory wars illustrate, the built representation of the Democratic Kampuchean era—epitomized by Tuol Sleng Genocide Museum and the Choeung Ek Center for Genocide Crimes— has occupied a politicized position vis-à-vis extant nation-building, past regime change, and contemporary Cambodian governmentality. Consistently configured along a precarious axis of politicized yet paradoxically generalized victimhood, Tuol Sleng and Choeung Ek operate as metonymic sites for a national narrative that strategically remembers the disastrous Khmer Rouge policies. Following suit, Cambodia's built memorial landscape labors to manufacture an albeit incomplete form of national memory amid competing post–Khmer Rouge liberation discourses, governmental calls to forget, and ongoing obfuscations in the UN/Cambodian War Crimes Tribunal.

Within this open-ended, contradictory context, the denial to grant collective reparations in the form of built memorials corresponds to a decades-long incomprehensibility regarding sustainable genocide remembrance. And the limitations of both sites vis-à-vis contemplative remembrance are drawn into even greater focus when considered alongside Cambodia's emergent atrocity-driven tourist industry. If in-country memorialization has yet to achieve reparative reconciliation, then the mass circulation of the Killing Fields history as a tale of unimaginable evil has made even more difficult contemplative remembrance. To that end, the present-day management of Tuol Sleng and Choeung Ek (and the contemporary state-sanctioned rehabilitation of former Khmer Rouge sites) is increasingly focused on tourism, which is driven by outsider perspec-

tives and foreigner desires. Such commodification—arguably a natural
outgrowth of Colonel Lam's emphases on atrocity exhibits and perpetrator inhumanity—functions as yet another impediment to collective
Cambodian genocide remembrance. This spectacularization of the Killing
Fields era draws into paradoxical focus the politicized history that circum-
scribes Tuol Sleng and Choeung Ek, which draws its affective power from
Khmer Rouge infamy and ongoing impunity.

Spectacular Cruelty: Atrocity Tourism
in Twenty-First-Century Cambodia

If, as Andreas Huyssen asserts, a society's memory "is shaped by such
public sites . . . as the museum, the memorial, and the monument," then
the built sites that epitomize Cambodia's tourism industry dramatically
and undeniably reinforce the unresolved dimensions of national remembrance.[85] Situated within a global imaginary and grounded in two distinct
moments, such an industry is principally reliant on a bifurcated heaven–
hell axis. Indeed, as Youk Chhang evocatively observes, "Cambodia is
known to the world for two things—Angkor Wat and the 'killing fields.'
Some believe one came from God and the other from hell."[86] This affective binary is evident in religious monuments to the thirteenth-century
apex of the Khmer empire and genocide memorials that bear witness to
the twentieth-century tragedy of Democratic Kampuchea.

Even with the seeming disjuncture between Cambodia's monuments
(rooted in state triumphalism) and mass graves (imbued with national
trauma), both forms of public remembrance are shaped by a connective
sense of national ruination. From majestic temple ruins to the stained
floors of former Khmer Rouge detention centers like Tuol Sleng, from
the recently rehabilitated Cambodian National Museum to the vast ne-
cropolis that is Choeung Ek, Cambodia's tourist industry is punctuated by
built ruins, stone remnants, and human remains.[87] While David Chandler
rightly maintains that twenty-first-century Cambodia is a country fixed to
"more distant periods" embodied by the likes of Angkor Wat, the nation
is—as previously discussed—simultaneously "scarred" by its more recent
Khmer Rouge history.[88] Such traces undergird a concluding consideration
of Cambodia's tourist industry, which builds upon a vexed characterization of Cambodian public memory by way of politicized tensions, competing narratives, and increasingly commodified remembrance.

The vast majority of Cambodia's foreign tourists inevitably make their way to Angkor Wat, located 5.5 kilometers north of Siem Reap. A tribute to classical Khmer civilization and a de facto shrine to the bygone Khmer empire, Angkor Wat is not only the largest standing temple in the world. The must-see spiritual destination is also a potent icon of Khmer identity, evidenced in heated public debates and violent clashes involving its cultural ownership (e.g., colonial contestations with France and contemporary disputes with Thailand).[89] Moreover, as Chandler observes, the monument's identifiable multitower outline is featured prominently on Cambodia's flag, making it "the only country in the world that boasts a ruin" in its national symbol.[90] Diplomatically, Angkor Wat was the primary draw and principal backdrop for former First Lady Jacqueline Kennedy's 1967 visit to Cambodia. Amid a multitude of photo-ops and state banquets, Prince Norodom Sihanouk reiterated—two years before U.S. bombings of the Cambodian countryside began—his nation's neutral stance with regard to the American war in neighboring Vietnam.[91]

Undeniably, Angkor Wat figures keenly in Cambodia's tourist economy, which is responsible for a fifth of the nation's gross domestic product.[92] On average, two million tourists annually visit the UNESCO World Heritage site, which—under the corporate auspices of Sokha Hotel Company, Ltd., a subsidiary of the Cambodian petroleum company Sokimex—maintains a healthy profit margin charging a minimum entrance fee of $20 (U.S.) per person.[93] The sheer number of tourist pilgrimages to Angkor Wat makes visible the monetary power of such architectural remains, bringing into focus a neoliberal economy typified by service labor, free-flowing foreign capital, and discounted commodities. For *tuk tuk* drivers, small business souvenir peddlers, and pay-by-the-hour tour guides dependent on throngs of tourists, the marketability of Angkor Wat enables a subsistence existence comprised of cheap fares, inexpensive wares, and low hourly wages.

Notwithstanding the spectacular visual, artistic, and capitalistic registers of Angkor Wat, an increasing number of visitors flock to sites affiliated with the Democratic Kampuchean era. From recently rediscovered killing fields in Kampong Chhnang province to Pol Pot's cremation site in Anlong Veng (a post-1979 Khmer Rouge base), from Tuol Sleng Genocide Museum and the Choeung Ek Center for Genocide Crimes to Siem Reap's Land Mine Museum, foreign tourists somberly make their way through Cambodian death sites, ex–Khmer Rouge strongholds, defunct torture centers, and former civil war zones.[94] Such outsider excursions make unquestionable a sightseeing fascination with the built remnants and human remains of Pol Pot time. As *National Geographic Today* writer Zoltan Istvan notes,

> In the chronicle of 20th century horrors, Cambodia ranks high. For much of the last three decades, Cambodia has suffered through war, political upheaval and massive genocide. Recently Cambodia has begun to revive. Its dark past is part of the reason: Tourist curiosity about Cambodia's genocide has become big business. ... "There are two things you must see in Cambodia," says Scott Harrison, a traveler from Australia. "Obviously one is Angkor Wat. But the other is the killing fields outside Phnom Penh."[95]

Though visitors to such sites number in the hundreds of thousands, not millions, this emergent atrocity tourism—a by-product of Cambodia's "political upheaval" predicated on a "dark past" and reliant on a widespread knowledge of "massive genocide"—reinforces an aforementioned hellish dimension to the nation's twenty-first-century service industry.[96] Given the large-scale losses suffered by Cambodians during the Democratic Kampuchean era, such spots are ubiquitous. To date, the DC-Cam has located (as part of its fifteen-year-long mapping initiative) 19,733 mass graves (defined as containing "four or more bodies"), 196 Khmer Rouge prison/ detention centers, and 81 survivor memorials.[97]

Indisputably, the growth of atrocity tourism in Cambodia is distressingly not unique. In particular, Cambodia's killing fields represent yet another stop in a long-standing practice of visiting places associated with unspeakable violence, state-authorized death, and state-sanctioned violence. As Philip Stone and Richard Sharpley remind, "death tourism" has included ancient world ventures to gladiatorial spectacles in Rome, tourist treks to postdisaster Pompeii, pilgrimages to public executions in medieval England, and guided expeditions of nineteenth-century Parisian morgues.[98] If the twentieth century is, as Elie Wiesel asserts, one of profound "indifference," it is also one of mass violence, and such unfeeling frames operate in tandem with large-scale human loss.[99] From the Armenian genocide to the Shoah, from the Dominican Republic to Rwanda, from Bangladesh to Bosnia, genocide remains an all-too-familiar outcome of nation-state authoritarianism.

What is more, the proliferation of death tourist sites in a century of genocide intersects with now-familiar macabre locations produced in the calamitous aftermath of political assassination, global war, and international terrorism. Such hindsight places include the likes of President John F. Kennedy's motorcade route in Dallas, Hiroshima's Peace Park, and the crash site for hijacked Pan Am Flight 103 in Lockerbie, Scotland. In a post-9/11 imaginary, atrocity tourist destinations consist of New York City's Ground Zero, the Pentagon Memorial in Washington, D.C., and Stonycreek Township just outside Shanksville, Pennsylvania, the tragic final location for United Airlines Flight 93.

These settings of mass violence and human catastrophe affectively correspond to Malcolm Foley and J. John Lennon's 1996 characterization of "dark tourism," which encapsulates "the presentation and consumption (by visitors) of real and commodified death and disaster sites."[100] Though understood within the field of cultural geography as a subgenre of mainstream tourism, dark tourism (aka macabre tourism, heritage tourism, thanatourism, doom tourism, morbid tourism, or atrocity tourism) is increasingly popular and profitable.[101] As the 1.3 million visitors who traveled to Auschwitz-Birkenau in 2010 highlight, genocide tourism is—in the twenty-first century—a thriving global business.[102]

This is not to suggest that these locations do not have other agendas (e.g., memorial, contemplative, or educational). Instead, the presence of individuals not intimately connected to specific histories of loss (i.e., tourists) necessarily obscures site purpose, blurs intentionality, and obfuscates impact. Such complications and concomitant commodification, manifest in increased admission prices, survivor-guided tours, and on-site souvenirs, underscore the capitalistic contours of contemporary Cambodian genocide remembrance, which is most recognizable in a built landscape punctuated by abandoned Khmer Rouge prisons and punctured by large-scale graves. Cambodia's atrocity tourist industry—increasingly comprised of monuments to Khmer Rouge leaders (e.g., Pol Pot's cremation site), memorials to the regime's victims (stupas), and artifacts of torture (as evident in Tuol Sleng Genocide Museum)—accentuate an economic investment in the Democratic Kampuchean period.

This morbid venture capitalism is epitomized by the privatization of Choeung Ek, Cambodia's largest killing field. In 2005, the Japanese-owned company JC Royal was given a thirty-year contract to manage the memorial site, allowing it to raise admission from $0.50 to $3.00 (U.S.) for foreign tourists, with the concomitant annual agreement that $15,000 would be paid to the municipality of Phnom Penh.[103] Between 2006 and 2007, the Choeung Ek Center for Genocide Crimes generated $621,936 in ticket sales, and the current UN/Cambodian War Crimes Tribunal promises to increase worldwide interest in the Killing Fields site.[104] As 2009 visitor profiles bring to light, Choeung Ek's audience is by and large non-Cambodian: out of an estimated 220,000 visitors, the vast majority (200,000) was foreign.[105]

Not surprisingly, due to the profit-making potential of these sublime spaces, Cambodian would-be entrepreneurs such as Nhem En (the former portrait photographer at Tuol Sleng Prison) have similarly accessed the Khmer Rouge era, confirming former Choeung Ek site manager Neang Say's declaration that "Cambodia has become a place where they use the bones of the dead to make business."[106] Expressly, as the August 2010 *Time Magazine* exposes, En is set to open a private museum in Anlong Veng that "will include, among other things, a walking stick, toilet seat, and sandals he claims belonged to Pol Pot." Though ostensibly committed to "help[ing] illuminate Khmer Rouge history for foreigners and young Cambodians alike," En nevertheless is "offering [his] museum for $2 million to anyone interested in buying it."[107] Uncannily, the mention of "two million" in En's asking price hearkens back to the annual number of tourists who visit Angkor Wat and the 1.7 million who perished during the Democratic Kampuchean era. In spite of the overt commercialism and disruptive everydayness of walking sticks, toilet seats, and sandals, En's museum, like other Khmer Rouge sites, uses the ghastly reputation of the Pol Pot–led regime within the Western (and Cambodian) imagination as legible embodiment of unadulterated, extraordinary evil.[108]

Such efforts to capitalize on the Killing Fields are not limited to enterprising individuals and foreign corporations. Recently, the Cambodian Ministry of Tourism announced plans to rehabilitate fourteen Khmer Rouge–era buildings in Anlong Veng. Imagined as a "theme park devoted to the Khmer Rouge," restored attractions will include Pol Pot's bungalow, a Khmer Rouge propaganda radio station, a munitions warehouse, and Khmer Rouge military general Ta Mok's lakeside compound.[109] Responding to criticisms of insensitive opportunism, Thong Khon (Cambodia's current Minister of Tourism) maintains, "It is right that the government should profit from remaking this historic place."[110] Such "remaking," predicated on the supposed commemorative reconstruction of Khmer Rouge history, is presently driven by the market desires of an atrocity tourist economy.[111] At the same time, with former members of the regime in various levels of government, including (most infamously) Cambodia's current head of state (Prime Minister Sen), the rehabilitation of Democratic Kampuchea by way of restored buildings and artifacts takes on the apolitical registers of what *Time Magazine* reporter Brendan Brady terms "an odd nostalgia for a most deadly regime."[112]

Set against these contexts, to remake—or remember—the Khmer Rouge era in the twenty-first century then is to access a state-authorized version of history that continues to be reliant on (and at times celebratory of) perpetrator notoriety. Within a distinctly Cambodian atrocity tourist milieu, such modes of disreputable remembrance ultimately monumentalize the spectacularly shocking policies, practices, and politics of the Pol Pot–led regime. Even with Youk Chhang's evocative assertion that "genocide should not be commercialized. It is already bad enough to have lived through genocide," Cambodia's Killing Fields are indubitably becoming, as Kevin Doyle characterizes, the country's new "revenue fields," fertile grounds for foreign investment, domestic development, and governmental support.[113] This disconcerting and opportunistic deployment of Khmer Rouge history, which explicitly eschews culturally sensitive contemplation in favor of sideshow profitability, coincides with the original curatorial agendas at work at Tuol Sleng Genocide Museum and the Choeung Ek Center for Genocide Crimes, which remain the two most visited atrocity sites in Cambodia.

The significance of these destination points—affectively measured through sympathy, empathy, and general feeling—is problematically mediated through a hyperactive global tourist practice. Indeed, as David Simmons narrates:

> "What do you feel when you look at these people?" asked the monk, gesturing toward the photos covering the walls of Tuol Sleng Genocide Museum. . . . I didn't have the heart to tell the monk that the photos and the amateurish paintings of various torture methods festooning the walls of Tuol Sleng left me largely unmoved. Why was this? Could it be the overkill of what we might term "atrocity tourism"? For although the outrageous conduct of the Khmer Rouge . . . surely earned them queue-jumping status at the gates of hell, the tourist circuit the world over is dotted with memorials to systemic inhumanity: the concentration camps of

Germany and Poland, Jerusalem's Holocaust Memorial, Thailand's Death Railway, and various assorted abandoned or converted prisons, torture chambers and other atrocity attractions.[114]

Simmons's evaluation of site value, drawn from the vantage point of atrocity tourist, not surprisingly privileges an outsider gaze that in the end ignores the issue of in-country (or nontraveler) remembrance. Likewise, Simmons's flippant remark about "queue-jumping status at the gates of hell," attributed to Khmer Rouge outrageousness, uncritically replicates the hyperbolic dimensions of Colonel Lam's curatorial agenda and contemporary atrocity tourism. As dismissive is the author's critique of "amateurish paintings of various torture methods," which fails to account for the fact that such work is a visual testimonial of crimes against humanity committed on-site. Indeed, these paintings were produced by aforementioned former Tuol Sleng prisoner Vann Nath, whose survival depended on his ability to produce—under extreme duress—portraits of Pol Pot.[115]

Hence, to revise Raymond Williams's well-known affective aphorism, such "structures *for* feeling" are presently curated for non-Cambodian viewers unconcerned with more expansive historical narratives and unaware of the nation's memory politics. As a result, these sites, which are increasingly invested in perpetuating (for tourists and for profit) an atrocity-driven memory of the Khmer Rouge, further dispense with Cambodian-centric reparative remembrance and collective memorialization.[116] Evoking notions of restoration and rehabilitation, such reparation rubrics acknowledge Khmer Rouge wrongdoing and simultaneously provide a public space for mourning and commemoration. Whereas the nation's current atrocity tourist economy relies on the de facto reenactment of perpetrator crimes for *foreign* consumption, what remains elusive—even after Khmer Rouge overthrow, Vietnamese liberation, post-PRK national rehabilitation, and UN tribunal—is a nation-wide, *domestic* contemplation of "these people," or Democratic Kampuchea's victims.

Toward Contemplative Commemoration: Cambodian American Memory Work

Apparent in the original rehabilitation and current usage of Tuol Sleng Genocide Museum and the Choeung Ek Center for Genocide Crimes, the present state of memory affairs in Cambodia is largely characterized by a contested landscape for survivors of Pol Pot time. Haunted by a genocidal past that has not been juridically reconciled, imbued with calls to strategically remember, and increasingly determined by the economic demands of the tourist marketplace, to remember the Killing Fields era in Cambodia is to necessarily engage a history of state-authorized violence, nationally sanctioned erasure, and internationally driven spectacle. In turn, the absence of viable, culturally sensitive memorials in Cambodia renders palpable an in-country crisis of memory. Such a crisis—suggestive of instability and impending catastrophe with regard to remembrance—foregrounds a closing consideration of Cambodian American memory work, which, because of refugee subjectivity and ruptured citizenship, is necessarily produced outside the confines of state-authorized remembrance. If Cambodian American cultural producers labor to remember the Killing Fields era, they are charged—due to their geopolitical distance from the country of origin—with the visionary task of diasporically reconstructing (and transnationally rehabilitating) a legible sense of cultural belonging and social citizenship. In other words, Cambodian American memory work is defined by practices of imagining otherwise that make possible a different articulation of survivor agency committed to the very practice of reparation. As legal rights activist Carla Ferstman (Director of REDRESS) clarifies, "[reparations are] the act of making whole the damage caused to an injured person and is based on the notion that when a wrong occurs there should always be an appropriate remedy that returns the injured to a similar state of affairs prior to the wrong."[117]

Such narratives of survivor agency and reparation are embedded in the curatorial agenda at work in Chicago's Cambodian American Heritage Museum and Killing Fields Memorial, located at 2831 W. Lawrence Avenue. A built monument to Cambodian culture and memorial to its Killing Fields past, the museum provides a template through which to consider Cambodian American identity formation and cultural production. The site currently operates under the aegis of the Cambodian Association of Illinois, a nonprofit establishment originally founded in 1976 as a refugee resettlement organization. To date, the Cambodian Association of Illinois provides social and education services to an estimated five thousand Cambodians and Cambodian Americans and is the only organization of its kind in the Chicago area.[118]

With the help of an anonymous donor, the Cambodian American Heritage Museum and Killing Fields Memorial opened its doors in 2004 and offers, on a daily basis, guided tours of its exhibits.[119] According to the association's Web site, the museum

> raises awareness of the Cambodian genocide and celebrates the renewal of Cambodian community and culture here in the United States. It provides an unforgettable educational experience and offers a place for reflection, healing and celebration of the human spirit. Featured are revolving exhibits that explore the history of Cambodia, the Killing Fields genocide and the journey of Cambodian Americans.[120]

If Tuol Sleng Genocide Museum and the Choeung Ek Center for Genocide Crimes are shaped by perpetrator criminality, characterized by sublime atrocity and delimited to the Khmer Rouge era, the Cambodian American Heritage Museum and Killing Fields Memorial is marked by a different emphasis and temporality. In particular, what is reiterated in the museum is a "history of Cambodia, the Killing Fields genocide and the journey of Cambodian Americans" that expands the before, during, and after schema of the stock Democratic Kampuchean narrative. Further, the site's exterior—which features a traditional Cambodian bas-relief facade—fuses Cambodian decorative architecture to an otherwise unremarkable office building. Consequently, the building reflects a transnational reenvisioning of space, which buttresses a reading of the museum as a distinctly Cambodian American site.

As is clear in the site's mission, central to the museum/memorial's agenda is its commitment to "reflection, healing and celebration of the human spirit." According to museum chairperson Leon Lim, the site represents a means "for people who lost their homeland, families, belongings, and culture to claim their identity and celebrate the lives they've found in Chicago."[121] Following suit, the Cambodian American Heritage Museum and Killing Fields Memorial is shaped by a diasporic sense of renewal inextricably linked to the refugee experience (the "Cambodian community and culture here in the United States"). At the same time, the context provided on-site (revealed by way of placards, exhibition notes, and museum staff) speaks to its more expansive educational mission inclusive of Cambodian and non-Cambodian perspectives. With its concomitant emphasis on "heritage" and "awareness," the museum offers visitors exhibits focused on Khmer culture (iterated through traditional arts, religion, and culinary practices), includes a short documentary film that recounts the post–Democratic Kampuchean refugee experience, and features displays concentrated on daily life in Cambodia.

Visitors are led through the exhibit by a member of the Cambodian Association of Illinois, who tells viewers the historical and cultural significance of various artifacts on display. Because the Cambodian government bans the exportation of ancient Khmer art, the museum showcases reproductions of pieces from Angkor Wat, which are created at the museum by Cambodian artists and staff members. Though the majority of the exhibits are located on one floor of the multistory office building, the tour does lead the visitor to these artist workshops, where one can see half-finished *apsara* statues, reproductions of classical Khmer art, and in-process constructions of high Cambodian architecture. The tour ends with the Killing Fields Memorial, a tall, multipaneled glass structure upon which are etched names of victims who perished in the Khmer Rouge era. As sightseers view the memorial, the tour guide—a Cambodian American refugee and survivor of the regime—narrates his or her own connection to the Democratic Kampuchean era. Visitors are repeatedly and consistently encouraged to ask questions; they are also given instructions with regard to proper religious observances and appropriate commemorative gestures.

The narrative produced by the Cambodian American Heritage Museum and Killing Fields Memorial is predominantly focused on the persistence of Khmer culture and memory in the face of war, genocide, and relocation. Indeed, what is emphasized time and again is the richness of Cambodian high art, the distinctive nature of Khmer traditional crafts, and basic pillars of Cambodian society: religion, family, and education. Whereas Tuol Sleng and Choeung Ek restage the Killing Fields era by way of Khmer Rouge atrocity, the Cambodian American Heritage Museum and Killing Fields Memorial reminds viewers of a more expansive history, which spans the time of Angkor Wat to the present. At the same time, the inclusion of the memorial engages on multiple levels the issue of loss. The names of the victims that appear on the memorial represent a more involved recovery project that aims to identify and commemorate the 1.7 million who died under the Democratic Kampuchean regime. Such remembrance—focused on survivors—is revealed in the museum's future plan to collect oral histories from Cambodian refugees.

Taken together, the Cambodian American Heritage Museum and Killing Fields Memorial represents a particular transnational archive that moves beyond the perpetrator-driven narrative of wholesale ruination promulgated by Tuol Sleng Genocide Museum and the Choeung Center for Genocide Crimes. As a consequence, the museum/memorial makes visible the stakes of Cambodian American cultural production, which likewise attempts to engender an extrastatal site for reparation and remembrance by making whole what has been lost, militating against master narratives of victimhood, and pioneering symbolic forms of justice. Diasporically envisioned, such memory work also exemplifies a transnational cartography shaped by a permeability that allows for alternative narratives of citizenship and genocide remembrance. If, as Kandice Chuh notes, "transnationalism recognizes contemporary flows of capital and information that seemingly find national borders irrelevant and 'patriotic' loyalties displaced from nation-states to differently configured collectivities," then such a category is, with slight revision, uniquely suited to both the Cambodian American Heritage Museum and Cambodian/Cambodian American refugees who, notwithstanding involuntary statelessness, continue to imagine a reparative and restorative home outside the confines of Cambodia and within the boundaries of the United States.[122]

CHAPTER 2

Screening Apology

Cinematic Culpability in *The Killing Fields* and *New Year Baby*

With trepidation, I ask the question that has been churning inside me since that distant April in 1975: "Can you forgive me for not being able to keep you safe in the French Embassy, for leaving Cambodia without you?" "No, no," he says, gripping my hand hard. "It's not like that. Nothing to forgive."

—Sydney Schanberg, "The Death and Life of Dith Pran," reprinted in *Beyond the Killing Fields: War Writings*

The work of healing a country really happens inside each Cambodian. As the Cambodian government and the international community struggle to find justice and healing, individual Cambodians, like those in my family, must do the same. For each of us, it is a different journey. For a very long time, I was stuck on the question: "What does it mean for my family or me to forgive the Khmer Rouge?"

—Socheata Poeuv, "Memory, Justice, and Pardon: What Does it Take to Heal?" *Justice Initiatives*

O N JANUARY 20, 1980, the *New York Times Magazine* published "The Death and Life of Dith Pran: A Story of Cambodia" by *Times* editor, columnist, and correspondent Sydney Schanberg. A Pulitzer Prize–winning journalist, Schanberg received earlier acclaim for his Vietnam War–era reportage. Expressly, the Singapore-based reporter chronicled the collateral damage of U.S. policy in Cambodia by critically detailing in-country volatility under the U.S.-installed Lon Nol regime (1970–75).[1] Notwithstanding Schanberg's previous Cambodian work, the *New York*

Times Magazine piece signaled—by way of perspective and tone—a profound departure for the seasoned war reporter. As the *Times* correspondent admits,

> I pause here to say that this chronicle, of all the stories I have
> written as a journalist, has become the hardest for me to pull out
> of my insides. To describe a relationship such as Pran's and mine
> demands candor and frankness about self, not romantic memories.
> I feel exposed and vulnerable.[2]

Indeed, "The Death and Life of Dith Pran"—the story line basis for Roland Joffé's Academy Award–winning film *The Killing Fields* (1984)—was an emotionally driven first-person remembrance of a friendship forged in the interstices of war, challenged by international nonintervention, and irrevocably impacted by the three-year, eight-month, and twenty-day reign of the Khmer Rouge.[3] Chronologically ordered, "The Death and Life of Dith Pran" takes place before, during, and after the 1975 establishment of Democratic Kampuchea and concentrates on the reporter's relationship with Pran, a former U.S. Army translator turned foreign press assistant.

At the titular level, Schanberg's story of "death and life" is reminiscent of the biblical Lazarus and the U.S. slave narrative (e.g., *Narrative of the Life of Frederick Douglass*), engendering a narrative expectation of resurrection, rescue, and rebirth.[4] Like nineteenth-century predecessor and fellow newspaperman William Lloyd Garrison, Schanberg introduces Pran to his readers, adhering to an established American tradition in which white masculinity is a legitimating subjectivity in minority stories of unimaginable imprisonment and dramatic liberation. Correspondingly, Schanberg corroborates (via first-person narration and incorporated interview) the Cambodian survivor's journey from Khmer Rouge killing fields (a legible site of enslavement) to Thai refugee camp (an identifiable place of transitional freedom). Schanberg summarizes from the very beginning that

> I began the search for my friend Dith Pran in April 1975. Unable to
> protect him when the Khmer Rouge troops ordered Cambodians
> to evacuate their cities, I had watched him disappear into the inte-
> rior of Cambodia, which had become a death camp for millions.
> Dith Pran had saved my life the day of the occupation, and the
> shadow of my failure to keep him safe—to do what he had done
> for me—was to follow me for four and a half years. Then, on

October 3, 1979, Dith Pran crossed the border to Thailand and freedom. This is a story of war and friendship, of the anguish of a ruined country and of one man's will to live.[5]

Haunted by an inability to protect his friend Dith Pran and the "failure to keep him safe," Schanberg concisely establishes the emotional and narrative stakes of his *New York Times Magazine* piece. However, while the journalist maintains that what follows is "a story of war and friendship, of the anguish of a ruined country and of one man's will to live," "The Death and Life of Dith Pran" is *not* a strict journalistic account of life before, during, and after the Democratic Kampuchean regime. Rather, the article is an anguished tale of guilt, abandonment, and reconciliation that, as a deeper consideration makes clear, fits a more expansive constellation of mixed feelings fomented in the disastrous aftermath of the American War in Vietnam, Cambodia, and Laos.

Notwithstanding Schanberg's above-mentioned self-account of individual difficulty and concomitant vulnerability, "The Death and Life of Dith Pran" was in substantial ways not unique. Moreover, despite apolitical authorial declarations to the contrary, the amity-driven exposé was still a politicized "story of Cambodia" that on one level dismissed Vietnam War tactics and criticized U.S. policies in the region. For example, Schanberg stresses in the opening pages of his op-ed that both he and Pran "cared little about local or international politics or about military strategy," instantiating a covert liberal critique of the Vietnam War by way of realpolitik (e.g., "international politics") and U.S. aggression (emblematized by "military strategy").[6] As "The Death and Life of Dith Pran" progresses, Schanberg reasserts this liberal humanitarian position, declaring that he was initially

> drawn to the story . . . [of pre–Khmer Rouge] Cambodia as a nation pushed into the war by other powers, not in control of its destiny, being used callously as battle fodder, its agonies largely ignored as the world focused its attention on neighboring Vietnam. . . . What propelled both of us was the human impact— the 10 year-old orphans in uniforms, carrying rifles almost as tall as themselves; the amputees lying traumatized in filthy, overcrowded hospitals; the skeletal infants rasping and spitting as they died while you watched in the all-too-few malnutrition clinics; and the sleepless, unpaid soldiers taking heavy fire at the front lines,

depending on the "magic" amulets they wore around their necks
while their generals took siestas after long lunches several miles
behind the fighting.[7]

Focused on "human impact" (manifest in descriptions of child soldiers,
fragmented Cambodian bodies, inadequate medical care, and corrupt military officials), Schanberg reiterates a collateral damage reading of the war
that discreetly marries U.S. foreign policy to impending humanitarian crisis. As significant, Schanberg's characterization configures sociopolitical
dissolution in Cambodia to "neighboring Vietnam" and echoes the tenets
of a contemporaneous liberal antiwar movement in the United States.

On another level, whereas Schanberg's "Death and Life of Dith Pran"
commences with a liberal evaluation of the nation's Vietnam War–era
position as "battle fodder," it struggles to maintain this assessment after the
Khmer Rouge takeover, which necessarily coincides with U.S. troop withdrawals in the region and a seeming conclusion to the Vietnam Conflict.
Such political endpoints give way to a more ambivalent imaginary shaped
by international nonintervention and postwar abandonment. As the opening epigraph establishes, Schanberg's chief concern with regard to Pran is
not the failure of U.S. foreign policy but that the war correspondent left
Cambodia without him. Such abandonment encompasses Schanberg's
failure to protect Pran from the collapse of the Lon Nol regime and the
rise of the Khmer Rouge. In so doing, the *Times* reporter assumes the role
of a U.S. soldier, who—given orders to return—must leave behind friends,
colleagues, and allies in the country of conflict. Simultaneously suggestive
of surrendering and withdrawal, the very act of *abandoning*—as discussed
by Schanberg and Pran—intersects with President Gerald Ford's 1975 decision to pull troops out of Vietnam and other parts of Southeast Asia.

Within the realm of American politics, the Vietnam War as catastrophic military event generates a host of interpretations that hinge on
support for political hawks and doves in the United States. For neoconser-
vatives, it is an alleged nonbacking of troops (militarily and domestically)
that is to blame for a U.S. loss. For liberals like Schanberg, the question
is one of policy, which asks whether American troops should have been
there at all and centers on the humanitarian impact of U.S. foreign policy
in Southeast Asia. Be that as it may, Schanberg's guilt over surrendering
Pran to the Khmer Rouge complicates the question of intervention in
the aftermath of authoritarianism and genocide. Indeed, the correspon-

dent's later characterization of the Khmer Rouge as a regime that "turned Cambodia into a nationwide gulag" accesses an anticommunist sensibility fundamental to cold war liberalism.[8]

Admittedly, these bifurcated politics largely remain in the background, and "The Death and Life of Dith Pran" repeatedly returns to the story of two friends separated by forces beyond their control. Even so, such recurring declarations of guilt (made plain in oft-mentioned remorseful statements and constant expressions of regret) cohere with an ambivalent post–Vietnam War script utilized by liberal cultural producers and conservative state actors. Epitomized by the representation of American soldiers and correspondents as confused, unwilling, and ultimately repentant actors in a chaotic cold war play, these redemptive memories reconfigure the war to match what many scholars note is a tactically forgetful narrative of precombat innocence.[9] From Michael Herr's journalistic *Dispatches* (1977) to director Michael Cimino's *The Deer Hunter* (1978), from Francis Ford Coppola's *Apocalypse Now* (1979) to Oliver Stone's *Platoon* (1986) and *Born on the Fourth of July* (1989), the American War in Vietnam (and, by unquestionable proxy, dirty wars in Laos and illicit campaigns in Cambodia) is remembered as the frenzied exception rather than the systematic rule of U.S. foreign policy.

Moreover, these cold war stories—focused on the state-authorized loss of U.S. innocence (linked to mandatory drafts, war resolutions, and hawkish governmentality)—undeniably privilege the tragic toll experienced by American, not Southeast Asian, bodies. Put alternatively, such revisionist reframing casts American soldiers and war correspondents as protagonists in a master narrative of embodied cold war victimhood. To be sure, Southeast Asian bodies figure keenly as background actors in this master narrative. According to Viet Nguyen, the Southeast Asian subject is chiefly relegated to a traumatized supporting role as "a powerless . . . silent figure whose presence is only of isolated significance in the movements of armies, nations, and capital, and one that is ultimately the object of others' politics."[10] Analogously, American subjects are, in amnesiac fashion, the tragic beneficiaries of "others' politics," despite their intimate political, social, and cultural connection to the interventionist nation-state.

As Marita Sturken and Yen Le Espiritu maintain, the Vietnam War as U.S. historical event is difficult to remember precisely because it failed from the beginning to engender a "good war" narrative "in which the United States [as exceptionalist] is . . . triumphant *and* moral."[11] Amid military missteps, within a milieu of human rights violations, and situated after the fall of Saigon, U.S. exceptionalism—reliant on an a priori characterization of the nation-state as unmatched moral paragon—was unviable unless the conflict was retroactively envisioned as a distinct rupture, an exception. Paradoxically, the peacetime rehabilitation of American wartime subjects fits a more expansive restoration of idealized American selfhood. Such sentimental citizenship (inclusive of liberal and conservative perspectives) is constructed through a reading of inherent democratic virtue pathologically interrupted by a set of inimitable circumstances: executive-level mismanagement (presidential folly), domestic discontent (expressly antiwar protest), and subsequent nonsupport (defunding and military withdrawals).[12]

These supposedly exclusive conditions presage Ronald Reagan's codification of a Vietnam Syndrome during his 1980 presidential campaign, wherein fiasco over there was attributable to a catastrophic lack of commitment over here. As Reagan proclaimed, "thousands of boat people have shown us . . . there is no freedom in the so-called peace in Vietnam. The hill people of Laos know poison gas, not justice, and in Cambodia there is only the peace of the grave for at least one-third of the population slaughtered by the Communists."[13] Missing from Reagan's declaration is the extent to which U.S. foreign policy and military intervention was directly responsible for making Vietnamese "boat people" through ideologically driven war. Furthermore, covert campaigns in Laos and illegal bombings in Cambodia unquestionably foreground the contemporaneous experiences of Laotian "hill people" (the Hmong) and mass violence in Democratic Kampuchea. Divergently, this cold war hindsight characterization of the American War in Vietnam prefigures a curative foundation for future interventionist policy.

Illustratively, in the aftermath of the first Persian Gulf War (1990–91), Reagan's Republican successor, George H. W. Bush, triumphantly averred, "By God, we've kicked the Vietnam Syndrome once and for all."[14] Consequently, President Bush—as Isabelle Pelaud rightly surmises— "gave the signal to future administrations that it is possible to continue intervening militarily, economically, and culturally in the Middle East, Latin America, Africa, and Asia."[15] Even with weighty foreign policy implications, the narrative foundation for the Vietnam Syndrome—predicated on loss, premised on grief, and negotiated through apologist frames— brings into focus a sentimental albeit strategic manipulation of traumatic wartime narratives that move beyond the borders of Vietnam and encompass Cambodia's killing fields. In turn, the affective reconfiguration of regrettable yet justifiable U.S. aggression calls attention to the contested terrain of U.S. cultural memory and the Vietnam War.

In the face of others' politics, what remains constant is the alchemical recuperation of the American subject from military aggressor to militant humanitarian. This affective transformation undergirds an in-depth consideration of Schanberg's "Death and Life of Dith Pran." Moreover, this emotional schema foregrounds a close reading of Roland Joffé's cinematic adaptation, *The Killing Fields,* which likewise employs a legible savior/victim frame that begins with realpolitik but concludes with apolitical answers to problems of U.S. imperialism, international nonintervention, and Khmer Rouge authoritarianism. In particular, a distinct humanitarian resolution—which eschews complex geopolitics in favor of amity-driven negotiations between Schanberg and Pran—renders visible an unintentional articulation of what I term cold war apologetics. Premised on a two-sided understanding of apology (as an expression of remorse and an excuse for problematic action), suggestive of a distinct temporality (the cold war), and rooted in argumentation (rhetoric), these apologetics seemingly reconcile (after the fact) the failures of U.S. foreign policy by way of an ostensibly universal humanism and humanitarianism. As the juxtaposition of "The Death and Life of Dith Pran" and Joffé's *Killing Fields* makes clear, each production (notwithstanding liberal cultural agendas) ends with an exceptionalist narrative of reunion, salvation, and redemption.

These tropes of universal humanism and humanitarianism are evident in reader reactions to "The Death and Life of Dith Pran." Specifically, Schanberg's amity-driven chronicle elicited a slew of positive reactions, emblematized by Nobel Laureate Elie Wiesel's short yet poignant response. In the *New York Times* "Letters to the Editor" section (published February 24, 1980), Wiesel averred, "I have rarely been so moved: Sydney Schanberg's treatment of suffering and friendship is masterful. I am leaving shortly for Cambodia. Mr. Schanberg's words will remain with me."[16] Wiesel's reaction was echoed by fellow reader Nelson A. Navarro (from New York City), who analogously opined, "For all the human tragedy that has been the fate of Cambodia—and the United States, and us all—the story of Sydney Schanberg's friendship for Dith Pran represents a redeeming human triumph." Navarro added, "People are capable of extreme cruelty; that we know only too well; but we tend to forget that they—we—

are also capable of so much love."[17] Acknowledging the dramatic power
of Schanberg's first-person account of Pran's "death" under Democratic
Kampuchea and his rebirth in a Thai refugee camp, Wiesel and Navarro's
readings of "friendship," "human tragedy," and "human triumph" troublingly rescript the article's apolitical conclusions, which emphasize uni-
versality over specific circumstance and privilege affect over U.S. foreign
policy failures.

Concomitantly, this romantic vision of reconciliation through apolitical friendship settles on the refugee subject (Pran), who in the end is the
model minority recipient of American asylum. Such humanitarian frames
inadvertently mask significant questions about American responsibility,
U.S. culpability, and international accountability, fomenting the amnesiac
registers of the Cambodian Syndrome with regard to the Killing Fields
era. Expressly, if the era of the Killing Fields is allegedly the unimaginable
outcome of others' politics, it is also a retroactive space to envision *our*
politics. When co-opted by conservatives, the rise of the Khmer Rouge
is not attributable to U.S. intervention; instead, it is the direct consequence—as war on terror hawks such as President George W. Bush
assert—of American troop withdrawals in the final stages of the Vietnam
War.[18] At the same time, the question of others' politics opens the door to
liberal frames of universal human rights and interventionist humanitarianism that address the effect—and not the cause—of conflict and crisis.

Moreover, if Pran's final location bespeaks an idealized saved position,
Schanberg's location as primary narrator and principle actor in both "The
Death and Life of Dith Pran" and *The Killing Fields* reinforces a dominant
position for the American subject. Affectively, Schanberg's guilt operates
in equal relation to Pran's traumatic story of survival. The journalist relates,
"in the months and years" that followed his departure from Cambodia,
he experienced a "recurring nightmare" wherein he "awak[es], thinking of
elaborate stratagems I might have used to keep [Pran] safe and with me.
I am a survivor who cannot cope with surviving."[19] Similarly, the task of
remembering Pol Pot time is afforded the *Times* correspondent, who, entrusted with the burden of documentation, controls the narrative means
of historical production. As Schanberg reveals in the opening paragraphs
of his *Times* account,

> Pran wants the story told of what has happened, and is still hap-
> pening, to his people. He wants to talk about the unthinkable
> statistic that Cambodia has become: an estimated three million

or more people, out of a population of seven million in 1975, have been massacred or have died of starvation or disease.[20]

In the above passage, although Pran "wants the story told," within the narrative imaginary of "The Death and Life of Dith Pran" the act of articulation falls on Schanberg.[21] Notwithstanding Pran's significant role in narrating the genocide to a large audience (after all, the Cambodian survivor is credited with coining the term "the Killing Fields"), he does so by way of Schanberg, who becomes both principle narrator and prominent state actor in "The Death and Life of Dith Pran" and *The Killing Fields* film.

In due course, Schanberg's central role assumes a proprietary register, which persists in concluding scenes involving a reunited Schanberg and Pran. As the introductory epigraph by Schanberg makes plain, integral to "The Death and Life of Dith Pran" is a circuitous, teleological story of apology, in which the reporter asks for forgiveness and the Cambodian survivor stresses that there is "nothing to forgive." Tellingly, it is the American Schanberg—and not the Cambodian survivor Pran—who becomes the chief recipient of reparative justice. Reminiscent of making whole what has been ruptured, this reparation renders complete Schanberg's relationship to Pran and assuages his guilt about leaving him behind. At the same time, "The Death and Life of Dith Pran" and *The Killing Fields* produce— via cold war apologetics—a master narrative of Democratic Kampuchea outside Cambodia that ultimately privileges (notwithstanding liberal and conservative politics) American subjectivity and leaves unattended larger issues of genocide remembrance, juridical nonaction, and Cambodian agency.

Within this open-ended, apologetic imaginary, documentarian Socheata Poeuv pointedly refocuses the attention of reparation and reconciliation on survivors of the Killing Fields era. If, as Elazar Barkan asserts, the "road to reconciliation begins with acknowledgement," and "apology reifies the memory of the conflict and validates the identity of victims *as victims*" (emphasis added), then Poeuv's stress on the ability (and inability) to forgive in the opening epigraph engenders a different site for reparation that rehabilitates survivors vis-à-vis a heretofore unexpressed Cambodian agency.[22] Specifically, whereas "The Death and Life of Dith Pran" and *The Killing Fields* are invested in apology as a means to a reconciled American end, Poeuv's *New Year Baby* (2006) is a film circumscribed by the filmmaker's evocative opening question, "What does it mean for my family or me to forgive the Khmer Rouge?"

Predicated on the regime's policy of forced marriage, *New Year Baby* commences with the revelation that Poeuv's siblings have a different father who perished during the Khmer Rouge era. This revelation of distinct paternity serves as a catalyst for a family trip to Cambodia, and the film follows Poeuv, her mother, her father, and her brother as they return to past residences in Phnom Penh, the Cambodian countryside, and former labor camps. As the film progresses, *New Year Baby* becomes a Cambodian American story of rupture and survivor resilience, set against a backdrop of familial trauma, collective remembrance, and communal healing. To be sure, what initially links "The Death and Life of Dith Pran" and *The Killing Fields* to *New Year Baby* is the extent to which the Democratic Kampuchean era (and, by necessity, the Cambodian genocide) is literally screened, strategically staged, and tactically projected by way of guilt, apology, and reconciliation.

Even with narrative and cinematic coherences (at the level of history, subject, and theme), asymmetrical points of historical entry contradistinguish Schanberg's article and Joffé's film from Poeuv's *New Year Baby*. Moreover, these temporal deviations determine a divergent set of apologetics by way of American, Cambodian, and Cambodian American bodies. For Schanberg and Joffé, the American War in Vietnam is a starting point and guiding frame for considering the Cambodian genocide, yet both texts problematically privilege American actors. Paradoxically, "The Death and Life of Dith Pran" and *The Killing Fields* narrate a largely apolitical story of life under the Khmer Rouge, revealed in each production's emphasis on individualized reconciliation and transcendent friendship. Alternatively, in *New Year Baby*, Cambodian subjects take center stage, and their personal negotiations with the recent genocide past underscore a collective problem with current modes of and contemporary routes to state-authorized justice. These polemics, rooted in processes of apology and forgiveness, presage an otherwise reading of reconciliation through the cinematic acknowledgment of survivor agency.

Restaging U.S. Culpability: Roland Joffé's *The Killing Fields*

Nearly four years after the publication of Sydney Schanberg's "Death and Life of Dith Pran," *The Killing Fields* premiered at New York City's Cinema 1 on November 2, 1984. As *New York Times* reporter Samuel Freedman observed in a prerelease commentary, *The Killing Fields* represented "the first attempt by a commercial film to grapple with the Cambodian geno-cide."[23] Distributed by Warner Bros., produced by David Puttnam (pre-viously of *Chariots of Fire* fame), and directed by British documentarian Roland Joffé, the film featured Sam Waterston as protagonist Sydney Schanberg. The American side of *The Killing Fields* cast was comprised of John Malkovich, Spaulding Gray, and Craig T. Nelson, who filled support-ing roles as a Western photojournalist, a U.S. diplomat, and an American military attaché, respectively. Amid cold war tensions in the Vietnamese-ruled People's Republic of Kampuchea and in light of ongoing struggles with still-active Khmer Rouge, *The Killing Fields* was filmed (on location) in Thailand. This geographic fact explains the cinematic (and potentially problematic) choice to cast Thais (not Cambodians) as displaced Phnom Penh residents, labor camp denizens, and Khmer Rouge cadres.[24]

Bruce Robinson's adapted screenplay closely corresponded to Sydney Schanberg's source text vis-à-vis setting (Cambodia, Democratic Kampuchea, and in the United States), temporality (before, during, and after the Khmer Rouge era), and sentimentality (comprised of guilt, re-morse, and redemption). The portrayal of Angka—as authoritarian, geno-cidal body politic—was made explicit in the film's revised title, which (to briefly recount) emerged from Pran's own characterization of Khmer Rouge labor camps, reeducation centers, and execution sites. Befitting Joffé's documentary film background, *The Killing Fields* was the product of meticulous research. Indeed, the film's director, producer, and screen-writer conducted comprehensive interviews with Schanberg and Pran. Likewise, Sam Waterston reportedly "spent almost a week with the *real* Sydney Schanberg and read all of his notebooks and dispatches from Cambodia" (emphasis added). In addition, Joffé read Pol Pot's writings, screened contemporaneous East German/Yugoslavian film footage of the regime, and interviewed Cambodian refugees in Thailand, Europe, and the United States. The final production—punctuated by chaotic cityscapes, barren landscapes, and shallow graves—brought together historical, indi-vidual, and collective remembrances of "life under the Khmer Rouge."[25]

In ostensible contrast, Haing S. Ngor—who eventually assumed Dith Pran's on-screen persona—purportedly "never even met the man he would recreate on film."[26] A regime survivor and recent Cambodian refu-gee, Ngor had no acting experience, yet his comparable story of survival, escape, and resettlement proved providential. As *Killing Fields* cast-ing director Pat Golden recalled, "months [were spent] . . . scour[ing] the Cambodian expatriate communities in California, New York, and Washington, D.C." before she found Ngor at a Cambodian wedding in Oxnard, California.[27] When the former Cambodian doctor finally completed a screen test, Golden, Puttnam, and Joffé were impressed by a seamless "authenticity" in his performance, no doubt the result of Ngor's own experiences in Democratic Kampuchean labor camps.[28] Such spaces were certainly traumatic for Ngor, who—like other Cambodian survivors—experienced incredible personal loss: his fiancée and the majority of his family were among the 1.7 million who perished under the regime.[29]

Not surprisingly, when Ngor assumed the role of Pran, he simultaneously relived his own story of survival.[30] This mimetic slippage is discernible in an account involving Ngor and a Thai actress (who played a child informant). Following a tense scene wherein Pran's garden is uprooted and summarily destroyed (as per an extreme policy of collectivization whereby individual ownership was strictly prohibited), Ngor reportedly ran off set. Soon after, Ngor stridently insisted to Joffé that the actress *was* a Khmer Rouge soldier, temporarily halting that day's production. As Freedman explains, Ngor was disturbed by the child's "flat, dead eyes," which reminded him of "the eyes of the thousands of children in the Khmer Rouge." According to the *New York Times* journalist, this recollection prompted an involuntary memory of "the horrors both he and Mr. Dith had actually endured."[31] By stressing a shared subjectivity—at the level of horrors and endurance, between Ngor and Pran—Freedman gestures toward the film's representational politics, which in part engendered an iconographic reading of the Killing Fields era through characterizations of interchangeable Khmer Rouge perpetrators and universal Cambodian victimhood.

If the Ngor/Pran conflation underscores a transposable figurative politics, then it also reaffirms the documentarian frames at work in *The Killing Fields*. To reiterate, the film's true-to-life depictions were the collective outcome of a *collected* Cambodian refugee experience. Such communal selfhood was composed of intimate contacts with state-authorized violence during the Democratic Kampuchean era. In related fashion, *The Killing Fields* (as cinematic production) from the beginning drew emotional power from Ngor's *authenticated* intimacy, evident in the actor's postproduction assertion that, "For me, movie not different. . . . I have enough experience in Communist times. I put emotion into the movie. We have a lot of scenes like in Khmer Rouge time. Everything the same."[32] Ngor's

ability to "put emotion into the movie" and relate authentic intimacy
was praised by critics and industry insiders. As *Time Magazine* reviewer
Richard Schickel declared, "Ngor . . . brings a natural gift and memories
of his own torments by the Khmer Rouge to this role."[33] Such inherent
commendation was echoed by an anonymous *Variety* critic who—notwithstanding the negative assertion that the film's "overall aesthetic . . .
does not go in for nuances of character"—maintained that Ngor was "a
naturally sympathetic and camera-receptive man" who "effectively carries
the weight of the film's most important sequences."[34] In light of such commendation, Ngor's performance (not surprisingly) garnered him the 1985
Academy Award for Best Supporting Actor.[35]

In his acceptance speech, Ngor restated for fellow attendees and millions of television viewers his meteoric rise from Cambodian refugee to
A-list movie actor. Accordingly, the doctor turned actor passionately
avowed,

> This unbelievable, but so is my entire life. I wish to thank all mem-
> ber of Motion Picture Academy for this great honor. I thank David
> Puttnam, Roland Joffé for giving me this chance to act for the first
> time in "The Killing Fields." And I share this award to my friend Sam
> Waterston, Dith Pran, Sydney Schanberg, and also Pat Golden, that
> casting lady who found me for this role. And I thank Warner Bros.
> for helping me tell my story to the world, let the world know what
> happened in my country. And I thank God Buddah that tonight I'm
> even here. Thank you very much. Thank you.[36]

Given the forum (the 57th Annual Academy Awards), Ngor's speech fit a
typical Hollywood script, wherein directors, producers, fellow actors, production companies, and casting agents are acknowledged. Even so, Ngor's
concluding lines—which credit Warner Bros. for helping him tell his story
to the world and letting the world know what happened in his country—
reinforce the film's narrative stakes, which were committed to publiciz-
ing (by way of cinematic storytelling and liberal politics) Cambodia's
largely forgotten genocide history. Consequently, the film—which to
date remains the most well-known production about the Cambodian
genocide—functions as the primary mode (i.e., master narrative) through
which the Killing Fields era is cinematically remembered and culturally
accessed within the dominant U.S. imagination.

The resonance of *The Killing Fields* as cinematic master narrative is to some extent attributable to its Vietnam War–era politics, apparent in the film's legible (albeit somewhat controversial) critique of U.S. foreign policy. In particular, Joffé's film maps an expansive cartography that fixes American policies of military aggression and international nonintervention to the disastrous rise of the Khmer Rouge. Furthermore, regardless of Ngor's previous categorization of "Khmer Rouge time," anticommunist sentiment is largely absent in *The Killing Fields*. Instead, the film complicates bifurcated cold war politics via a critical interpretation of and direct engagement with U.S. militarism. Apropos a cinematic exposé, such representations are evident in aftermath scenes of American bombings, real-time footage of President Nixon's denial of a Cambodian invasion, and Schanberg's past and present statements concerning U.S. military intervention and concomitant culpability.

Even so, Joffé's public responses to politicized criticism, coupled with the film's use of Southeast Asian war tropes and frames, inadvertently recast Cambodia (and by proxy, its history) as a multivalent sideshow vis-à-vis the American War in Vietnam. Within a milieu of foreign policy critique, contemporaneous conservative and moderate viewers questioned whether *The Killing Fields* was an anti-American film. In response, the British director clarified,

> The film isn't anti-American; it's anti-ideology. . . . The argument
> is that the degree of bombing on a peasant country creates a kind
> of distress and a fury. The average age of the Khmer Rouge troops
> that came into Phnom Penh was 17, and those troops had
> 75 per cent casualties. That would psychologically affect you. What
> the film is saying is that the world isn't filled with strange and
> bizarre acts for no reason.[37]

Stressing that *The Killing Fields* "isn't anti-American" but rather "anti-ideology," Joffé dialogically situates U.S. foreign policy and attendant realpolitik alongside Khmer Rouge authoritarianism. Correspondingly, the United States is, despite markedly different political registers, ideologically connected to the Khmer Rouge. Alternatively, Joffé's claim that the "average age of the Khmer Rouge troops . . . was 17" presages an adolescent reading of child soldiers. This characterization of assumed naiveté coheres with Joffé's previous allusion to Cambodia as a "peasant country," calling forth a first world/third world binary. In a more progressive vein, Joffé unflinchingly attributes the rise of the Khmer Rouge to U.S. militarization, foregrounding a cause-and-effect relationship between "distress," "fury," and "strange and bizarre acts."

Nevertheless, the film's causal critiques of cold war politics are made less stable by the director's subsequent depiction of Pol Pot, which chiefly relies on a hierarchical, pathological reading of Brother Number One. As Joffé maintains,

> I think the most terrifying thing in Pol Pot's writing . . . was the outstanding mediocrity and crudeness. One realized a mind that mediocre couldn't see the ridiculousness of his ideas. It was close to being psychotic. The other thing I detected in Pol Pot was an intense nationalism and traces of paranoia—paranoia of the West, of Vietnam, of Thailand, even of China. Pol Pot had the idea of rebuilding the ancient peasant empire of Angkor Wat. He became an expression of the terror and hysteria of a whole country just as Hitler did.[38]

Emphasizing Pol Pot's "outstanding mediocrity and crudeness," Joffé depicts the Angka leader through hyperbolic declarations of genocidal evil, rooted in mentions of profound psychosis, paranoia, terror, and hysteria. On one level, Joffé's characterization, which cartographically castigates Pol Pot's paranoia via "the West," "Vietnam," "Thailand," and "China," all the same stresses the international politics at play before, during, and after the Khmer Rouge era. These histories bear the mark of French colonization; likewise, such pasts are made politically complicated by U.S. militarization, the Vietnam War, and the Kampuchean-Vietnamese War. Moreover, Joffé rightly acknowledges Chinese support of the regime and recognizes Thailand's postconflict role (e.g., refugee camps).

On another level, notwithstanding Pol Pot's irrefutable role in the making of the Cambodian genocide, Joffé's portrayal inadvertently emphasizes a reading of "ridiculousness" that fails to account for how the regime's reign of terror was institutionally facilitated, militarily supported, and internationally enabled by large-scale global indifference. What is more, the director's assertion of extreme folly unfairly and inaccurately indicts those who were conscripted (without choice) into the Khmer Rouge and forced to live under the tenets of the Democratic Kampuchean regime. Last, but certainly not least, Joffé's analogous framing of Pol Pot and Hitler relies on a nonspecific although recognizable political shorthand. Such economic treatments of despotism problematically conflate dictatorial communism with authoritarian fascism despite prevailing historical realities. Indeed, fundamental to the far-right politics of fascist ideology was an all-encompassing disavowal of the left, making at least politically unfeasible a connection between Pol Pot and Hitler.

Nevertheless, Joffé's response makes visible a culturally viable analogy rooted in the polemical interstices of genocide-oriented memory work. Unquestionably, remembering (and, in the case of *The Killing Fields*, restaging) state-authorized violence often involves an interrogative and historicized reconsideration of how it could happen and why it occurred. Following suit, these causal factors determine a critical examination of *The Killing Fields*, which (as cinematic text) aims to remember the rise and fall of the Khmer Rouge in the imagistic aftermath of the Vietnam War.[39] Concomitantly, Joffé's comments, concerned with and concentrated on ideology, simultaneously promulgate a diagnostic reading of cold war doctrine that intersects with the unsettled question of U.S. culpability and Khmer Rouge responsibility through pathology. If the very act of diagnosing involves an evaluation of one's history and a concomitant assessment of causal factors, then *The Killing Fields* likewise investigates the Cambodian case through two interconnected, prerevolutionary narratives: the American campaign in Southeast Asia and the Cambodian civil war (between Lon Nol soldiers and the Khmer Rouge).

These investigative frames are evident in the theatrical trailer for *The Killing Fields*, which—given the genre—conveniently outlines (in truncated fashion) the film's primary political and cultural stakes. Aurally, the preview commences with Waterston's summation of Cambodia, wherein the *New York Times* reporter solemnly narrates the burst nature of the Vietnam War:

Cambodia. To many Westerners, it seemed a paradise. Another world, a secret world. But the war in neighboring Vietnam burst its borders, and the fighting soon spread to neutral Cambodia. In 1973, I went to cover this sideshow struggle as foreign correspondent of the *New York Times*. It was there, in the war-torn countryside amidst the fighting between government troops and the Khmer Rouge guerilllas, that I met my guide and interpreter, Dith Pran. A man who was to change my life in a country that I grew to love and pity.

Illustratively, the trailer opens with three scenes screened in relatively rapid succession. These include a vignette featuring a lone female figure who labors in an isolated rice paddy, a cinematic portrait of a child (wearing a military helmet) who sits atop a water buffalo, and a shot involving four black helicopters in a wide blue sky. Pertaining to the first image, the frame, overwhelmed by the expansive green of a rice paddy and high palm trees, bespeaks a stock Southeast Asian topography found in Vietnam War films. This generic landscape focus is rendered geographically specific by Waterston's verbal declaration that "Cambodia" was "to many Westerners . . . a paradise," instantiating an idyllic appraisal of the nation in line with Joffé's previous characterization of a "peasant country."

The trailer then shifts to another rural scene involving the above-mentioned child figure. Straining under the weight of an adult-sized military helmet, the child focuses his attention on a forming storm cloud in the distance. This scene (which, like the voice-over, actually opens the full-length film version) features Waterston's observation that Cambodia was "another world, a secret world." Consequently, the *Killing Fields* actor reinforces an interpretation of the Southeast Asian country by way of non-Western alterity. When situated against the director's adolescent characterization of Khmer Rouge soldiers, the figure of the child epitomizes an analogously naive configuration. The actor's mention of "a secret world" becomes more significant when placed adjacent to covert bombings of the Cambodian countryside under the Nixon administration. Transitionally, the foreboding nature of the storm cloud prefigures the next trailer image, timed to fit Waterston/Schanberg's contention that "the war in neighboring Vietnam burst its borders, and the fighting soon spread to neutral Cambodia." Taken together, Waterston—within the span of approximately ten seconds—charts Cambodia's recent political past, from pre-1970 neutrality to increasing volatility under the Lon Nol regime.

These historical frames underscore a national (and international) trajectory from peacetime nonalignment to forced wartime involvement. Visually, this narrative is perceptible via an idealized agricultural scene (the rice paddy vignette). Mediating such frames is an implied militarization (the helmeted child) that ultimately concludes with an overt representation of the American military-industrial complex. The somber registers of Waterston's opening voice-over cohere with the monotonous beat of Mike Oldfield's stark score. As the trailer progresses, this solitary sound is gradually overwhelmed by the disruptive din of helicopter blades, which function as aural signifiers of both U.S. military intervention and approaching civil war. Parenthetically, in view of the film's focus on wartime atrocity and genocide, Oldfield proved an especially interesting compositional choice: prior to *The Killing Fields,* Oldfield scored the 1973 horror classic *The Exorcist.*

While Waterston solemnly relates that "the war in neighboring Vietnam burst its borders," the preview moves to a scene involving four black Huey helicopters, which exemplify the multinational reaches of the American War in Vietnam. Predictably, what follows are supporting images of war and militarization. As spectacular explosions erupt in undisclosed countryside locations and Phnom Penh streets, smoke and debris overwhelm background shots. As guerrilla troops march in single file over a scorched landscape, Schanberg and Pran dart behind sandbag barricades to avoid sporadic gunfire. This metonymic treatment of combat through image and shot corresponds to and strengthens Waterston's politicized characterization of Cambodia as a "sideshow struggle." The mention of conflict coincides with an image of Waterston/Schanberg's passport photograph, reiterating the journalist's movement across borders, and foregrounds a closing narrative focus on Dith Pran (as portrayed by Haing S. Ngor).

A frantic Waterston/Schanberg furiously types in a nondescript hotel room, and Pran, armed with a concerned facial expression, enters the frame via stage left. Pran's cinematic entrance coincides with Waterston's final assertion that the foreign press assistant was "to change my life in a country that I grew to love and pity." Along these lines, Waterston (as Schanberg) configures Ngor (as Pran) through a foreign-born country love and amity-driven sentiment. Immediately following Waterston/ Schanberg's affective declaration, the trailer shifts to excerpted scenes that involve brief exchanges between Schanberg and Pran, representations of U.S. withdrawal (helicopters readying for landings atop an embassy building), barren portraits of Khmer Rouge labor camps, snapshots of New York City (associated with Waterston/Schanberg), and shots of Democratic Kampuchea (linked to Ngor/Pran).

Even with this visual particularity, the theatrical trailer ultimately fails to engender a transparent narrative engagement with Cambodia's genocidal history. Instead, the preview (and, by necessary extension, the entire film) stresses a country on the brink of dissolution and chaos. As significantly, such decontextualized emphases repeatedly quote dominant (and Pulitzer Prize–winning) photographic representations of the American War in Vietnam. Indeed, as deeper contextualization and a close reading

of three scenes highlight, *The Killing Fields* continually draws from a recognizable Vietnam War photographic archive, epitomized by images of
public executions, harried evacuations, black helicopter fleets, and village
massacres. As a result, the express intent of the film—to cinematically remember the Killing Fields—is in some measure obscured, buttressing a
reading of cold war apologetics. Inclusive of culpability and simultaneous
justification, such apologetics address the prima facie conditions of war
without a sustained consideration of legacy, memory, and ongoing trauma.

A Useable Past: The Vietnam War and Screening *The Killing Fields*

In "The Wall, the Screen, and the Image: The Vietnam Veterans Memorial,"
Marita Sturken initially evaluates American postwar public remembrance
using Sigmund Freud's characterization of "screen memory." Such memory, as Sturken summarizes, "functions to hide highly emotional memory"
that "conceals while offering itself as a substitute."[40] Rooted in revision,
shaped by inaccurate reflection, and based on retroactive characterization, screen memory becomes the sutured sublimation of remembrance
and forgetfulness. Underscoring its multivalent function as noun and
verb, Sturken notes that a "screen" represents a "surface that is projected
upon" and pertains to "an object that hides something from view, that
shelters or protects." Militarily, a screen refers to a specific troop formation "used to cover the movements of an army."[41] Situated adjacent this
memory-oriented milieu, Joffé's film about the Democratic Kampuchean
era analogously offers itself as a politicized, screened memorial. Grounded
in the history of the American War in Vietnam, concentrated on American
and Cambodian bodies that journalistically cover army movements, and
invested in recuperating savior/survivor frames, *The Killing Fields* projects
a mode of genocide remembrance that "hides from view" a concomitant
forgetting.

Expressly, the film's emphasis on U.S. culpability vis-à-vis cold war realpolitik potently reminds viewers of the disastrous impact of American
policy in Cambodia and Southeast Asia. Nevertheless, as the preceding
analysis of the theatrical trailer underscores, the movie's imagistic reliance on a recognizable Vietnam War archive unintentionally obscures a
complex set of in-country politics integral to Pol Pot time. This historical
and historicized elision is observable in Roger Ebert's review, wherein the
noted *Chicago Sun-Times* critic observed:

The American experience in Southeast Asia has given us a great
film epic (APOCALYPSE NOW) and a great drama (THE DEER
HUNTER). Here is the story told a little closer to the ground, of
people who were not very important and not very powerful, who
got caught up in events that were indifferent to them, but never
stopped trying to do their best and their most courageous.[42]

By critically locating *The Killing Fields* alongside Coppola's *Apocalypse Now*
and Cimino's *The Deer Hunter,* Ebert utilizes an interchangeable appraisal
of Cambodia's violent past and the catastrophic failure of the Vietnam War
through the "American experience in Southeast Asia." Along these lines,
Ebert's evaluation replicates the interpretive work in Sydney Schanberg's
"Death and Life of Dith Pran," which similarly privileges American—not
Cambodian—bodies.

Additionally, Ebert's summation that *The Killing Fields* is principally
about "people who were not very important and not very powerful" and
individuals "who got caught up in events that were indifferent to them"
restages the Cambodian genocide via an instantly familiar Vietnam War
account. In situating *The Killing Fields* within a cinematic pantheon of
other American experiences in Southeast Asia, the *Chicago Sun-Times*
reviewer unintentionally eschews historical specificity (Pol Pot time) in
favor of a flattened genre consideration (the "typical" Vietnam War film).
These compacted analyses are in part attributable to the relatively quick
and constant circulation of Vietnam War films in the years following the
April 30, 1975 Fall of Saigon. As Eikoh Ikui argues, from *Taxi Driver* (1976)
to *Rolling Thunder* (1977), from *Coming Home* (1978) to *The Deer Hunter,*
and from *Apocalypse Now* to *First Blood* (1982), films about the Vietnam
War increasingly make visible an *Americanized* investment in traumatic
remembrance.

Historically, such assimilated narratives culturally countered contemporaneous foreign policies of "Vietnamization" under the Nixon administration. According to Ikui, *The Deer Hunter* in particular "personalized
the war itself in the figures of [its] heroes," which in emblematic fashion
"transformed the Vietnam War into an 'American' war."[43] Admittedly, this
foreign policy revision also involved a problematic class politics linked
to Vietnam Syndrome dynamics. As Robert G. Lee maintains, "the myth
that America lost the war in southeast Asia because it had been betrayed
by the liberal elite mobilizes a populist working-class rejection of liberal

economic and social policy and lays the foundation for an attempt to re-store American hegemony by revitalizing an undivided American peo-ple."[44] Following suit, the restoration (or rehabilitation) of U.S. hegemony involved an indivisible characterization of the Vietnamese, foreground-ing *The Deer Hunter*'s sideshow treatment of Vietnamese bodies as inhu-mane, cruel, and illegible subjects. In slight contrast, Joffé's film eschews working-class solidarity in favor of bourgeois camaraderie, exemplified by Schanberg and Pran's like-mindedness with regard to U.S. foreign policy and the Khmer Rouge, Schanberg's occupation (as *New York Times* cor-respondent), and express familial connections (as married men with children).

Even with classed differences, the inimical characterization of the Vietnamese in *The Deer Hunter* inadvertently prefigures a similar depic-tion of the Khmer Rouge in *The Killing Fields,* who for the most part lack reason, individualized thought, and empathy.[45] In the same way, the trau-matic recuperation of working-class American soldiers affectively echoes the middle-class Schanberg's rehabilitation from self-interested *New York Times* reporter to compassionate humanitarian. As a closer examination of three scenes makes clear, these narrative emphases locate the Cambodian genocide within a larger Americanized narrative of military folly and mili-taristic disaster. Equally important, the allusion to and eventual dismissal of U.S. culpability in the film's concluding moments fits an ambiguous ma-trix of nonpolitical humanitarian politics fundamental to a nascent cold war neoliberalism. Embedded in an undeniable critique of U.S. foreign policy, such neoliberalism privileges a decidedly nongovernmental solu-tion to the Khmer Rouge period. The overt expression of these neoliberal politics aptly takes place in the stateless parameters of the refugee camp, the setting for the film's final scene.

Continuing with Sturken's screen-oriented consideration, *The Killing Fields*'s eventual disavowal of state culpability remains hidden amid its symptomatic treatment of the American War in Vietnam, which spans both liberal and conservative characterizations of a Vietnam Syndrome. Unquestionably, *The Killing Fields* as cinematic narrative is a pathological story of state-authorized violence and individualized trauma. On one level, such diagnostic frames are revealed through a specific medical motif—the Red Cross—that typifies a nongovernmental stateless site of international humanitarianism. From U.S. bomb sites to the Khmer Rouge takeover of Phnom Penh, from its absence in the Killing Fields to its hyperpresence in Thai refugee camps, the appearance of the Red Cross operates as a neo-liberal index upon which to evaluate mass violence, authoritarianism, and liberation. On another level, *The Killing Fields* also maps—through implicit and explicit allusions to portraits of violence and suffering contained in iconic Vietnam War photographs—a host of factors (à la symptoms) integral to a medically driven cinematic representation of both U.S. foreign policy and state-authorized violence under the Khmer Rouge.

Exemplifying this link between ideological war and authoritarian regime is Joffé's restaging of the Neak Leung incident, which occurs early in the *Killing Fields* narrative. A thriving commercial town roughly thirty-eight miles southeast of Phnom Penh, Neak Leung was the site of a disastrous military miscalculation. Specifically, on August 6, 1973, a B-52 bomber dropped its twenty-ton load on the town center, killing 138 civilians and wounding an additional 268 Cambodians. Declared by U.S. embassy officials as an accident, the tragic story of Neak Leung was at the time broken by Schanberg, who with Pran's help was able to rush to the site in the immediate aftermath of the bombing.[46] Returning to the film, what cinematically precedes this Neak Leung incident is a mundane scene involving Schanberg (Waterston) and Pran (Ngor). Having bribed Cambodian officials, the reporter and his assistant make their way up the Mekong River atop a police boat, neatly framed by lush vegetation and clear blue water.

In dramatic contrast, the next scene involves Neak Leung, wherein the bright greens and blues of the previous shot disappear, replaced by darker tones of dirtied gray, smoldering black, and muted white. The camera settles on three men who carry a stretcher upon which the body of a bloodied young woman lays. Pictorially, the dark red blood on the woman's body is consistent with the image of the Red Cross, which appears on white armbands and vests. The stretcher and medical insignia establish the central stakes of a triage scene replete with medical evaluation, prioritization, and diagnosis. Amid a treacherous terrain of overturned cars, splintered wood fragments, and exploded concrete, the three men (with unconscious woman in tow) move diagonally to the top of the frame toward a make-shift hospital. The physical obliteration of the landscape is iterated in the anguished cry of a child, which increases in volume as the unidentified medical party nears the crude infirmary.

As Schanberg and Pran reach this destination, the camera shifts to a high-angle view, bringing into wider focus a landscape of upturned earth, ubiquitous mud, and endless rubble. This chaotic imaginary functions as a primary setting for military personnel, women, and children, who slowly make their way through the debris. In the middle of the frame is a large, water-filled crater (the epicenter of the bombing) that (along with the tent hospital) functions as the shot's focal point. Such background details and foreground movements (composed of environmental debris, wounded bodies, and field hospitals) hearken back to postbattle scenes like the one depicted in Larry Burrows's now famous Vietnam War photograph titled "Reaching Out." Originally part of a longer series of images (wherein Burrows followed a marine troop during Operation Prairie), "Reaching Out" appeared in the October 28, 1966 issue of *Life* magazine.[47]

Burrows's photographic composition—which is in color and consists of muddied military bodies in varying stages of battle distress—focuses (by way of central axis) on two figures: a wounded African American soldier (U.S. Marine Gunnery Sergeant Jeremiah Purdie) and an unidentified white figure seated in the foreground. This secondary figure—who sits with left arm outstretched and eyes open—is covered in mud and is presumably dead (given his blank stare). The photograph's title references Purdie's physical movement, wherein the wounded marine (supported by his fellow troop members), with arms raised, seemingly marches toward the reclining white figure. Sans captioning, the exact location for the photograph is initially unclear, though subject dress (military uniforms), its date of publication, and a background of Southeast Asian flora suggest an undisclosed battle location in Vietnam. Such war-driven readings of space and place not surprisingly correspond to the photograph's *actual* setting: an American first-aid camp south of the demilitarized zone. The absence of helicopters, identifiable medical personnel, and hospitals engenders a spatial ambiguity juxtaposed with markedly clear affective gestures. Illustratively and dramatically, as an unidentified *Life* magazine writer evocatively averred, "Reaching Out" was a "Hieronymus Bosch–like portrait of chaos, courage, and desolation."[48]

Whereas the opening moments of the Neak Leung scene are reminiscent of Burrows's "portrait of chaos, courage, and desolation," what cinematically follows prompts a reading of another iconic Vietnam War image: Eddie Adams's February 1, 1968 black-and-white photograph of a Vietcong execution. Taken during the early stages of the Tet Offensive, Adams (an Associated Press photojournalist) captured General Nguyen Ngoc Loan's fatal shooting of Nguyen Van Lem at the point of bullet impact, and the image was among those credited with strengthening an already growing antiwar movement in the United States. Central to the photo's political power was the troublingly intimate connection between photographer and subject. Indeed, as Susan Sontag surmises:

> There can be no suspicion about the authenticity of what is being shown in the picture taken by Eddie Adams in February 1968. . . . Adams's picture shows the moment the bullet has been fired; the dead man, grimacing, has not started to fall. As for the viewer, this viewer, even many years after the picture was taken . . . well, one can gaze at these faces for a long time and not come to the end of the mystery, and the indecency, of such co-spectatorship.[49]

Whereas Adams's image bespeaks the "indecency, of such co-spectatorship," the ensuing scene involving Schanberg, Pran, and a group of Lon Nol soldiers cinematically revises this tableau to fit the parameters of moral reportage. What precedes this militarized encounter is a brief exchange between Schanberg, Pran, and an unidentified woman. As Schanberg and Pran make their way through the bomb site, they encounter a number of Neak Leung's residents, including the above-mentioned young woman, who asks whether the pilot of the plane has been arrested. This question is directed at Schanberg, who is—as a close-up of the young woman's skeptical face makes clear—guilty by way of national association.

The unidentified woman, Schanberg, and Pran are interrupted by the sound of a military jeep, and the camera shifts to the vehicle, which contains four Lon Nol soldiers and two Khmer Rouge prisoners. With guns pointed and amid declarative shouts, the Lon Nol soldiers shove the two Khmer Rouge combatants out of the jeep and are summarily posed for execution. With shirts torn and torsos exposed, the prisoners' hands remain tied behind their backs; subsequently, they are forced into a kneeling position. Schanberg—who has previously admitted that he has run out of film—nonetheless pulls out his camera and pretends to take photographs. This documentary action agitates one of the Lon Nol soldiers, who quickly moves in the direction of the *Times* reporter. Yelling "no camera, no camera," the soldier—dressed in drab green military fatigues—points his gun at Schanberg. The correspondent and Pran are quickly ushered to another location, away from the public execution site. As Schanberg and Pran walk toward the left side of the frame, two gunshots are heard.

When situated adjacent the Eddie Adams image, the interaction between Schanberg and the Lon Nol soldiers assumes the registers of a revised reenactment. Accordingly, Schanberg (as ethical photojournalist)
uses his camera to interrupt and potentially stop the execution. As a result, Schanberg is a failed objective journalist who succeeds as a human
rights interventionist. Nevertheless, the execution is halted only temporarily, and Schanberg cannot—in the face of state power—enact permanent change. Moreover, notwithstanding divergent journalistic motives,
both Adams and Schanberg (to varying degrees) are de facto witnesses
to a violent breakdown in juridical order inextricably linked to the U.S.
presence in Southeast Asia. Whereas Adams's photograph explicitly engages—by way of the military body and the political prisoner—a political
alliance between American and South Vietnamese forces, the portrayal of
Schanberg in *The Killing Fields* makes visible a similar bilateralism between
the American government and U.S.-backed Lon Nol soldiers.

To read the Neak Leung bombing as a U.S. military mistake disallows
a triumphant reading of U.S. foreign policy in Southeast Asia. However,
problematically at stake is the degree to which the Vietnam War determines Joffé's retelling of the Killing Fields era. Concurrently, the use of
Vietnam War frames presages the film's later engagement with mass atrocity under the Khmer Rouge. In particular, the film's title (which attests
to state-authorized violence and execution during the Angka regime) is
viscerally illustrated in a scene involving Pran, who has recently escaped
a labor camp. Clothed in tattered black pants and shirt, Pran (flanked on
both sides by water) makes his way along a narrow, muddy embankment.
The camera follows the Cambodian escapee as he carefully navigates
an inhospitable terrain of dead trees, sharp branches, and light brown
sludge. The climax of the scene occurs when Pran falls into a shallow
ditch filled with skulls, bones, and decomposing bodies. Mike Oldfield's
score, which up to this point has maintained a monotonous single beat,
assumes a fevered pitch (replete with screeching violins) as the camera
shifts to a dramatic close-up of a child's skeleton. The next frame involves
the entire length of the levee, filled with rows and piles of still-clothed
skeletal bodies, which includes a close-up of Pran's distressed expression. The scene concludes with individualized shots of bloated corpses
in the water and follows Pran as he hurriedly moves to the end of the
embankment.

Notwithstanding the specific sociopolitical terrain of the Khmer Rouge era, this scene—which deliberately concentrates on the Cambodian body corpus to underscore the horrific policies of the Khmer Rouge body politic—hearkens back to a well-known image of a different Southeast Asian wartime atrocity. Indeed, the ordered yet harried placement of bodies (in piles and rows) calls forth a set of images taken of the My Lai and My Khe massacres. On March 16, 1968, almost a month after Eddie Adams's iconic photograph, U.S. troops (specifically Charlie Company of the 1st Battalion, 20th Infantry Regiment, 11th Brigade, 23rd Infantry Division) gathered over three hundred unarmed men, women, and children and brutally murdered them in shallow irrigation ditches. U.S. Army photographer Ronald L. Haeberle, assigned to Charlie Company, documented the event, which infamously included portraits of recently killed Vietnamese civilians.[50] If the My Lai/My Khe photographs (released in 1969) galvanized an antiwar movement in the United States, they also form an imagistic archive of unbounded, amoral, and unethical military violence. The visual coherences between the My Lai photo and the *Killing Fields* scene render even less specific the politics of and dynamics under the Khmer Rouge, whose actions fit into a generic American narrative of human rights violation and mass violence.

Such disruptions—wherein international human rights violations occur at will—contribute to a pathological reading of the Khmer Rouge. Consequently, *The Killing Fields,* even with its intended concentration on the Cambodian genocide, is informed by a dominant, syndrome-driven reading of the Vietnam War. Such a syndrome encompasses, contains, and criticizes extreme dogma, wrongheaded military action, and disastrous regime changes according to established Vietnam War rubrics. This is not to suggest that the film is unconcerned with the sociopolitical landscape of Democratic Kampuchea. With regard to title and plot, *The Killing Fields* realistically restages (by way of setting, acting, and cinematography) the conditions under which the Khmer Rouge assumed power, reenacts the experiences of those who lived under the Khmer Rouge, and revisits the frenzied dissolution of Democratic Kampuchea. Nevertheless, the film's implicit reliance on particular photojournalistic images indubitably accesses a recent useable past (the Vietnam War) that renders illegible an explicit Cambodian history.

Alternatively, the diagnostic frames that undergird Joffé's depictions of Khmer Rouge soldiers and the Democratic Kampuchean era intersect with the film's concluding rehabilitative agenda, which affectively echoes Schanberg's source text through truncated apologies and forgiveness. The film's recuperation of Cambodia's genocide memory encapsulates an identifiable rescue narrative fixed to Schanberg (as American savior) and Pran (as Cambodian victim). If the film's critique of U.S. foreign policy and Khmer Rouge ideology is pathologically constructed, then its consideration of humanitarian crises (and potential solutions) is likewise medically construed. These diagnostic frames figure even more keenly when situated against an affective terrain of remorse. Specifically focused on Schanberg's guilt, the film's redemptive tale of regret and reunion produces a closed genocide narrative in which state-authorized violence is acknowledged with no direct call for juridical action.

The final scene, which takes place outside the realm of others' politics, occurs in a refugee camp (specifically a Red Cross rehabilitation center) and commences with a man lying in a hospital cot. The camera then shifts to another figure in a wheelchair that slowly moves left to right. The next shot settles on Pran, who assists an amputee with his prosthesis. Pran readies a medical bandage but is interrupted by a nurse, who tells him that he has a visitor. The attendant reunification between Schanberg and Pran is foreshadowed by John Lennon's idealistic ballad "Imagine," which initially plays in the background; as the scene progresses, the sentimental song increases in volume and eventually becomes the film's closing track. As Pran looks out, the camera moves to Schanberg, who slowly emerges from a white taxi parked by a Red Cross hospital. The next shot cuts to Pran, who, with tears in his eyes, rushes to Schanberg. At the same time, the lyrics of John Lennon's "Imagine" become more distinct, and the initial reunion between Schanberg and Pran takes place as the former Beatle lyrically disavows wholesale nation-state formations and patriotism.[51] As if following Lennon's peace directive, Schanberg and Pran fittingly embrace in the affective confines of a nongovernmental, humanitarian space.

Hearkening back to Schanberg's "Death and Life of Dith Pran," the *New York Times* correspondent timidly asks, "Do you forgive me?" In quick response, Pran confidently avers, "Nothing to forgive, Sydney. Nothing to forgive." Analogous in form and content to Schanberg's source text, Pran's answer on one level underscores the movie's anti-ideological stance, which ultimately finds a humanitarian solution that exists outside the purview of others' politics. On another level, Schanberg's apologetic question represents a truncated expression of regret that, in light of Pran's response, proves distressingly unnecessary. Without full disclosures of guilt and direct statements of wrongdoing, such a question nevertheless prompts a reparative action from Pran, who answers in the negative. Like "The Death and Life of Dith Pran," what is at last privileged is an individualized reading of reconciliation that ends not at the level of policy but rather on the allegedly universal power of friendship.

Reimagining Culpability: Socheata Poeuv's *New Year Baby*

Whereas Joffé's *Killing Fields* optimistically concludes within the problematic confines of a depoliticized Thai refugee camp, Cambodian American Socheata Poeuv's autobiographical film, *New Year Baby,* commences with a decidedly more complicated aftermath reading. Produced by Charles Vogl and edited by Sandra Christie, Poeuv's debut film opens with a black screen upon which the following Khmer Rouge principle (rendered in a stark white typeset) appears: "If you preserve secrecy, half the battle is won." Evoking a clandestineness and combativeness emblematic of the authoritarian Angka regime, the proverb's emphasis on tactical forgetting (the preservation of secrecy) foreshadows what thematically materializes and structurally emerges in *New Year Baby.* Correspondingly, Poeuv's documentary—reliant on survivor memory instantiated by intergenerational inquiry—militates against familial silences and strives to connect survivors and their children by way of historical reclamation, collected family stories, and collective remembrance.

Expressly, *New Year Baby*'s family plot, which begins in Dallas, Texas, and moves quickly to Cambodian cities and villages, traverses an incomplete refugee story of survival, and the film is very much a contemporary narrative even in light of its negotiation with the Democratic Kampuchean past. Simultaneously, the film's narrative trajectory—which begins in the Cambodian American present and navigates the Democratic Kampuchean past—is cartographically coordinated through an initial setting in the United States and a subsequent location in Cambodia. Correspondingly, Poeuv's film cinematically eschews a linear temporality, relying instead on a disjointed retelling that foments an identifiable transit for and legible site of 1.5-generation refugee postmemory. Drawing on Marianne Hirsch's characterization of 1.5- and second-generation memory work, this intergenerational remembrance is "powerful . . . precisely because its connection to its object or source is mediated not through recollection but through an imaginative investment and creation."[52] As a result, *New Year Baby* is grounded in an artistic impulse that labors to produce, via documentary footage, animation, and real-time interviews, a distinct refugee genealogy.

Nonetheless, these genealogical registers are destabilized from the out-set by the aforementioned parental revelation that Poeuv's two sisters are in fact her deceased aunt's children and her brother is from her mother's prerevolutionary marriage. Further, Poeuv is—as *New Year Baby* later makes known—the product of a forced marriage orchestrated during the Khmer Rouge era. As Poeuv recalls in a 2008 *Huffington Post* op-ed,

> My parents never talked about their story of survival until one Christmas day five years ago, when they made a confession to me. They told me that even though they had raised me, my brother, and sisters as one nuclear family, we were not nuclear at all. In fact, we are a patchwork quilt. In effect, my family was formed during the Cambodian genocide.[53]

Poeuv's admission, characterized as a "confession," renders unfeasible a harmonious kinship narrative. In the same way, *New Year Baby* explores the legacy of Khmer Rouge authoritarianism through a fragmentary fam-ily structure that resembles a "patchwork quilt . . . formed during the Cambodian genocide." Rooted in an organized assemblage of disparate parts, this patchwork image becomes an apt metaphor for *New Year Baby*'s overall narrative, which deconstructs what has come before and sutures together after-the-fact fragmentation.

Even more significant, this filial formation is incontestably the cata-strophic consequence of Khmer Rouge biopolitics, signaling (to divergent ends) Michel Foucault's well-known meditation on the organic nature of state-sanctioned power. Specifically, such biopolitics rely on a "set of mechanisms through which the basic biological features of the human species became [during the eighteenth century] the object of a political strategy."[54] Notwithstanding the French poststructuralist's original his-torical emphasis (the Enlightenment era), initial conceptualizations of the nation (between sovereign state and biopolitical entity), and prelimi-nary location (the Western racist state), these biologically determined ap-paratuses unquestionably encapsulate the Democratic Kampuchean era. In other words, such biopolitics are evident in Khmer Rouge policies in-tended to regulate, police, and produce (through family frames) idealized Democratic Kampuchean citizens.

From involuntary parent/child separations to the forced segregation of wives and husbands, from the prohibition of affective kinship names to the proliferation of state-dictated marriages, the Khmer Rouge regime

was irrefutably interested in a familial disintegration and state reintegra-
tion attendant to a wide-ranging year zero agenda. Nevertheless, as Achille
Mbembe critically reminds, "to exercise sovereignty is to exercise control
over mortality and to define life as the deployment and manifestation of
power."[55] Moreover, the management of death and the related (de)classi-
fication of life form the foundation for what Mbembe terms "necropolitics," an archetypical "power formation that combin[es] the characteristics of the racist state, the murderous state, and the suicidal state."[56] These
necropolitics—which reveal a political economy grounded in difference,
a polity circumscribed by mortality, and a sovereignty rehearsed via execution—fit the authoritarian parameters of a Democratic Kampuchean
nation-state. Focused on a complete elimination of the inimical (the
Cham, Khmer Khrom, doctors, and other enemies of the people), concentrated on a draconian collectivization that disallowed even subsistence
provisions, and typified by the constant dismissal of the West and Western
medicine (e.g., antibiotics), the Khmer Rouge as sovereign entity managed
life through proscriptive and imminent schemes of death. Within this devastated domestic milieu, *New Year Baby*—a text born out of Democratic
Kampuchean policies that functions as a testament to fatal sovereignty—
is a biopoliticized kinship story that challenges the necropolitics (and, by
de rigueur extension, Angka's necropoliticians) responsible for bringing
Poeuv (and other Cambodian Americans) into being.[57]

   New Year Baby opens with the Khmer Rouge, yet swiftly locates its
cinematic attention on the Cambodian American refugee. Immediately
after the previously discussed black frame, *New Year Baby* shifts to a syn-
copated series of individual shots that gradually materialize and eventually overwhelm the screen. Aurally accompanied by composer Gil Talmi's
subtle score, the precise placement of these cinematic portraits—which
assume the shape of an orderly rectangular album—is formalistically
reminiscent of the previously discussed S-21 photographs.[58] Even so, such
snapshots, in which smiling Cambodian/American subjects hold small
chalkboards that bear handwritten first and last names, are decidedly different from the Tuol Sleng images vis-à-vis purpose, register, and geopolitical location. After all, identified by number and tragically fixed to the
confines of Democratic Kampuchea's notorious prison, those depicted in
the S-21 photographs are (as Peter Maguire evocatively characterizes) "facing death."[59] Irrefutably the victims of the Khmer Rouge regime, the Tuol
Sleng detainees bear necropoliticized witness to state-sanctioned torture
and execution.

Alternatively, the portraits that open *New Year Baby*—filmed in Long Beach, California—exemplify a more hopeful (albeit biopolitical) aftermath embodied by the children of Cambodian survivors. As Poeuv states, Long Beach—home to the second largest number of Cambodians in the diaspora—coheres with a more expansive directorial vision of a "new generation on the shores of a new country."[60] Set against this migratory context, the aforementioned signs, linked to refugee camp life, originally contradistinguished newly arrived denizens from those slated for sponsorship. With regard to the film, these physical markers operate as a visual metonym for displacement (from the country of origin), a pictorial motif of impending relocation (to the country of asylum), and a material artifact that testifies to an about-to-be-formed Cambodian American-ness. Consistent with implicit next generation optimism, the next shot eschews a set of particularized representations in favor of a communal portrait of 1.5-generation Cambodian Americans. Notwithstanding group framing, the camera eventually settles on director Poeuv, who occupies the screen's center axis.

These sanguine themes—suggestive of new lives and rebirths—exemplify Poeuv's preliminary voice-over, which clarifies the documentary's intergenerational stakes and reifies the director's role as primary narrator and chief protagonist. As the above-mentioned portraits fill the black rectangular screen, Poeuv summarizes,

> We are part of a baby boom generation. We were born after our parents lost everything in Cambodia. Once they came to America, our parents put the past behind them and never talked about it. In my family, I am known as the lucky one. Years later I realized how lucky I really am.

Accessing a successional characterization (as a member of a "baby boom generation") circumscribed by parental loss, Poeuv instantiates a traumatized reading of history, epitomized by a sense of left-behindedness, silence, and chance. Concurrently, Poeuv's mention of luck—grounded in a cinematic revelation of reproductive provenance—contrasts with an inauspiciousness representative of life under the Khmer Rouge. Such collocation is temporally at work in the director's admission that she would realize, "years later," how lucky she really was. As this brief evaluation of both visual and auditory signifiers brings to light, *New Year Baby* opens with generational pronouncement yet largely struggles with familial articulation. It likewise commences with an Americanized 1.5 generation but is principally preoccupied with the insurmountable task of understanding the first generation's experiences in Cambodia.

Amid this appositional, intergenerational milieu, New Year Baby is not surprisingly a work intimately concerned with the complicated relationship between history, memory, and family formation. As someone born after her "parents lost everything in Cambodia," Poeuv is a 1.5-generation witness to profound parental silence and a refugee subject haunted by her "lucky" status. These oppositional identities evenly inform New Year Baby's tripartite narrative. As early archival footage and the inclusion of animated vignettes make clear, the film begins with a biopolitical thesis fixed to how histories are written and traumatic stories retold. Furthermore, a necropoliticized reframing of the past—represented by staged apologies between former Khmer Rouge cadres and their victims—proves (in the end) an unviable path to reconciliation. Last but certainly not least, the film's transnational conclusion, which involves a return to prerevolutionary tradition as a means to present-day healing, signals a decidedly more optimistic space for what Poeuv provocatively notes is essential for justice: memory.[61]

To recapitulate, New Year Baby's plot takes place during the Khmer Rouge era (1975–79), involves a family's exodus to a Thai refugee camp (1979–80), and encompasses their lives in the United States (1980–present). Altogether, Poeuv's debut film endeavors to make whole a fragmented story of loss, displacement, relocation, and reunification. Fittingly, given the documentary's accentuation on profound disruption, New Year Baby imagistically starts in the stateless parameters of the refugee camp. Following the protagonist's assertion that she was "lucky," the film shifts to a close-up of a black-and-white photograph that depicts the director as an infant. As the camera pans out, the protagonist's mother also appears in the frame. With baby in lap and a slight smile on her face, Poeuv's mother glances downward, affectively evoking an iconic mother-and-child tableau. Embodying the role as chief narrator, Poeuv simultaneously discloses that she was born during the Cambodian New Year in a Thai refugee camp. As the mother/child portrait fades, black-and-white photographs of her parents, two sisters, and brother come into view, concretizing the film's biopolitical focus through family frames.

Accordingly, the before/after link between Democratic Kampuchean history and refugee subjectivity is codified via documentary footage of life under the Khmer Rouge, which occurs after the screening of family photographs. This archive is primarily composed of real-time images of Pol Pot, visual representations of the evacuation of Phnom Penh, pictures of labor camps, and portraits of mass graves. These representations—which incorporate visual representations of chaos, exploitation, and death—make visceral state-authorized mass violence and an en masse regulation of Cambodian bodies consistent with Angka authoritarianism. On the one hand, such footage prefigures a cinematic move from the biopolitical to the geopolitical through a historicized articulation of national grief. In turn, these historical frames subsequently connect first-generation survivors to their 1.5-generation children.

On the other hand, *New Year Baby* is marked by a transnational register that emerges from an after-regime rupture. Concomitantly, Poeuv—as a Cambodian American postgenocide subject—struggles to reconcile the disremembered past with a decidedly less certain familial present. This reconciliation labors to reassemble a fragmented history by way of memory work and generates a mimetic project that is strategically disjointed. As Poeuv clarifies:

I said, "Okay, I think I'm going to Cambodia with my parents. I am going to bring a camera and shoot them, follow them." And all these artistic choices happened piecemeal along the way. That's why I feel it's strictly my film. To a lot of purists, film people, it feels like I didn't come forward with one vision. But, because there are so many looks, so many textures, and things like that, the story is about the journey and how it all happened.

Accordingly, *New Year Baby* is very much a textured narrative that stridently refuses to adhere to a single focus. Punctuated by a series of failures, reimaginings, and abrupt meanderings, the film directly engages a mode of collected remembrance that engages uprooted (and unrooted) family members.

For example, Poeuv's brother—who was born in-country during the Democratic Kampuchean era—returns to Cambodia and quickly realizes he is for the most part illegible to aunts, uncles, and cousins who speak Khmer, a mother language he has long since forgotten. For Poeuv's mother, Phnom Penh as reclamation site proves analogously indecipherable. As the matriarch attempts to show Poeuv her prerevolutionary apartment, she finds that it is no longer there. Exacerbating an ambiguous reading of built loss is the fact it remains unclear to mother, director, and viewer if the structure no longer exists or its location is simply forgotten. These moments of cultural and spatial forgetting contrast with vivid memories of loss, which are most evident in familial recollections of those who perished under the regime.

Such traumatic remembrance is strikingly plain in a scene involving Poeuv and her father, who travel to Preah Mliu. A former Khmer Rouge labor camp, Preah Mliu is both the site of her aunt's death and the place where her parents met. This contemporary return to life under the Khmer Rouge is prefigured by a conversation between director and subject. As the two motor through the Cambodian countryside, the director asks her father, "Why do you think there are more bad guys now?" In response, Poeuv's father opines, "After the Khmer Rouge killed the people . . . the Khmer Rouge still stay. So the bad karma cannot see bad karma." Grounded in a Buddhist belief of moral causation and ethical reparation, the patriarch's reading of contemporary Cambodia implicitly acknowledges the ongoing absence of juridical consequence for former Khmer Rouge officials and cadres. Concurrently, the father's assertion that "bad karma cannot see bad karma" corresponds to an ongoing nonreconciliation that perpetuates a form of karmic blindness. Intratextually, the father's contention (that "the Khmer Rouge still stay") also foreshadows later confrontations and encounters with excadres.

As significantly, this exchange anticipates an emotionally charged encounter with Democratic Kampuchean necropolicies via a visit to the deceased aunt's Preah Mliu gravesite. A regime victim of forced relocation, overwork, draconian collectivization, and famine, Poeuv's aunt had, according to the father, nothing to eat and quickly succumbed to disease. As the scene shifts from car to former Khmer Rouge labor camp, the camera follows Poeuv and her father as they slowly make their way through the nondescript countryside village. Reminiscent of her mother's earlier search for a prerevolutionary home, Poeuv's father points to an empty lot where his labor camp domicile once stood. As the scene progresses, the absence of a built structure contrasts with the paradoxical presence of a makeshift sepulcher. The two eventually stop at a worn cement latrine near to which Poeuv's aunt (her mother's sister) is buried.

While Poeuv looks in the direction of her relative's unmarked grave, the father recalls, "Last time Ma and I came to Cambodia she wanted to come by, but didn't. Ma wanted to unbury her, but they often say if the soul seems at peace, then we should let her rest." By narrating the mother's previous (albeit unfulfilled) desire to "come by" and her impulse to "unbury" her sister, Poeuv's father potently characterizes an open-ended familial trauma. All the same, the assertion of "peace" and "rest" inadvertently forecloses an unburial of both the aunt's body corpus and the Khmer Rouge past. These passive foreclosures—which simultaneously remember the atrocities of the Angka regime yet fail to engender a sustained commemoration or revised action—are affectively understandable in light of individualized tragedy and large-scale human loss. Nevertheless, when situated adjacent a larger genocide amnesia (e.g., Prime Minister Hun Sen's 1998 notorious imperative to Cambodians that they should "bury the past"), such foreshortened narratives unintentionally perpetuate an incomplete articulation of the traumatic past.

Resonant with Poeuv's initial "piecemeal" characterization, such unfinished memory work is a recurring motif in *New Year Baby*, which repeatedly grapples with intergenerational, familial silences and incomplete utterances. This partial knowledge of this past—which foregrounds more expansive questions of "how" and "why"—consistently haunts the filmmaker, who early on confesses that she "knew more about the Holocaust than the Khmer Rouge" and that she "knew even less about my family." On one level, this lack of knowledge underscores the extent to which the Holocaust was and remains—by way of jurisdiction (Nuremberg), cultural production (films, documentaries, and memoirs), and education—the most recognized and well-documented genocide event of the twentieth century.

On another level, this epistemological crisis—which underscores a profound conflict at the level of reference, revelation, and articulation—undergirds a uniquely nondocumentarian aesthetic choice. *New Year Baby* includes a series of interspersed animated vignettes conceived and drawn by Paul Fierlinger.[62] The son of Czech diplomats, known as one of the founders of "independent animation," and a specialist in "hand-drawn, paperless 2D animation," Paul Fierlinger had previously created and produced over seven hundred animated shorts, commercials, and films.[63] Most relevant to *New Year Baby* is Fierlinger's *Drawn from Memory*, which premiered at the Sundance Festival in 1995.[64] Originally commissioned by PBS's American Playhouse in 1993, *Drawn from Memory* (an animated, full-length film) depicted Fierlinger's coming-of-age and adult experiences under state-sanctioned authoritarianism.

Born in 1936, Fierlinger was admittedly a faraway witness to the Nazi occupation of Czechoslovakia. At the time, his parents were on assignment in Japan. Unable to come home due to fascist occupation, Fierlinger became a child exile in the United States for the duration of World War II. Soon after the war, Fierlinger returned to Czechslovakia where, according to the animator, he "lived for twenty years in communism, under the same totalitarian system" as Poeuv's parents and relatives.[65] Situated adjacent this political and politicized context, Fierlinger (an eventual émigré) was intimately familiar with the oppressive histories that circumscribe *New Year Baby's* plot and principle characters. In an interview conducted by Poeuv, Fierlinger contended that he "understood the feelings and the fears that control people."[66] Such affective proclamations made the Czech expatriate a seemingly ideal collaborator for the refugee-oriented film.[67]

Even so, Poeuv's use of animation extends beyond affinity and comparative like-mindedness. In particular, Poeuv's aesthetic choice was likewise the result of her first-time filmmaker status and influenced by the realities of an incomplete archive. As the director maintains,

> I was learning every step of the way. So the reason why I decided on animation—that I would want animation in the film—was because there were certain stories that I wanted to tell, and there was no raw material for me to work with. . . . There were no photographs of that story. I didn't want to use archival footage, because we were specifically using archival footage to set up the historical background. Reenactments were out of the question.[68]

Faced with the paucity of "raw material," manifest in the nonexistence of photographic evidence, Poeuv's incorporation of animated sequences demonstrates an incontrovertible archival absence. As a close examination of one vignette brings to light, Fierlinger's animation enables an alternative engagement with "certain stories" in *New Year Baby*. Such imagined narratives, created through translation, dependent on interpretation, and reliant on personal recollections, paradoxically cohere with and deviate from an established historical linearity. Indeed, through line, color, and drawn metaphor, Fierlinger accesses an affective recapitulation born out of forced relocation, traumatic upheaval, and ostensibly unspeakable loss. Unlike Roland Joffé's *Killing Fields*, which mimetically restages

Democratic Kampuchea through Vietnam War imagery and reenactment, *New Year Baby* is divergently committed to a multivalent rehabilitation of individual pasts via affective remembrance.

These recuperative efforts are apparent in an early scene wherein Poeuv (and her family) travel to Cambodia following the mother's unsettling revelation. Within the claustrophobic real-time confines of a plane and with a *Lonely Planet: Cambodia* guide in hand, Poeuv acknowledges,

> I had no memories of Cambodia. So, I read every book I could find about its history. Growing up in America, I only heard of it as an afterthought of the Vietnam War. In order to stop the Viet Cong from smuggling weapons through Cambodia, America dropped more bombs on Cambodia than were dropped on Japan during World War II. The Khmer Rouge—the red Cambodians— emerged from the jungles to overthrow the government.

Poeuv's contention that she "had no memories of Cambodia" renders visible an unsettled transnational location, which prefigures a lack of remembrance "growing up in America." Moreover, apropos the director's allusion to "Vietnam War" postscripts, what follows is a series of historically specific images: threatening black helicopters, spectacular jungle explosions, marching Khmer Rouge soldiers, and a chaotic Phnom Penh cityscape, replete with armed soldiers and disoriented civilians.

Reminiscent of Sydney Schanberg's "Death and Life of Dith Pran" and Roland Joffé's *Killing Fields,* Poeuv's explication and *New Year Baby*'s cinematic montage narrate an undeniable relationship between U.S. foreign policy and the rise of the Khmer Rouge. Notwithstanding political and representational correspondences to Joffé's film (i.e., overt criticisms of U.S. foreign policy), *New Year Baby* is different in its familial focus, evident in the narrative shift from archival footage to animated short. This cinematic change occurs alongside Poeuv's vocalized observation that "On Cambodian New Year in 1975, [the Khmer Rouge] marched into the capital city Phnom Penh and told every citizen to leave. My parents were there." Poeuv's date pronouncement ("Cambodian New Year") instantiates a cultural reading of April 17, 1975 by way of prerevolutionary holiday. This intimacy is grammatically confirmed through the collapse of public ("every citizen") and private ("my parents"). Accordingly, Poeuv foments an intergenerational connection between history and memory that commences with an official narrative (inclusive of time and location) yet concludes with a familial characterization of witnessing.

Pictorially, Poeuv's assertion that her "parents were there" is retold vis-à-vis an animated sequence, composed of slight lines, solid colors, and a clear background/foreground delineation. Aurally, as Fierlinger's vignette progresses, the narrative shifts from Poeuv's commentary to her mother's voice-over. Recounting the evacuation, the mother (amid outdoor sounds of children playing and birds taking flight) relates, "We have [the] radio on and we heard the radio announcing by Khmer Rouge, say 'we took over.'" The mother's verbal account is subtitled, which constitutes (via printed text) a complementary narrative mode. As Poeuv's mother continues, Fierlinger's animated vignette opens with a domestic Phnom Penh scene. As the shot moves left to right, a calendar and a radio appear in the far left of the frame, visually confirming Poeuv's original date assertion and her mother's concomitant remembrance. In addition, a small female child moves from the radio to an open window, through which a flock of black-brown birds is discernible.

This background figure is promptly joined by a smaller child; a young woman in a patterned skirt occupies the foreground. As Poeuv's mother continues, Talmi's minimalist score starts; in the meantime, the young woman transforms into a black-brown bird. The two children are correspondingly converted, and the three avian figures take flight, exit through the open window, and join the aforementioned flock. This transmogrification is reiterated throughout the entire vignette. From *cyclo* drivers to outdoor vendors, from couples to extended families, human forms quickly give way to indistinguishable black-brown birds. A potent metaphor for a migration from cityscape to countryside, the black-brown birds—which compositionally call to mind a government-issue Khmer Rouge uniform—foreshadow an analogous selfhood transformation (from Cambodian citizen to Democratic Kampuchean subject). In a more geographic vein, as the animated short moves from domicile to street, from street to market, and from market to countryside, the sheer number of birds figuratively makes concrete the en masse evacuation of the city. Interrupting the mother's voice-over, the father (speaking in Khmer), asserts, "The citizens of Phnom Penh were leaving. One or two million."

Amid a landscape of abandoned domiciles, unattended shops, and unmanned *cyclos*, the mother is reintroduced as primary narrator, testifying that "Everybody panic[ked]. And you scared to death when you see the black uniform." Such anxious frames are visually concretized through an increased flock movement out of the city and into the countryside. Notwithstanding an impressive coordination of winged movement, some birds exhaustedly fall to the ground. Although the final destination is initially unclear, the flock of birds eventually lands in a lush rice paddy punctuated by six enormous iron cages (five in the background and one in the foreground). Whereas some birds roost in cages, others settle on the edge of the paddy. More distressing, two rows of dead birds occupy the foreground. Such images of death presage the director's concluding assertion that "The Khmer Rouge wanted to create a classless society. They forced everyone into labor camps. They cancelled Cambodian New Year and renamed April 17th Cambodian liberation day." Incontrovertibly, Poeuv's closing statement, set against an enclosed landscape marked by cages and ravaged by death, critically undermines Khmer Rouge claims of "liberation."

Taken together, this narrative of large-scale turmoil, which typifies the Khmer Rouge takeover of Phnom Penh and the entire nation, is drawn according to first-generation witnesses (Poeuv's mother and father) and 1.5-generation survivors (Poeuv). Aesthetically, this intergenerational focus, coupled with Fierlinger's strategic use of animals (birds) as a metaphor for sociopolitical disruption, illuminates Poeuv's direct engagement with Art Spiegelman's *Maus: A Survivor's Tale.* As the director relates,

> For me . . . *Maus* was the most authentic narrative I'd ever read about my experience of being second-generation survivors. . . . I wanted it to be a very rich film that wasn't just about the facts of what happened to my family, but to discuss certain themes, and play with those themes. And, one of the themes is memory.[69]

Concentrated on her "experience of being [a] second-generation survivor," Poeuv locates herself within the expansive narrative fabric of the Cambodian genocide.[70] Indeed, though she was born after the dissolution of the Khmer Rouge regime, she nevertheless acknowledges the legacy of trauma and state-authorized violence through family frames. Hence, thematically committed to "memory," Poeuv's assertion that *New Year Baby* was not "just about the facts of what happened to my family" coincides with the multivalent narrative agendas at play in Spiegelman's second-generation story of the Holocaust. Like Poeuv, Spiegelman's project was, from the outset, a familial endeavor.

Accordingly, if, as *New York Times* journalist Esther B. Fein observes, Spiegelman's most famous work "began as neither art nor history" but as an "attempt to get closer to his father," then Poeuv's use of animation is analogously rooted in parental silences and family frames.[71] Such coherences and negotiations are apparent in Spiegelman's admission that

> *Maus* for me . . . is a way of telling my parents' life and therefore coming to terms with it. . . . . Another aspect of the way I've chosen to use this material is that I've entered myself into the story. So the way the story got told and who the story was told to is as important [as] my father's narrative. To me that's at the heart of the work.[72]

Emphasizing a bifurcated position as both narrator and story subject, Spiegelman's *Maus* provides a larger narrative template for Poeuv's *New Year Baby*, which similarly engages a fluid reading of witness and witnessing. Although the title establishes from the beginning the director's central role, what emerges as the film progresses is an increased emphasis on "who the story was told to." To that end, Poeuv's documentary includes several shots of the director and a parent in the same frame, wherein the latter narrates a remembrance to the former. By the same token, several shots involve close-ups of family members who narrate to Poeuv (and, by proxy, the viewer) offscreen.

Notwithstanding the direct examination of interpellated viewpoints through intergenerational frames, *New Year Baby* is necessarily connected to a set of biopoliticized inquiries that involve forced migrations, involuntary separations, and state-dictated marriages. Within this biologically driven milieu, Fierlinger's animated vignettes (which include illustrations of plants, rice paddies, animals, and cages) provide an allegorical script through which to read the authoritarian management of life emblematic of Democratic Kampuchean politics. Concomitantly, Fierlinger's utilization of death imagery makes discernible the natural outcome of Khmer Rouge necropolitics. From dying plants to deceased birds, from abandoned cityscapes to bleak labor camps, Fierlinger's work visually corresponds to reel-time parental revelations and familial remembrances predicated on rupture and loss. In turn, such recollections foreground larger questions about individual culpability, state responsibility, and collective reconciliation.

Suggestive of an action that renders the past consistent with the present, reconciliation equally depends on a schema of accountability, which encompasses a related willingness to accept and atone for charges of wrongdoing. This relationship between accountability and reconciliation is most visible by way of apology, which—as mentioned previously—codifies a particular relationship between victim and perpetrator through the affective expression of remorse. If *New Year Baby* as documentary text is dedicated to suturing together a fragmented past in order to rationalize contemporary family frames, it is further committed to exploring the possibilities and limitations of apology. This tripartite consideration of apology, culpability, and reconciliation is evident in two connected scenes that involve two former Khmer Rouge cadres and their victims.

As Poeuv and her father leave Preah Mliu, the director narrates a desire for "more answers," which leads to a meeting with Mom Tep, an ex–Khmer Rouge hospital supervisor. Prior to this fateful encounter, the father has emphatically expressed his unwillingness to engage former regime leaders. Poeuv ignores this paternal directive, and what follows is a brief exchange with Mom Tep. As Poeuv asks the former cadre why she joined the Khmer Rouge, an unnamed Cambodian translator occupies the right-hand side of the frame. The conversation between director and cadre is decidedly unremarkable until the translator interjects, stating that his mother and several of his family members, who were Mom Tep's patients, perished during Pol Pot time. Following this revelation, Poeuv asks the ex–Khmer Rouge to apologize to the translator. Halfheartedly, Mom Tep asks for forgiveness but stresses that what happened was chiefly the fault of high-level Khmer Rouge leadership. The director asks the translator if he will accept the apology, and he answers in the negative.

These denials of accountability foreshadow a second scene involving another ex–Khmer Rouge cadre, who tends to his small farm plot as Poeuv, accompanied by her father, asks him about his regime role. The former cadre maintains the Khmer Rouge had superior agricultural practices, though he quickly acknowledges that the number of deaths that occurred under the regime was a problematic issue. Further, even though the ex–Khmer Rouge confesses that "killing was done," he assumes—like Mom Tep—no direct role in the suffering of others. Tellingly, Poeuv's father remains silent; in contrast, Poeuv takes on the role as interrogator, which—in this criminal context—assumes a prosecutorial register. Ineffectively, Poeuv pushes the onetime cadre to answer to allegations of arranged marriages, forced relationships, and Khmer Rouge brutality, but to no avail. In response, the former cadre accesses the ongoing UN/Cambodian War

Crimes Tribunal, insisting that its importance lies in its ability to rightfully prosecute those responsible. Dramatically, Poeuv's father collapses after these two exchanges, and the director admits that she feels "terrible."

The predictably vexed relationship between perpetrators and victims—which Poeuv attempts to ameliorate by way of forced apology—illustrates a potential limitation at the level of state-authorized justice, which similarly attempts to juridically elicit accountability through guilty verdicts and admissions of wrongdoing. Notwithstanding Poeuv's desire for answers and collective reconciliation, each cadre refuses to cooperate within the sincerity-driven parameters of apology. As Elazar Barkan and Alexander Karn productively assert,

> In the best cases, the negotiation of apology works to promote dialogue, tolerance, and cooperation between groups knitted together uncomfortably (or ripped asunder) by some past injustice. A sincere expression of contrition, offered at the right pitch and tenor, can pave the way for atonement and reconciliation by promoting mutual understanding. . . . Practiced within its limits, apology can create a new framework in which groups may rehearse their past(s) and reconsider the present.[73]

Accordingly, Poeuv's "negotiation of apology" fails due to an overdetermined agenda that naively privileges closure instead of further "dialogue, tolerance, and cooperation." Equally important, each cadre's refusal to take responsibility—coupled with a wrong "pitch and tenor"—perpetuates a nonreconciled reading of the Khmer Rouge past. Indeed, as Poeuv concedes in a subsequent interview, she wanted "to see them take responsibility, but it was disappointing and dissatisfying."[74]

Responding to such apologetic failures, *New Year Baby* closes with a markedly different path toward reconciliation. Situated against the biopoliticized history of the Khmer Rouge, the film's reclamation of two life ceremonies is rooted in a potent subversive impulse. Returning to the site of Poeuv's birth (the Thai refugee camp), the father reveals that his chief regret is that he was unable to hold a birth ceremony for his daughter. Intended to celebrate life and secure prosperity, this Theravada Buddhist ritual normally occurs when a child is one month old. Consequently, Poeuv facilates a retroactive observance of the ritual that affectively affords her father a sense of religious closure. Whereas the birth ceremony represents a symbolic form of redress via prerevolutionary tradition, the film's con-cluding scene—which takes place in the family's Dallas home and features a wedding cake—involves an American marriage practice. Indeed, if *New Year Baby* commences with refugeed rupture, it ends—through revela-tion, reclamation, and practice—with a distinctly Cambodian American conclusion.

Taken together, *New Year Baby* revises and subsequently employs what Lisa Lowe observes as a now-recognizable "Asian American critique" that epitomizes a transnational evaluation of race, power, and nation. As Lowe contends, such an assessment "asks us to interrogate the national ontol-ogy through which the United States constructs its international 'others'" and maps the ways in which the "nation-state has . . . sought to transform those others into subjects of the national."[75] Poeuv extends this critique to encompass the United States and Cambodia. Correspondingly at stake in *New Year Baby* is the ontological issue of how Poeuv's family was domesti-cally, internationally, and transnationally produced within the spectrum of U.S. foreign policy, state-authorized loss (under the Khmer Rouge), and the Cambodian genocide. With early allusions to American bombings and an overall emphasis on Cambodian American refugees (who assume politicized identities as national nonsubjects, or international others), the film explicitly charts the bifurcated legacies of U.S. imperialism and Khmer Rouge authoritarianism on those formed in the aftermath of war, mass violence, and necropolitical regulation.

As a result, Poeuv's refugee actors—which include the filmmaker and are composed of her mother, father, sisters, and brother—are historically embedded in what Lowe asserts is a "tireless reckoning."[76] Calling to mind infinite acts of itemization and suggestive of prolonged, unyielding effort, this "tireless reckoning"—foundational to an intelligible Asian American critique—foregrounds an unflagging iteration of traumatic pasts alongside nonreconciled presents.[77] Still, as Jodi Kim maintains, Asian American critique must—especially when situated adjacent to the cold war—simultaneously be "conceptualized as an *unsettling hermeneutic* that provides a crucial diagnosis."[78] In so doing, Kim engenders a rereading of *New Year Baby* as a multivalent, judicious, and juridically driven text. Like Roland Joffé's *Killing Fields, New Year Baby* explores and makes visible critical genealogies of U.S. imperialism that involve a remapping of and reengagement with Khmer Rouge authoritarianism.

Even with this thematic coherence, *New Year Baby* is decidedly less concerned with a pathological, global characterization of the Khmer Rouge. Instead, the documentary's "crucial diagnosis" hinges on an evaluation of survivor memory and a layered assessment of traumatic legacy. Because of its *individualized* focus on refugees, Poeuv's film destabilizes essentialized readings that produce a universal refugee subject (à la Schanberg's "Death and Life of Dith Pran"). Rather, the category of refugee—which contains a chaotic history of rupture, displacement, and relocation—functions (to access and revise Grace Kyungwon Hong's conceptualization of "women of color") as an "analytic" on which to diagram the limitations of state-authorized justice.[79] Hence, the above-mentioned imperial genealogies intersect with a set of transnational familial relationships that bring to light a Cambodian genocide past and underscore an American refugee present. In related fashion, the documentary film alternatively accentuates the still unsettled terrain of transitional justice through the active remembrance of the Khmer Rouge vis-à-vis biopower and necropolitics. As a close examination of *New Year Baby* makes clear, these subjects must concomitantly reckon with militarized histories, genocidal genealogies, and traumatized legacies through a principally vexed apologetic imaginary.

CHAPTER 3

Growing Up under the Khmer Rouge

Cambodian American Life Writing

The Angkar *is the mother and father of all young children, as well as adolescent boys and girls.*

—Khmer Rouge slogan, *Pol Pot's Little Red Book: The Sayings of Angkar*

As a survivor, I want to be worthy of the suffering that I endured as a child. I don't want to let that pain count for nothing, nor do I want others to endure it.

—Chanrithy Him, *When Broken Glass Floats: Growing Up under the Khmer Rouge*

I N JUNE 2000, a quarter century after the Khmer Rouge takeover of Phnom Penh, the *New York Times* published a review of two Cambodian American memoirs: Loung Ung's *First They Killed My Father: A Daughter of Cambodia Remembers* and Chanrithy Him's *When Broken Glass Floats: Growing Up under the Khmer Rouge.* Titled "Memories of Genocide," Joshua Wolf Shenk's literary appraisal opens with an allusion to the Khmer Rouge–driven forced evacuation of Cambodia's cities. As the writer turned critic surmises,

> Most left on foot and, after walking for days in the scorching heat, received another order from soldiers: to write their "biographies." It was a simple ruse to ferret out intellectuals to be executed. But it also hinted at a crucial theme of the Khmer Rouge's genocidal regime: an obsession with the control of stories. . . . Now the stories

are being told by survivors. . . . Cambodia does not yet have its
Anne Frank or Elie Wiesel, two storytellers who bore so hard into
the particulars of their experience that they could speak for anonymous millions. Perhaps Ung and Him had these models in mind, as
both chose to narrate their stories in present tense, from their point
of view as children.[1]

Alluding to state-authorized "biographies" and cognizant of the totalitarian regime's "obsession with the control of stories," Shenk gestures toward
a central mode in contemporary Cambodian American writing: Killing
Fields–era memoirs. Situated within a catastrophic milieu of war, genocide, and familial loss, *First They Killed My Father* and *When Broken Glass
Floats* are topically linked, comprised of childhood memories emblematic
of growing up under the Khmer Rouge.

Correspondingly, *First They Killed My Father* and *When Broken Glass
Floats* begin with a pre–Khmer Rouge setting, replete with idyllic scenes
of city and family life. Each narrative then shifts to the large-scale evacuation of Phnom Penh (or other major Cambodian metropoles) and en
masse relocation of its denizens to agricultural labor camps. Camp life—
and the traumatic details of such an existence—occupies the bulk of both
autobiographies. Concomitantly, the camp space, typified by a Khmer
Rouge authoritarianism personified by countless cadres who constantly
surveil and punish, is the principal panoptic setting for child protagonists
who bear firsthand witness to execution, starvation, overwork, disease,
and torture. In each memoir's concluding chapters, the 1979 Vietnamese
invasion of Cambodia foregrounds an out-of-country migration to Thai
refugee camps. These noncitizenship sites become a final narrative resting place for protagonists who await refugee sponsorships to the United
States.

As Shenk suggests, such memory-oriented returns assume revisionist
registers when placed adjacent to Democratic Kampuchean directives to
forget the past, forgo familial relationships (as the opening Khmer Rouge
saying makes clear), and exist in a tabula rasa revolutionary present. In
tactical Janus-faced fashion, by recollecting a pre- and postrevolution-
ary Cambodia, Ung and Him produce an identifiable cold war cartography (inclusive of U.S. bombings of the Cambodian countryside) and
reconstruct a Democratic Kampuchean imaginary. Further, like other
Cambodian American cultural producers, both authors highlight a postgenocide subjectivity (wherein Cambodian refugees are transformed

into Cambodian Americans) and, most significantly, agitate for juridical action (in the absence of domestic trial or international tribunal). Chronologically ordered, *First They Killed My Father* and *When Broken Glass Floats* formalistically echo other Cambodian American memoirs that, as Teri Shaffer Yamada notes, employ a distinct "autobiographical chronotype" composed of three time periods: before April 1975 (prerevolutionary Cambodia), 1975–79 (Democratic Kampuchea), and after 1979 (wherein protagonists flee the Vietnamese-occupied People's Republic of Kampuchea for Thai refugee camps).[2] From Dith Pran's edited anthology *Children of Cambodia's Killing Fields* (1999) to *Daughter of the Killing Fields* (2005) by Theary C. Seng, from *On the Wings of a White Horse: A Cambodian Princess's Story of Surviving the Khmer Rouge Genocide* (2006) by Oni Vitandham to Martha Kendall and Nawuth Keat's *Alive in the Killing Fields: Surviving the Khmer Rouge Genocide* (2009), Cambodian American life writing time and again accesses this before, during, and after Khmer Rouge continuum.

Notwithstanding structures unique to Cambodian American life writing, Shenk's second assertion—which maintains that "Cambodia does not yet have its Anne Frank or Elie Wiesel, two storytellers who bore so hard into the particulars of their experience that they could speak for anonymous millions"—troublingly eschews the tenets of a distinct life-writing genre in favor of a now-familiar Holocaust referent. Shenk evaluates the efficacy of childhood remembrances of genocide by way of canonical narratives like Anne Frank's eponymous diary and Elie Wiesel's *Night* trilogy, accentuating the dominant role such productions play in the mass reception of non-Holocaust texts. This reception accretes more significance within a contemporary literary marketplace increasingly flooded by what Kay Schaffer and Sidonie Smith characterize as stories of "traumatic remembering," part and parcel of a turn-of-the-twenty-first-century "memoir boom." As Schaffer and Smith contend,

> Exemplary of the literature of traumatic remembering in the West have been Holocaust stories and all that has come to signify "the Holocaust" as the emblematic limit case of human rights abuse in the twentieth century. So important and influential have Holocaust stories become, and so ingrained in Western audiences invoking a pattern of response, that this signal event has become the template for all forms of traumatic telling, response, and responsibility within the contemporary field of human rights.[3]

If the Holocaust is the "signal event" that has "become the template for all forms of traumatic telling, response, and responsibility," then memoirs about the Shoah—as Shenk's valuation makes clear—become totalizing prototypes upon which stories of genocide and state-sanctioned violence are measured. Such autobiographical indices obscure very real differences between Jewish productions and Cambodian American life writing with regard to history, politics, and state-sanctioned justice. Most obvious, the disjuncture between hindsight prosecution (the trials at Nuremburg) and still-to-be-served justice (the ongoing U.N./Cambodian War Crimes Tribunal) weakens Shenk's original comparative claim because two different agendas are at play. For those who recall the Holocaust, at stake is a "never again" modality facilitated through a juridically acknowledged remembrance (e.g., *Yad Vashem*); for Cambodian American writers who recollect the Killing Fields era, the issue is an instantiating "remember again" impulse intended to catalyze unrealized juridical processes.

Less apparent is the extent to which Shenk's critical appraisal ignores the specific traumatic contours of Cambodian American life writing. Shenk's childhood comparison fails to account for asymmetrical juridical histories; it is likewise undermined by a misreading of narrative rupture, thematic purpose, and extenuating sociopolitical contexts. For example, Shenk insists that each memoir lacks a coherent (or authentic) narrative voice. In particular, Shenk criticizes *First They Killed My Father* and *When Broken Glass Floats* on the flat assumption that each author carelessly uses incongruous adult reasoning. Accordingly, Chanrithy Him's memoir is extravagantly "tinged with melodrama" and the author "seems to strain to relate the immediacy of a time so long ago." Shenk moreover asserts that Him "tries to impose an adult's logic and values on a world that, to a child, must have seemed impossible," which he later argues lessens the narrative impact of her autobiography.[4] Similarly, Shenk alleges that Ung's "child narrator sometimes seems like a puppet whose strings are held by the adult author," a reading ostensibly substantiated by the author's use of political terms like "cadre" and "coup," indicative of grown-up characterizations. In turn, such insights supposedly make her memoir "disingenuous."[5]

From the beginning, this less-than-generous reading of *First They Killed My Father* and *When Broken Glass Floats* is suggested in the review's title. In stressing "memories" and not "memoirs" of genocide, Shenk stimulates an incomplete and fragmented reading of each text. Nevertheless, it is precisely such interrupted childhood memories of genocide, influenced by war, shaped by authoritarianism, and marked by unimaginable suffering, that demand a reading of Cambodian American literature through alternative frames. As Ung and Him attempt to make sense of national rupture, forced familial separations, parental executions, and lost childhoods in *First They Killed My Father* and *When Broken Glass Floats,* respectively, the inclusion of adult commentary brings to light an undeniably politicized context forged in the interstices of conflicted Cambodian nationhood, replete with foreign-born realpolitik and comprised of unthinkable violence. Simultaneously, the tactical use of a child perspective—which calls forth legible frames of innocence—inadvertently destabilizes allegations of U.S. innocence via midcentury campaigns in Southeast Asia.

For these reasons, the desire to combat such historical amnesias in the face of genocide is of paramount significance in Cambodian American Killing Fields narratives. In his introduction to *Children of Cambodia's Killing Fields,* survivor Dith Pran provocatively argues:

> It is important for me that a new generation of Cambodians and Cambodian Americans become active and tell the world what happened to them and their families under the Khmer Rouge. I want them never to forget the faces of their relatives and friends who were killed during that time. The dead are crying out for justice. Their voices must be heard. It is the responsibility of survivors to speak out for those who are unable to speak, in order that genocide and holocaust will never happen again in this world.[6]

Pran's declaration to "never to forget the faces of their relatives and friends" directly challenges individual and communal impulses to dis-remember (deliberately and unintentionally) the tragic realities of the Khmer Rouge era. Equally important, Pran's desire that "a new generation of Cambodians and Cambodian Americans become active" by "tell[ing] the world what happened" underscores a testimonial manifesto linked to intergenerational juridical protest. This collective impulse—to represent the Cambodian experience between 1975 and 1979 (the period of Democratic Kampuchea)—eschews a strict reading of autobiography as an individual life story and instead situates Cambodian American memoir within the rubric of collective (and collected) articulation.[7]

Indeed, *First They Killed My Father* and *When Broken Glass Floats* highlight that memoir—a genre that potentially enables survivors and their children to "speak out for those who are unable to speak"—proves an apt literary vehicle for such "cries for justice." However, as a closer analysis of both memoirs makes clear, this juridical agenda—grounded in an evidentiary narrative of Khmer Rouge abuses and crimes—instantiates particular limitations at the level of subjectivity and articulation. Expressly, if *First They Killed My Father* and *When Broken Glass Floats* detail Khmer Rouge crimes, each autobiography is (as subsequent critiques over authenticity and authorship underscore) subject to practices of judicial cross-examination. These cross-examinations are apparent in the contested reception of each work, which include allegations over fabricated narratives and claims of uncertain authorship. Even so, the critiques levied in each work (e.g., against U.S. foreign policy and Democratic Kampuchean authoritarianism), coupled with the compulsion to remember the Killing Fields, function as multivalent diagnoses of the failure of American exceptionalism and Khmer Rouge collectivization.

These debates, diagnoses, and criticisms bring to light the main charge before Cambodian American life writing, which is rooted in a specific responsibility: the verbalization of justice through individual account and collective remembrance. Remembering a Cambodia that, after 1975, ceases to exist as a "once-gentle land"(drawing on Chanrithy Him's country-of-origin characterization) attaches to each production the additional task of making visible a certain absented presence. Suggestive of an event that has occurred but remains unacknowledged, the absented presence of the Killing Fields era resembles what Avery Gordon argues is integral to haunting and other "ghostly matters." As Gordon explains:

> If haunting describes how that which appears to be not there is often a seething presence, acting on and often meddling with taken-for-granted realities, the ghost is just the sign, or the empirical evidence if you like, that tells you a haunting is taking place. The ghost is not simply a dead or missing person, but a social figure, and investigating it can lead to that dense site where history and subjectivity make social life. . . . Being haunted draws us affectively, sometimes against our will and always a bit magically, into the structure of feeling of a reality we come to experience, not as cold knowledge, but as transformative recognition.[8]

Correspondingly, it is the ghost of the Killing Fields—an absented presence or social figure that draws into dramatic focus violent histories, large-scale memorialization, and refugee citizenship—that, regardless of geographic distance and temporal gap, continually haunts Cambodian American writers who autobiographically attempt to structure feelings via an unreconciled genocidal past.

Likewise invested in a transformative recognition evident in the eventual vocalization of alternative juridical sites, Chanrithy Him and Loung Ung inevitably begin their respective memoirs with individual haunting experiences fixed to this seething past. For instance, stating that "in 1990 Cambodia still remains home to political unrest. Pockets of the Khmer Rouge still fight," Him admits, "The Khmer Rouge are a continent away, and yet they are not. Psychologically, they are parasites, like tapeworms that slumber within you, living passively until something stirs them to life."[9] Similarly, in *First They Killed My Father*'s epilogue, Ung confesses, "In my new country, I immersed myself in American culture during the day, but at night the war haunted me with nightmares."[10] Taken together, at stake in *When Broken Glass Floats* and *First They Killed My Father* are interrelated ghostly matters, traumatic impulses inclusive of commemoration (for those lost) and reconciliation (for those living). At the same time, Him and Ung reconstruct and reimagine—through family frames—the socially destructive dimensions of Khmer Rouge policy, which separated parents from children through relocation, reeducation, and execution. These family frames and childhood remembrances reproduce the Killing Fields era as a cast of social figures: unseen U.S. military personnel, ubiquitous Khmer Rouge cadres, and disappeared family members.

Returning to Joshua Wolf Shenk's critique, these social figures are imagined and reproduced within the interstices of childhood remembrance and adult reflection. Consequently, the ghost of the Cambodian genocide is visible in after-the-fact interpretation, past/present commemoration, and concomitant juridical interpolation. This ghostly reading engenders an analysis of both memoirs through trauma narrative, embodied frame, and triage practice. If, as Cathy Caruth reminds, the "originary meaning of trauma itself (in both English and German), the Greek *trauma*, or 'wound,' originally refer[red] to an injury inflicted on a body," the notion nevertheless is most legible via affective rubrics that make plain profound emotional injury.[11] Analogously, fundamental to the psychoanalytic definition of trauma is the extent to which it is comprehended, or embodied, and whether it can (or cannot) be narrativized. As Caruth argues, trauma is

> much more than a pathology, or the simple illness of a wounded psyche: it is always the story of a wound that cries out, that addresses us in the attempt to tell us of a reality or truth that is not otherwise available. This truth, in its delayed appearance and its belated address, cannot be linked to only what is known, but also to what remains unknown in our very actions and our language.[12]

Reminiscent of Dith Pran's above-mentioned call to action, it is the "story of a wound that cries out" that typifies *First They Killed My Father* and *When Broken Glass Floats,* two trauma narratives focused on "a reality or truth that is not otherwise available." Set against a backdrop of juridical nonreconciliation, Ung's and Him's interrupted childhood remembrances are undeniably rooted in the "delayed appearance" of justice and "belated address" of Khmer Rouge crimes of genocide.

Within this traumatic milieu, crucial to Cambodian American cultural production then is an ongoing evaluation of state-inflicted injury and mass-scale loss. As Cambodian survivor Pin Yathay, author of one of the first accounts of the Killing Fields, solemnly outlined, "the tragedy of Cambodia has not yet run its course nor will it for generations. . . . Millions have died . . . [a] culture has almost vanished, a social system disintegrated."[13]

Mindful of multigenerational impacts, Cambodian American childhood narratives about the Democratic Kampuchean era undertake a mode of memory work ultimately mediated through transnational triage. Drawing on James Kyung-Jin Lee's exploration of triage vis-à-vis governmentality and biopolitics, Cambodian American authors (who necessarily articulate ruination by way of individual trauma and familial loss) retroactively render a contrapuntal "diagnosis infused with power" and a "decision made with authority" independent of state-sanctioned reconciliation efforts. Indeed, as Lee suggests, triage "is not healing, but is a way to healing . . . [it is] a tool for making order out of chaos, and most important, for assigning value to that order."[14] Cambodian American writers Loung Ung and Chanrithy Him reproduce a distinct sense of agency through the strategic and tactical reorganization (or triaging) of political, social, and familial chaos.

Expressly, the destabilization of U.S. exceptionalism, the revelation of large-scale indifference, and the lack of access to state-authorized justice delineate the primary parameters of postgenocide, postmigration Cambodian American selfhood. Such a restructuring restages criminality, reassesses causality, and recalibrates culpability. In the process, Cambodian American autobiography militates against multisited erasures and constitutes an otherwise space (à la Gordon's haunting discourse) for memory, reparation, and justice. Situated against and adjacent to these politicized contexts, Cambodian American literary production is invested in an antiforgetting project that transnationally spans the United States and Cambodia. Put otherwise, Cambodian American writers—in their respective literary recollections of the past—repeatedly use the literary labor of memory (i.e., memoir) to expose catastrophic U.S. policy, lay bare international indifference, and underscore contemporary juridical inaction.

Qualifying Genocide: Cartographies, Culpability, and Cambodian American Memoir

Alluding to "anonymous millions," Joshua Wolf Shenk reveals the extent to which genocides are at once measured through quantitative frames. Nonetheless, it is the multifaceted *qualification* of genocide via politicized, affective remembrance that brings to light a narrative tension between singular recollection and collective memorialization in Cambodian American life writing. As an April 2000 *New York Times* synopsis of Cambodian American life writing by Richard Bernstein evokes, the almost two million who perished in Cambodia's Killing Fields represent "a horrifying number, but so large as to seem almost like an abstraction, like the distance to the nearest star."[15] Bernstein's remark about "abstraction" and "distance" emphasizes certain geographic realities and multidecade time passages. After all, the nearly 8,600 miles that separate Cambodia (as traumatic epicenter) from the United States (as principal reception site), coupled with the twenty-year divide between the 1979 dissolution of Democratic Kampuchea and the millennial publication of Ung's and Him's memoirs, potentially makes less urgent a reading of the Killing Fields as a relevant and remembered genocide event.

Notwithstanding geography and history, Ung and Him are chiefly concerned with a qualitative retelling of Cambodia's genocide through contrapuntal childhood moments. Indeed, as Loung Ung recalls in a 2005 *New York Times* op-ed titled, "A Birthday Wrapped in Cambodian History,"

While children elsewhere in the world watched TV, I watched public executions. While they played hide-and-seek with their friends,
I hid in bomb shelters with mine; when a bomb hit and killed my
friend Pithy, I brushed her brains off my sleeve. I will never forget
the day they [the Khmer Rouge] came for my father. They said
they needed him to help pull an oxcart out of mud. As he walked
off with the soldiers, I did not pray for the gods to spare his life. I
prayed only that his death be quick and painless. I was 7 years old.[16]

Whereas childhood is sentimentally conceived as a time free from worry,
strife, and violence, Him's desire to "be worthy of the suffering . . . [she]
endured as a child" and Ung's fatal game of "hide-and-seek" (which ends
in her friend Pithy's death) uncannily makes clear the degree to which innocence gives way to trauma. Indeed, both Him and Ung lose their childhoods and are forced to grow up under the Khmer Rouge. Hence, such
childhood memoirs give way to a decidedly traumatic bildungsroman
chiefly comprised of personal losses (the deaths of family members) and
sociopolitical costs (the removal of state-authorized citizenship).

This particular utilization of the bildungsroman is problematically fixed
to what Joseph Slaughter notes is a long-standing connection between the
form and human rights, which—"since the Atlantic movement for the abolition of the slave trade"—has been "one of the primary carriers of human
rights culture" that has "travel[ed] with missionaries, merchants, militar-
ies, colonial administrators, and technical advisors."[17] Correspondingly,
yet also to different degrees, both authors privilege a decidedly iconoclas-
tic childhood narrative about the Democratic Kampuchean era. The indi-
vidualization of communal trauma is made more immediate and pressing
amid amnesiac frames wherein U.S. bombings are strategically forgotten,
the genocide is discounted (as an "autogenocide"), and international
justice is—as the ongoing machinations over the contemporary UN/
Cambodian War Crimes Tribunal illustrate—for the most part absent.

Nevertheless, Ung and Him initially recall the genocide in quantitative
fashion, which on one level confirms the status of each memoir as evidentiary text. Explicitly dedicated to the 1.7 million Cambodians who died
under the Khmer Rouge, Chanrithy Him's *When Broken Glass Floats* and
Loung Ung's *First They Killed My Father* establish from the beginning the
human cost of Democratic Kampuchean policies, making possible a read-

ing of both memoirs as legible literary memorials. If a memorial is both commemorative and contemplative, then Ung's and Him's autobiographies publicly acknowledge and reevaluate national, familial, and individual loss. In the process, these Cambodian American cultural productions attest to what Martha Minow observes is the affective potential of literary memory work: to "name those who were killed . . . depict those who resisted . . . and those rescued . . . accord honor and confer heroic status . . . [and] express shame, remorse, warning, shock."[18] Be that as it may, though Him and Ung access past childhood memories, their political projects are simultaneously predicated on a still-elusive present-day prosecution of surviving ex–Khmer Rouge leaders and cadres.

Within this justice-to-be-served milieu, a linear (or chronological) narrative corresponds to the judicial agenda at work in each text, which joins the significant challenge to remember the past to contemporary struggles for justice. Given that only one Khmer Rouge official has successfully been charged, tried, and convicted in the current UN/Cambodian War Crimes Tribunal (Kaing Guek Eav, aka Comrade Duch, the head warden of the notorious S-21 detention center), each memoir (published seven years before the official start of the tribunal) establishes an alternate route to justice forged not in courts of law but staged in literary, more fluid courts of public opinion. In an alternate but linked vein, the construction of Cambodian American memoir via the instability of place is epitomized by the seemingly unending movement of protagonists from city to country, from labor camp to refugee camp, from Southeast Asia to North America. This movement in and out of country cements each memoir's transnational dimensions, wherein Ung and Him articulate the transformation of Cambodian protagonists into diasporic refugee subjects. Returning to memorial frames, such work on one level operates—in the glaring light of nonjuridical action—as a placeholder for (or marker of) loss that has yet to be negotiated by way of state-authorized processes.

On another level, these movements expand the purview of U.S. autobiography beyond a literary mapping of the self to encompass a transnational cartography of culpability and equally complex political subjectivity. Equally important, such productions reveal a mode of retroactive nation-building that foregrounds a specific, pre- and postgenocide Cambodian citizenship claim. Accordingly, Him opens *When Broken Glass Floats* with the following poetic enunciation:

When broken glass floats, a nation drowns,
Descending to the abyss.
From mass graves in the once-gentle land,
Their blood seeps into mother earth.
Their suffering voice resounds in the spirit world,
Shouts through the soul of survivors,
Determined to connect to the world:
Please remember us.
Please speak for us.
Please bring us justice.[19]

Him's use of collective pronouns—for example, "their" to refer to victims whose "blood seeps into mother earth" and whose "suffering voice resounds"—immediately establishes the relationship between the living and the dead, the traumatized survivor and the deceased victim. Despite death, those who perished under the Khmer Rouge regime are all the same "determined to connect to the world" through "survivors" entrusted with the enormous task—or, to draw briefly from Pran's directive, *responsibility*—of genocidal remembrance.

The repetition of "please" and the use of italics in the concluding lines of the above poem foreground an intended relationship between writer and audience. Beseeched by those lost to "remember," "speak," and "bring us justice," Him positions herself as a witness (through memory and speaking) and a prosecutor (an embodied vehicle for justice). Concurrently, these calls to action are extended to the reader, who analogously functions as juridical spectator and—given the subsequent testimony that composes most of the narrative—a de facto jury member. To a different but still connected degree, Ung's opening claim in *First They Killed My Father* that "if you had been living in Cambodia during this period, this would be your story too" confirms her membership to an ostensibly universal Cambodian genocidal narrative.[20] Likewise, the second-person use of "you" and inclusive "too" gestures to a soon-to-be concretized juridical relationship between author and reader.

Cambodian American cultural production is further guided by refugee subjectivities born out of Khmer Rouge totalitarianism and cold war foreign policy, which in turn undercut sentimental notions of Democratic Kampuchean nationhood and idealized U.S. exceptionalism.[21] The issue of justice at the forefront of Cambodian American cultural production marries U.S. civil liberties (inclusive of free speech claims and due process subjectivity) to universal human rights. This reading of Cambodian American memoir connects to what Schaffer and Smith argue is a context of an "evolving culture of rights." Drawing on the testimonial registers of the 1948 Universal Declaration of Human Rights, the two cultural critics rightly assert that "personal witnessing plays a central role in the formulation of new rights protections, as people come forward to tell their stories in the contexts of tribunals and national inquiries."[22] Marked by "personal witnessing," *First They Killed My Father* and *When Broken Glass Floats* operate in slightly different frames, in a still-to-be realized tribunal imaginary.

Alternatively, the hybridity of Cambodian American identity—born out of Cambodian and U.S. subjectivity—presages and echoes in some way the fused nature of the UN/Cambodian War Crimes Tribunal, which similarly attaches international human rights to domestic Cambodian law. Thus, the very locus of Cambodian American selfhood presciently addresses the formation of contemporary trial formation in the country of origin. Even more relevant, the tactical use of American autobiography as self-making narrative is transformed into a story of self-destruction via U.S. bombings of the Cambodian countryside and subsequent U.S. support for the Khmer Rouge. Consequently, Him and Ung unintentionally draw upon a particular politics of resistance and critique embedded in American autobiography. Drawing on a previously mentioned example, if *Narrative of the Life of Frederick Douglass* (1846) revised—via autobiographical slave story—sentimental citizenship-building tropes to levy a potent critique against romantic democratic virtue, then Ung's and Him's memoirs analogously call attention to the catastrophic failure of cold war policies in Southeast Asia. Implicitly, the lack of U.S. involvement between 1975 and 1979 is apparent in each memoir's omission of any mention of the United States after the Khmer Rouge takeover of Phnom Penh in 1975. Following the fall of the Democratic Kampuchean regime, the United States reemerges as an asylum site only in the concluding moments of *When Broken Glass Floats* and *First They Killed My Father.*

Countering cold war claims of U.S. superiority and moral responsibility on the world stage, Him and Ung draw limited but nonetheless concentrated attention to U.S. military policy in Cambodia. Explicitly, these critiques are manifest through maps of and direct mentions of U.S.

bombings in the region. Illustratively, a map of Southeast Asia (which includes Cambodia, Vietnam, Laos, and Thailand) appears in the front matter of *When Broken Glass Floats*. Indicative of an expansive U.S. foreign policy during the late 1960s and early 1970s, the map's coordinates gesture toward Laotian dirty wars waged from Thai air force bases, epicenter military campaigns in North and South Vietnam, and—most important—illegal bombings of the Cambodian countryside along the alleged Ho Chi Minh Trail. Comingled with well-known Cambodian cities (e.g., Phnom Penh, Takeo, and Battambang) are B-52 target sites, which are identified by way of a map key in the lower left-hand corner ("B-52 'Menu Targets,' 1969–1970"). Labeled "Breakfast," "Lunch," "Dinner," "Supper," "Snack," and "Dessert," these locations bear the euphemistic mark of a larger U.S. campaign titled Operation Menu.[23] A dotted line extends from Takeo (Him's home city) to Khao-I-Dang (a post–Khmer Rouge refugee camp in Thailand) and intersects at distinct points in Phnom Penh and Cambodia's Northwest Province.

Taken together, the map demarcates three key spatial/temporal sites in Him's memoir: the B-52 bombings and the subsequent Khmer Rouge takeover of Phnom Penh; the time of the Killing Fields (in Northwest Province labor camps); and the post–Democratic Kampuchean migration (to Thailand). The narrative use of such site-oriented and historical referents are buttressed by the inclusion of newspaper articles from the *New York Times* and the *Economist,* which directly attest to the political situation in Cambodia before, during, and after the Killing Fields era by way of contemporaneous reportage. For example, the fourth chapter of Him's memoir commences with a May 6, 1975 *New York Times* headline, "Victors Emptying Cambodia Cities, U.S. Now Believes." The caption is followed by an excerpt that reads: "Washington, May 5—State Department officials said today they believed the Cambodian Communists had forcibly evacuated virtually the entire population of Phnom Penh soon after they took power in the capital early last month."[24] These alternative modes of documentation strengthen a sustained engagement with U.S. foreign policy and international nonresponses to an impending humanitarian crisis. Subversively, such reportage militates against amnesiac readings of the period that insist that no international action was taken out of a profound ignorance of Khmer Rouge totalitarian policies and practices.

At the same time, *When Broken Glass Floats* outlines a specific coalition of nation-states connected to Cambodia's destabilization during the latter part of the 1960s and the mid-1970s. This geography—composed of multiple countries—illustrates the complicated political terrain that will, as subsequent chapters in the autobiography reveal, lead to the disastrous formation and implementation of Democratic Kampuchea. The metaphoric articulation of this geography initially occurs through the aptly spectral image of a comet. Him narrates, "When the tail of the comet pointed to a particular place, Cambodia would be drawn into war with that country."[25] She then interrupts the memoir's temporality with a present-day assertion that

> I look back now as a survivor educated in America. I've sought
> out answers to questions I raised as a little girl. Trying to make
> sense of what happened. Trying to understand the players in the
> Vietnam conflict and those who took advantage of the situation,
> pulling Cambodia—the pawn, they called it—into the whirlpool
> of destruction.[26]

Him's inclusion of the Vietnam Conflict reiterates the narrative dimensions of the above-mentioned map and combats a particular amnesia within the United States about the Cambodian genocide. This memory work is reinforced by Him's observation that the comet "had more than one tail"—one that pointed to Vietnam and "one . . . invisibly pointed to the United States."[27] The use of "invisibly" in relation to the United States complicates a simplistic reading of the genocide in terms of isolationist or domestically contained dynamics. Embodied cartographically and expressed literarily, the connection between U.S. foreign policy, the Vietnam War, and the political destabilization of Cambodia is reconfirmed and expanded through the narrative inclusion of U.S. bombings, which are linked to the subsequent rise of the Khmer Rouge.[28]

Divergently, the map of Cambodia that appears in Ung's *First They Killed My Father* is temporally and geographically fused to the Khmer Rouge era, a reading substantiated by its delineation of Democratic Kampuchean zones (by way of directional coordinates such as "NW," "W," "SW," and "E"). Cambodia occupies a central position in the map, which—as in the case of *When Broken Glass Floats*—also includes Thailand, Laos, and Vietnam. Notwithstanding these other nation-state representations, the question of responsibility is primarily attributed to the Khmer Rouge regime that has geopolitically segmented Cambodia. However, Ung does address—albeit briefly—the role of U.S. foreign policy in the making of the Khmer Rouge. As she critically notes:

> The war in Vietnam spread to Cambodia when the United
> States bombed Cambodia's borders to try to destroy the North
> Vietnamese bases. The bombings destroyed many villages and
> killed many people allowing the Khmer Rouge to gain support
> from the peasants and farmers. In 1970, Prince Sihanouk was over-
> thrown by his top general, Lon Nol. The United States–backed Lon
> Nol government was corrupt and weak and was easily defeated by
> the Khmer Rouge.[29]

Tellingly, this admission of U.S. culpability occurs after the Khmer Rouge takeover of Phnom Penh. Though seemingly incidental, the evaluation of U.S. foreign policy embedded in Ung's recollection renders explicit a critique of cold war politics. On another level, Ung—unlike Him—includes dates as subtitles to chapter headings. For example, chapter 1 is titled "Phnom Penh, *April 1975*" and concerns a pre–Khmer Rouge Cambodia; chapter 3 ("Takeover, *April 17, 1975*") encompasses the Khmer Rouge evacuation of Phnom Penh; and subsequent chapters incorporate this pattern. The inclusion of dates attaches a historicity to Ung's personal narrative, further substantiating its function as evidentiary text.

All in all, in both *When Broken Glass Floats* and *First They Killed My Father,* the issue of international responsibility with regard to Cambodia's genocide foregrounds the argumentative potential of memory work, which recalls—in complex fashion—a historical narrative that necessitates reconsideration and reevaluation. Indeed, such revised narratives of nation-state culpability directly dispute President Richard M. Nixon's April 30, 1970 pronouncement that U.S. bombings were conducted not "for the purpose of expanding the war into Cambodia but for the purpose of the war in Vietnam."[30] Through their explicit engagement with U.S. foreign policy, Him and Ung produce an oppositional reading of U.S.–Cambodia relations prior to the start of the Khmer Rouge regime. This reading reimagines and reinscribes the centrality of U.S. foreign policy in the making of the Khmer Rouge. Consequently, Him and Ung (to varying degrees) counter discourses of U.S. exceptionalism as expressed through idealized cold war frames of democratic virtue, nonintrusive containment, and purportedly benign warfare.

Daughterhood, Family Frames, and Postnational Memory

Comprised of state-authorized histories of violence, Cambodian American memoir largely reimagines agency through a postgenocide citizenship and engagement with juridical activism. Central to the articulation of citizenship is the use of daughterly frames, which make visible a postgenocide communal membership (in Cambodia and within the Cambodian diaspora). Key to this citizenship formation is familial affiliation, which functions as an index of personal and national loss during the Khmer Rouge regime. The engagement with family frames is immediately apparent in Him's and Ung's memoirs.

For instance, *When Broken Glass Floats* opens with the following: "In dedication to *Pa* and *Mak,* I honor you. Chea, my idol who enriched my life. Tha, Avy, Vin, and Bosaba, who will live forever in my memory, I love and miss you dearly. For Cheng, who helped me escape the death camp."[31] This dedication is preceded by an "author's note," which confirms the familial scope of Him's narrative project in its emphasis on collaborative telling:

> Although I have photographic memories of what happened in my childhood as early as when I was three, some of the events in this book were recounted to me as I grew up and filled in by my relatives. To protect some people, I have changed their names in this book.[32]

Him's confession that her autobiography is shaped by familial stories signals a return to memory as a collective narrative process made more difficult by deterritorialized refugee subjectivities. Such remembrance correspondingly militates against a practice of disremembering, which—as previously discussed—takes the form of survivor silence and the absence of justice on the world stage.

Echoing a similarly collaborative trajectory, *First They Killed My Father* commences with a familial dedication:

> In memory of the two million people who perished under the Khmer Rouge regime. This book is dedicated to my father, Ung; Seng Im, who always believed in me; my mother, Ung; Ay Choung, who always loved me. . . . To my sisters Keav, Chou, and Geak

because sisters are forever; my brother Kim, who taught me about courage; my brother Khouy, for contributing more than one hundred pages of our family history and details of our lives under the Khmer Rouge, many of which I incorporated into this book; to my brother Meng and sister-in-law Eang Muy Tan, who raised me (quite well) in America.[33]

In *When Broken Glass Floats* and *First They Killed My Father,* family members epitomize and personify large-scale loss. Each dedication assumes an elegiac register, manifest in the listing of names, relations, and community members. Such familial pronouncements cohere with the inclusion of family trees in each memoir's front matter. Set amid a Cambodian/Democratic Kampuchean backdrop, these family trees—which bring together genealogy and geography—afford the reader the morbid task of mapping those who died and those who survived the regime. Indeed, elegiac frames confirm the multifaceted memorialization efforts constitutive of *First They Killed My Father* and *When Broken Glass Floats.* Correspondingly, such literary memorials necessarily connect the loss of family members to the dissolution of prerevolutionary life. Therefore, central to each dedication is the articulation of large-scale loss, the negotiation of dislocation, and the exploration of mass state-authorized violence through, by, and within familial frames.

Simultaneously, as 1.5-generation Cambodian American authors, Him and Ung deconstruct and revise traditional notions of a bildungsroman—a coming-of-age narrative focused on moral, psychological, and intellectual development—through stories of growing up under the Khmer Rouge that encompass memories of moral decay, trauma, and confusion. Drawing on the cultural capital that thematically accompanies the bildungsroman, Chanrithy Him and Loung Ung further legitimize their position as daughters of Cambodia to speak for the nation and about the genocide. Without mothers and fathers, a fact confirmed in both visual and verbal imaginaries, Him and Ung speak to the national trauma of Cambodia via their respective roles as daughters, subverting normative modes of narrative transmission from parent to child. Additionally, their status as de facto Khmer Rouge orphans coincides with their nonstate status as contemporary refugees. Taken together, through the deployment of familial frames, wherein citizenship location is related to mother, father,

brother, and sister—and within the space of familial disruption—each author rescripts and reincorporates personal, familial, and national memories of the Killing Fields era.

Initially, daughterliness seems incidental, a superficial category
that describes Ung's and Him's identities within the family unit.
However, the characterization of the family as political unit sets in motion a reading of the daughter as enfranchised subject. Alternatively,
the filial self-characterization of daughter becomes more politically
significant when juxtaposed with contemporaneous Khmer Rouge
policies. This chapter's opening epigraph, which unequivocally positions Angka in a parental role, illustrates the desire of the nation-
state to destabilize and destroy affective modes of belonging in service of total Democratic Kampuchean allegiance. As Ben Kiernan
forcefully reminds, the Khmer Rouge "mounted history's fiercest ever
attack on family life . . . children were no longer affiliated with their parents, but to *Angka*, the Khmer Rouge's ruling organization."[34] The revised
function of the nation-state as parent is evident in Him's recollection that

> Family ties were suddenly a thing of suspicion. Control was every-
> thing. Social ties, even casual conversations, were a threat. *Angka*,
> the organization, suddenly became your mother, your father, your
> God. . . . To question anything—whom you could greet, whom
> you could marry, what words you could use to address relatives,
> what work you did—meant that you were an enemy to your new
> parent.[35]

Sucheng Chan advances the focus on the Khmer Rouge's assault against
the family unit in her assertion that previous words for "mother" and
"father" were replaced with the more communist-centered "comrade."[36]

Equally, Loung Ung confirms this observation in *First They Killed My
Father*, recalling that, during the Khmer Rouge regime,

> children will change what they call their parents. Father is now
> "Poh," and not Daddy, Pa, or any other term. Mother is "Meh." I
> hold on to Pa's finger even tighter as the chief rants off other new
> words. The new Khmer have better words for eating, sleeping,
> working, stranger; all designed to make us equal.[37]

All the same, Ung resists—in her retelling—the Khmer Rouge directive in her continued use of intimate family addresses. Similarly, Him writes,

> Every day the Khmer Rouge set new rules. Now they want to control the words out of our mouths. We have to use the rural terms of address, calling our mothers *Mae*, and our fathers *Pok*. Our other option is to call our parents "comrade," a strange, detached word that, by the sound of it, makes me laugh. *How absurd!* In our culture, we have four or five words to describe the act of eating, to designate an older person, a monk, or a king.[38]

The lexical shift, coupled with policies that physically separated children from their parents, brings to light the extent to which Democratic Kampuchean citizenship was coded through the denial of familial affiliation at and beyond the level of address. Since the model citizen under the Khmer Rouge was defined through disremembering (of previous regimes, social structures, and classed identities), children, who temporally carried the fewest memories, were configured as idealized revolutionary subjects.

Therefore, the characterization of daughters as witnesses to atrocity, genocide, and national ruination resists the Khmer Rouge by way of memoir and memory work. The traditional script of idealized Cambodian womanhood—wherein daughters take on established female roles within and outside the home—is recuperated to challenge Khmer Rouge familial ideology. Him and Ung include episodes involving caring for children, providing food for the family, and, most significant, maintaining familial connections through remembrance. Addressing specific forms of this "memory resistance," Chanrithy Him writes,

> Though the Khmer Rouge can control every other aspect of our lives, they cannot scrub out our minds, polish away our intellect like an empty brass pot. In the midst of the daily fear of Khmer Rouge village life, it is a delicious secret. And I'm proud to witness it.[39]

As family members die through execution and from disease, each author constructs literary memorials that speak to the intimacy of family dynamics. As brothers, sisters, and mothers are separated from one another, Him and Ung reflect on the passage of time and the totalitarianism of the Khmer Rouge regime. Following the assumed execution of her father, Him writes,

Now time becomes hard to measure. We mark its passage in terms of who has died and who is still alive. Time is distilled and recalled by death. *Before Vin died . . . After Pa was executed. . . .* This is how we talk. Before Yiey Srem's death, I'm able to walk and see her briefly. Such visits are rare, even though our extended family members live close to each other. We have to weigh our desire for such contact against the risk of being punished for exhibiting "family intimacy"—a connection the Khmer Rouge frowns upon.[40]

As the above passage epitomizes, it is through the loss of family members, which reinscribes parent–daughter, brother–sister modalities through a survivor/nonsurvivor binary, that Him and Ung recount the passage of time. As suggested by Ung's title, the temporal frame that encompasses the genocide begins with her father's death, even though it is Ung's sister Keav who is the first to die under the Khmer Rouge regime. However, the inclusion of father and the quick connection to a daughter of Cambodia— who, most importantly, remembers—reinforces readings of daughterliness and family frames. Notwithstanding the absence of a familial connection in Him's title, the constant reference to family members and family trauma reinforces her similar position as a daughter of Cambodia.[41]

For this reason, the maintenance of familial codes and the insistence by each author that she is a daughter of Cambodia and *not* a daughter of Democratic Kampuchea cultivate alternative national narratives that challenge Khmer Rouge directives to disremember.[42] Covertly, the assumption of traditional gendered roles—exemplified in dutiful daughters—simultaneously speaks to dominant characterizations within the United States about the role of family in the task of nation-building. The prominence of not only mother and father as signifiers of Cambodia but husband and wife as identifiable pre–Democratic Kampuchean categories indirectly caters to cold war characterizations of the communist—and by extension, communism—as antifamily. The middle-class subject position embodied by both Him and Ung contributes to this relatively conservative reading. Indeed, both authors recount images of home wherein mothers prepare traditional meals in comfortable domestic spaces.

Analogously, these domestic spaces are characterized through identifiable class signifiers. Ung, describing her home prior to the Khmer Rouge takeover of Phnom Penh, clearly announces her class position early in the memoir, stating:

Inside our apartment, Kim, Chou, Geak, and Ma sit watching television in the living room while Khouy and Keav do their homework. Being a middle-class family means that we have a lot more money and possessions than many others do. When my friends come over to play, they all like our cuckoo clock. And while many people on our street do not have a telephone, and though I am not allowed to use one, we have two.[43]

The mention of a television, cuckoo clock, and telephones establishes the Ungs as a middle-class family, a point corroborated by the author's own socioeconomic admission. The acquisition of wealth—underscored by what Ung notes is "a lot more money and possessions"—engenders a vision of pre–Khmer Rouge Phnom Penh as a space of capitalist enterprise and success. Him echoes Ung's nostalgic capitalist characterization of pre-revolutionary Cambodia in her observation that

Pa was a good husband and father. At twenty-five, he was successfully supporting a growing family. In truth, my father and mother surprise not only his parents but also Mak's. A home was a status symbol, a measure of making it. Even their parents wondered, "Where did they get the money to build a house this big?"[44]

As Him claims, the home emerges as a potent "status symbol, a measure of making it." The articulation of "making it"—reminiscent of the American dream—is couched according to a capitalistic understanding of success, which is further confirmed by the size of the house.

If, as Rachel C. Lee notes, the "the American national narrative of 'home' encourages home ownership as a part of capitalist production," then Him's and Ung's home visions are legible to a U.S. readership and therefore suggest an intended audience.[45] Such home visions set up a contrasting characterization of life after the Khmer Rouge, wherein individuals are forced to eschew capitalist production in favor of extreme collectivization.[46] The strategic inclusion of middle-class modalities highlights a potential danger embedded in the nationally inflected milieu of testimonial cultural production. As Jenny Edkins reminds, "the potential of testimony to resist is not often realized in contemporary practices. Survivor testimony is appropriated and co-opted in projects of state-building or money-making."[47] Nonetheless, essential to When Broken Glass Floats and

First They Killed My Father is the corresponding role of the genocide in the configuration of familial memory and the creation of communal memory work. Such memory work is two-sided in its resistance to Khmer Rouge directives to forget and amnesiac U.S. politics that potentially lead to further erasure. As children who grew up under the Khmer Rouge, Him and Ung rely on the immediate family frame to relay, comprehend, and triage trauma and loss. At the same time, Him and Ung's strategic use of conservative home notions engenders—albeit problematically—a wider U.S. readership not cognizant of Cambodian history and cultural practices but familiar with heteronormative middle-class values.

The intergenerational aspects embedded in such practices of commemoration are to varying degrees suggestive of Marianne Hirsch's notion of "postmemory," which "characterizes the experience of those who grew up dominated by narratives that preceded their birth, whose own belated stories are evacuated by the stories of the previous generation, [and] shaped by traumatic events that can be neither understood nor recreated."[48] Applied to analyses of second-generation children of Holocaust survivors, Hirsch's work on intergenerational trauma is instructive, prompting a productive rethinking of genocidal memory beyond the first-generation level of witness. As Hirsch remarks, family photographs are emblematic sites for such intergenerational memory, for they "contain, perhaps more obviously than the names and narrative fragments handed down . . . the work of postmemory."[49] Recognizing the centrality of the familiar in such photographs, Hirsch highlights the potential of transmitting genocidal remembrance at the level of both the intergenerational and the intracommunal. Fixed to what Roland Barthes maintains is the didactic relationship between image as artifact and victim as photographic subject, Hirsch's postmemory schema depends on the family as recognizable referents in personal albums.[50] The human value of family photos dramatically shifts within a genocidal context.

Accessing Robert G. Lee's argument that the family is "the primary metaphor of the nation" (a notion substantiated by the abundance of kinship terms that linguistically determine citizenship and allegiance), the family frames embedded in genocidal narratives thus have the capacity to make visible national annihilation.[51] The photographic images and genealogical referents contained in *When Broken Glass Floats* and *First They Killed My Father* bring to light a specific body-count reading that tragically involves family members lost and victimized during the Khmer

Rouge period. Such images include vacation photographs, group portraits, individual portraits, and more formal images taken at refugee camps. The written story that precedes the visual narrative—replete with accounts of the execution of fathers, the death of family members, starvation, disease, and forced labor—collapses the political and politicized spaces between family and nation. Mindful of such collapses, these family photographs carry multiple meanings: they signify idealized notions of belonging, are the pictorial embodiment of citizenship, and operate as memorials to the prerevolutionary Cambodian nation-state. The photographic albums included in *When Broken Glass Floats* and *First They Killed My Father* also motion toward the aftermath of the genocide in depictions of each author and surviving family members in refugee camps. The absence of images taken during the era of Democratic Kampuchea underscores the recollective burden assumed by the written word.[52]

Notwithstanding the value of Hirsch's concept of postmemory in evaluating—through cultural production—intergenerational familial trauma, at stake for Chanrithy Him and Loung Ung is not so much the issue of traumatic transmission between generations. Instead, the traumatic memory is transnational, not intergenerational, in scope. Supplanting the primacy of the previous generation in second-generation traumatic narratives in favor of an analysis of the previous nation, 1.5-generation Cambodian American genocidal narratives address the unique position of artists who were child witnesses to state-authorized mass violence. Likewise compelling, each writer's specific political location as a refugee forces an analysis of postnational rubrics that influence mixed feelings around return and reconciliation.

These postnational dynamics are reflected in the concluding moments of both *When Broken Glass Floats* and *First They Killed My Father*. In her memoir's closing passage, Him writes,

> In my duffel bag, there are other pictures, tattered photographs I managed to keep safe during the Khmer Rouge time, moving them from the roof of one hut to the next. They travel with me to America, along with the indelible memories of Cambodia's tragic years; of *Pa* and *Mak*; of Chea, Avy, and Vin; of twenty-eight members of my extended family and countless others who have perished. . . . We are like the dust of history being blown away. . . . We are leaving behind Cambodia, ground under the wheel of the

Khmer Rouge, and flying to America. There, we will face other challenges, other risks, in a new place in which we have to redefine ourselves, a kind of reincarnation for us all.[53]

The "pictures, tattered photographs" are attached to acts of resistance during Pol Pot time, substantiating their value as artifacts of memory and reminders of pre–Democratic Kampuchean selfhood. What is more, Him's declaration that she will travel to America with "indelible memories of Cambodia's tragic years" promulgates a reading of postnational loss. Articulating such loss through the metaphoric "dust of history," Him reconfirms for the reader that the Cambodia of her youth is now an absented presence that persists only in nostalgic, imagined memories. Even with the seemingly hopeful observation of "reincarnation," Him's relocation to America carries "other risks" and requires postgenocidal redefinition. To be sure, Him's conclusion offers no true sense of reconciliation, a troubling open-endedness made clear in the memoir's preface, wherein the author, situated in an American present, is haunted by memories of the Khmer Rouge. Nor do the final moments of the memoir establish a physical means for return. After all, Cambodia has, according to Him, been "ground under the wheel of the Khmer Rouge."

For Loung Ung, the physical ability to return is explored in *First They Killed My Father*'s epilogue. All the same, Ung—like Him—must contend with the legacy of the Khmer Rouge on contemporary notions of selfhood and affective belonging. Admitting that while in the United States she fantasized about "how it would feel to return to where [she] belonged," Ung acknowledges that she dreams of "a place where everyone speaks my language, looks like me, and shares the same history."[54] However, Ung cannot completely "return home" because of her postnational subject position, which marks her not as a Cambodian but as a Cambodian American. Correspondingly, her return to Cambodia is marked by misstep and estrangement. For example, upon her return, Ung wears "loose-fitting black pants, brown T-shirt, and black Teva sandals," prompting her brother Khouy and sister Chou, along with her uncles and aunts, to frown at her appearance. Immediately realizing she "looked like a Khmer Rouge," Ung confesses, "All my fantasies of instant connection were crushed. My family and I reacted awkwardly to each other and they kept their many warm arms at their sides."[55] Despite the declaration that she is a daughter of Cambodia at the beginning of her memoir, Ung assumes an alienated prodigal role in its concluding moments. Though the scene ends with a seemingly individual act of reconciliation—wherein Chou takes Ung's hand and leads her to the car—a reading of affective alienation persists in the author's initial admission that "instant connection" is impossible.

The lack of closure that marks the author's return is reinforced by Ung's observation that "our fingers clasped around each other naturally as if the chain was never broken."[56] The inclusion of "as if," suggestive of interpretation formed through imagination, relies on the condition that the "chain" (or connection) between the two sisters has in fact been broken. In so doing, Ung makes visible a post–Democratic Kampuchean rupture that persists in the face of amnesiac policy, time passages, and geopolitical distance. All things considered, these ruptured narratives—embedded in both Chanrithy Him's *When Broken Glass Floats* and Loung Ung's *First They Killed My Father*—foreground an uprootedness that shapes the turn-of-the-twenty-first-century Cambodian American experience. Forcibly relocated in and out of country, Him and Ung are two daughters of Cambodia who, deprived of parents by the Khmer Rouge, dispossessed in their country of origin, and haunted by a genocide past in their assumed country of asylum, remain transnational orphans.

Nonreconciled Conclusions: Controversy, Jurisdiction, and Memoir

Armed with juridical agendas, Cambodian American life writing directly engages the public sphere. Accordingly, Cambodian American memoir is subject to public expectations that reinforce the extent to which (in a more universal vein) all autobiographies are politically constructed, deliberately ordered, and strategically manipulated. Notwithstanding the particular juridical activism at work in each memoir, controversies involving *When Broken Glass Floats* and *First They Killed My Father* foment a less celebratory reading of each text. In *When Broken Glass Floats,* at stake was a question of whether Him's work was single-authored or collaborative. In the case of *First They Killed My Father,* accusations of racism and hyperbolic accounts marred the reception of Ung's text among Cambodian American readers. As each controversy suggests, the responsibility of representing genocide and mass-scale trauma unquestionably intersects with a public sphere shaped by expectations of sole authorship, corroborated authenticity, and ostensibly rigid factuality.

Soon after the publication of *When Broken Glass Floats,* a debate over authorship erupted. The case principally involved Eugene, Oregon, reporter Kimber Williams, who claimed she had closely collaborated with Chanrithy Him in the production of her memoir. Not named as a contributor nor identified in the acknowledgments, Williams contended that she coauthored the text. Ironically, given the book's juridical registers, the reporter threatened legal action. This issue over authorship was the focus of a November 1994 article in the *Willamette Week* (a Portland, Oregon, paper). Titled "Broken Promises," journalist Debra Gwartney's article juxtaposed an excerpt from the *Eugene Register Guard* (written by Williams) with a passage from *When Broken Glass Floats.* What follows is an excerpt from Williams's article and Him's memoir, respectively:

Chanrithy Him loved to watch her father work the magic. It happened when the tight fingers of asthma would grip her lungs. Despite her frantic gasps, the air was stuck. Quickly, her father would open his drawer of medicine, grab a vial, a syringe. The magic worked. She could breathe again. Nothing was more amazing to her—one minute taking her last breath, the next minute running to play.[57] (Williams)

My father knew magic. I felt him work his magic when the heavy fingers of asthma clutched my lungs. I would sit up and gasp for air, but everything was stuck. Quickly, my father would open his drawer of French medicine, grab a vial and a syringe. Then the magic worked, it always did. It was amazing to me. One minute I was taking my last breath, the next minute I was running off to play.[58] (Him)

The title of Gwartney's piece—"Broken Promises"—at once establishes in legal fashion an assumed contract (or promise) between reporter Williams and subject turned author Him. Previously discussed former *New York Times* reporter Sydney Schanberg, whose Pulitzer Prize–winning series, "The Life and Death of Dith Pran," was the narrative basis for the 1984 *Killing Fields* film, figured keenly in the controversy. Schanberg had—prior to such allegations—written a publicity blurb for Him's memoir. Amid a heated back-and-forth between Him and Williams, Schanberg rescinded his earlier praise and eventually sided with the Eugene, Oregon, reporter. Stating that he had "substantial proof that Williams collaborated with

Him," Schanberg declared, "Nobody can take that story away from her . . . I don't think she realizes that. . . . There's no shame in calling upon others to help you. The only embarrassment is to not acknowledge it when people help you."[59] In the face of undeniable consistencies between Williams's article and Him's memoir, what emerges from Schanberg's comments is a more compelling contemplation of ownership vis-à-vis genocide narrative. Him declined to speak publicly about the controversy, but her lawyer, Michael Ratoza, contended that Williams had never "written a book in her life but would like to, so she's riding on Chanrithy Him's coattails." Ratoza further argued, "Williams never lived in Southeast Asia; she never experienced the tragedies my client experienced."[60] Insisting that Him's subject position as a Cambodian American refugee afforded her exclusive ownership, Ratoza's reliance on experience as a defense coheres with Sydney Schanberg's conciliatory acknowledgment that Him's story "could not be taken from her."[61]

Accordingly, at issue for Ratoza and Schanberg (notwithstanding different agendas) was not the prima facie veracity of Him's story but rather its legitimacy as a written narrative. For Schanberg, the question over authorship involved production but not content; for Ratoza, Him's position as writer was inextricably fixed to her identity as a Cambodian American. Schanberg and Ratoza's divergent readings of content and production—which converge at the point of identity politics and personal history—highlight a rupture between internally guided remembrance and the external values of a U.S. marketplace, or public sphere. Expanded beyond law and justice, this particular conflict over authorship makes visible the transnational dimensions of Cambodian American life writing focused on Cambodia and produced in the United States. Even with allegations of plagiarism, Him's story remains valuable with regard to genocide remembrance. After all, U.S. bombings did occur; the Khmer Rouge did exist; the genocide did happen.

Nevertheless, in terms of its reception, *When Broken Glass Floats* as autobiographical (not ethnographic) product is by and large destabilized. What is more, Him's text—or rather, the controversy over it—brings to the fore a complementary consideration of how Cambodian American genocide narratives are authenticated. Sydney Schanberg's role in the controversy—as an authority on Cambodian genocide narratives—confirms his prominent position as a foundational figure and de facto Cambodian American cultural broker. In other words, if Schanberg is founding father (by way of his first accounts of the genocide) and ultimate expert (due to his *New York Times* connection to the Killing Fields era), he is also charged with a problematic taste-making directive wherein memoirs about the Khmer Rouge are deemed worthy, appropriate, or potentially legitimate.[62] Schanberg's critical position with regard to Cambodian American memory work assumes—on an extreme level—a mode of gatekeeping, whereby such narratives are monolithically vetted and validated.

This concomitant issue of potentially essentialized narratives and authenticity foregrounds the controversy that faced Loung Ung following the publication of her memoir. Sino-Cambodian American Ung's self-articulated position as one whose story "mirrors that of millions of Cambodians" is in part undermined by her repeated declaration that she is a member of an ethnic Cambodian minority group. Indeed, as the narrative progresses, this self-characterization takes on an increasingly racialized dimension. Reiterating that her mother is Chinese and her father is Chinese Cambodian, Ung repeatedly ascribes "light" and "dark" characteristics as significant markers of difference. For example, Ung describes her mother as having "Chinese" features—"perfectly arched eyebrows, almond-shaped eyes; tall straight Western nose; and oval face"—and juxtaposes these features with her father, who has "black curly hair, a wide nose, full lips, and a round face."[63] Reliant on a distinct binary (between light and dark), Ung's narrative perhaps inadvertently adheres to dominant U.S. ethnoracial logic that directly and indirectly privileges whiteness over blackness. The employment of racialized constructs is one reason why the now-defunct Khmer Institute, a nonprofit organization committed to promoting the study of Cambodian American knowledge production and Khmer-related issues, questioned Ung's authorial authenticity and demanded that the writer respond to allegations of racism.[64] The status of Cambodian as other is correspondingly articulated throughout *First They Killed My Father*, and Ung goes so far to attribute the treatment of her family to a Khmer Rouge sense that they are "racially corrupt," even though leaders of the regime (such as Pol Pot, Nuon Chea, and Ieng Thirith) were likewise Chinese-Khmer.[65]

Alongside Ung's ethnoracial claims, those critical of *First They Killed My Father* attack her class background and politics. Expressly, she by and large celebrates (and then commemorates) her former middle-class status with little attention to those from poorer backgrounds.[66] To be sure, largely absent in *First They Killed My Father* are the countless Cambodians who inhabited a lower socioeconomic position than that of her family. When such figures appear in the memoir, Ung repeatedly dismisses them as simply (and problematically) "ignorant." As Ung alleges, the peasant population was more apt to commit crimes against her family because, in the words of her father, the villagers wish to "make us the first scapegoats for their problems."[67] The enumeration of the treatment of her family, which involves several episodes of abuse and comments about her "foreignness," buttresses claims of scapegoating within the text.[68] As the Khmer Institute vehemently criticized,

> Although Ung's book is sub-entitled "A Daughter of Cambodia
> Remembers," it is apparent that she neither truly considers herself
> "a daughter of Cambodia" (except for the purpose of publicity)
> nor does she with any kind of accuracy "remembers." Unlike the
> acclaim and support given to the movie "The Killing Fields," many
> survivors of the Democratic Kampuchea regime find this book
> inaccurate, distasteful, and insulting. We believe in this case that
> misinformation is more dangerous than no information. It is sad
> that a person would distort and sensationalize such a tragic experi-
> ence for personal gain. It dishonors the memory of the 1.7 million
> people who died and the legitimate stories of countless others who
> have and still suffer because of the Khmer Rouge.[69]

Taking to task Ung's daughterly characterization by way of race, ethnicity, and class, the Khmer Institute complicates the representational politics at work in *First They Killed My Father*, which were chiefly absent in mainstream appraisals of the memoir in the likes of *Publishers Weekly*, which assert its value according to representative experience.[70] The veracity of Ung's narrative was further undermined by the details included in it. From unfeasible accounts of child soldiering (wherein a seven-year-old Ung is able to hold an AK-47) to a prerevolutionary trip to Angkor Wat (which the Khmer Institute deemed impossible because of civil war checkpoints and blockades), Cambodian American critics maintained that Ung's memoir was exaggerated, hyperbolic, and troublingly fabricated.

In contesting the veracity of the text as accurate memoir, the Khmer Institute ultimately called into question Ung's daughterly assertion that she was a true citizen of Cambodia.[71] Illustratively, the debate over literary authenticity foregrounds a more politicized discussion of Cambodian American citizenship, genocide remembrance, and belonging. Indeed, the Khmer Institute's critique utilizes a language of political citizenship and affective belonging to rhetorically deconstruct Ung's transnationally con-

structed claim of Cambodian nationality. In doing so, the institute replicates—to a different, indigenous degree—a verification mode analogous
to Sydney Schanberg's response to Chanrithy Him's *When Broken Glass
Floats.* Even so, this verification potential represents one reading of the
Ung/Khmer Institute debate. On another level, these contestations illuminate unreconciled racial rubrics (which maintain the primacy of whiteness), nonreconciled juridical frames (an identifiable tribunal), and the
politics of representing mass-scale loss.

Central to criticisms about *First They Killed My Father* was its legitimacy vis-à-vis the Cambodian genocide, which was marred by alleged racial bias and misrepresentations of Cambodia's Khmer Rouge past. Within
a delicate juridical space, such biases and misrepresentations carry the
political potential to undermine declarations of victimhood and impede
(by way of truth telling) juridical activism. The critique of Ung's reliance
on black/white modalities and her privileging of middle-class subjectivities also make visible the class and racial inequalities in the United States
in that they also underscore the prevalence of such inequities among
an American readership that willingly consumes such productions. At
the same time, the actuality of the Cambodian genocide is, in light of
the memoir's best-selling status, effective among an outsider readership
drawn to *First They Killed My Father*'s melodramatic narration and ethnoracial legibility. The debates that followed the publications of Him's and
Ung's memoirs highlight the stakes of Cambodian American life writing,
wherein telling becomes a necessarily politicized act. Although Ung and
Him break potent silences with regard to the Khmer Rouge era, they do
so in a polarizing and largely unreconciled milieu comprised of competing
national agendas (in the United States and Cambodia) and inclusive of
survivors, victims, and perpetrators.

To be sure, scandals involving autobiographical veracity—and the
connected politics of traumatic representation—are not limited to
Cambodian American literary production. In fact, two years prior to the
publication of *When Broken Glass Floats* and *First They Killed My Father,*
a well-publicized authenticity case hit the front page of the *New York
Times.* The subject of this autobiographical exposé was Guatemalan indigenous rights activist and 1992 Nobel Peace Prize recipient Rigoberta
Menchú, whose self-titled autobiography *(I, Rigoberta Menchú)* was under
attack. Assembled from early 1980s interviews conducted by Venezuelan
sociologist Elisabeth Burgos-Debray, *I, Rigoberta Menchú* detailed the
eponymous subject's harrowing experiences growing up during the

Guatemalan Civil War (1960–96).[72] More than a decade after its 1983 publication, the memoir's veracity was the focus of David Stoll's 1998 tell-all, *Rigoberta Menchú and the Story of All Poor Guatemalans*. An American anthropologist, David Stoll spent a decade fact-checking the memoir's claims and interviewed those who personally knew the Menchú family and who were from the subject's home village. Notwithstanding Menchú's assertion that hers was the "story of all poor Guatemalans," Stoll stridently maintained that Menchú's story was in part an egregious fabrication.

Taking to task Menchú's self-ascribed uneducated status, undermining the politicized dimensions of her family's land struggles, and disputing the details of her brother's death, Stoll ultimately concluded, "By presenting herself as an everywoman, she has tried to be all things to all people in a way no individual can be. . . . [Readers must be able] to distinguish between what can be corroborated and what cannot, what is probable and what is highly improbable."[73] Among Stoll's larger contentions was that the memoir was propagandistic; the anthropologist vociferously alleged that *I, Rigoberta Menchú* served—in its celebration of leftist political consciousness—a problematic Guatemalan guerrilla agenda. Soon after the publication of Stoll's exposé, Menchú was repeatedly asked to answer to Stoll's allegations. Acknowledging she had omitted particular details, Menchú revealed that she had "mixed her own experiences with those of others to draw attention to Guatemala's violence."[74]

The mixture of Menchú's "own experiences with those of others to draw attention to Guatemala's violence" corresponds to similar articulations in *When Broken Glass Floats* and *First They Killed My Father*. What is more, these narrative mixtures—which attempt to raise awareness to facilitate social change—make visible the extent to which intimate remembrances of representational suffering are received within a more expansive public sphere, or jurisdiction. Indeed, Leigh Gilmore's notion of jurisdiction, which reimagines the public sphere via the "mechanisms of judgment that pervade it," productively traces how such "oppositional texts" represent "extrajudicial 'trials'" by way of "ethics, truth telling, and scandal."[75]

Apropos the autobiographical intentions that undergird Menchú, Him, and Ung's respective works, central to the reception of *I, Rigoberta Menchú*, *When Broken Glass Floats*, and *First They Killed My Father* is to varying degrees the extent to which trauma (inclusive of self, family, and nation) is reproduced and received. As Gilmore explains, jurisidictional conflicts over how to represent trauma and gender, and who may do so and with what limits, may occur whenever personal accounts are introduced into the public sphere, but particularly when those accounts concern the relation between personal injury and collective politics and make a claim for the representativeness of one's experience of, or perspective on, violence. Insofar as an individual who speaks of injury emerges as the subject of an autobiographical practice, and insofar as that subject makes a claim on public attention through the dissemination of that practice, a juridical project is immediately enjoined.[76]

Focused on the gendered autobiographical relationship between the personal, the collective, and the representative, Gilmore's engagement with "jurisdictional conflicts" and "juridical projects" underscores the difficulty facing authors invested in nonreconciled political movements. Within a milieu marked not by state-authorized justice but state-sanctioned silence, to represent trauma as a means to a juridical end is evaluated (or judged) according to dominant claims of authenticity and, as the *I, Rigoberta Menchú* critique brings to light, a troubling universal standard for human rights narratives. Such authentically driven judgments privilege absoluteness with regard to clearly delineated authorship, precise remembrance, and uncomplicated subjectivity.

Concomitantly, as the Menchú, Him, and Ung controversies nonetheless underscore, the inherent danger of such debates is that macrolevel histories of violence are eschewed in favor of microdegree debunking. In other words, though elements of Menchú's account may have been manipulated, what nevertheless remains is a nonreconciled, nonreparationed story of violence born out of racialized colonization and racist colonialism. Likewise, although Chanrithy Him's *When Broken Glass Floats* and Loung Ung's *First They Killed My Father* are less stable authentic narratives, they nonetheless bring to light the forgotten disastrous impact of U.S. foreign policy, the calamitous legacy of the Khmer Rouge, and the unresolved history of the Killing Fields era in the juridical arena. In so doing, *When Broken Glass Floats* and *First They Killed My Father* still succeed—in spite of such controversies—as qualified literary memorials to the Cambodian genocide and as conflicted monuments to a still-forming Cambodian American selfhood.

CHAPTER 4

Lost Chapters and Invisible Wars

Hip-Hop and Cambodian American Critique

He who protests is an enemy; he who opposes is a corpse.

—Khmer Rouge saying, *Pol Pot's Little Red Book:*
The Sayings of Angkar

My brother started talking about our culture and where he came from. He opened up, talking about the Khmer Rouge. He talked about being in camp, where he had to sneak out to get food knowing that if he would have been caught, it was an automatic death sentence. Something changed. I mean, I heard about this stuff before, but my parents never talked about it. . . . I'm sure every time they mention it they get flashbacks. I mean . . . imagine seeing your relatives, your brothers, and your sisters killed in front of you . . . [and] there's my brother telling me that you have to know where you come from to know who you are.

—Prach Ly (aka praCh), in "Hip Hop Memoirs:
An Interview with Khmer American Rapper praCh"

APPROXIMATELY TWENTY MILES from downtown Los Angeles, Long Beach's business district is a veritable "Little Phnom Penh." Located on Anaheim Street between Atlantic and Junipero Avenues, "Cambodia Town," as it is officially known by city planners, visitors, and residents, boasts numerous Khmer-owned jewelry stores, clothing outlets, donut shops, and restaurants.[1] Civically, culturally, and demographically, Long Beach contains a Cambodian consulate (one of only three in the United States), Theravada Buddhist temples, and the largest Cambodian

American population in the United States.[2] Approximately fifty thousand Cambodians and Cambodian Americans live in Long Beach, making the SoCal port city a certifiable Cambodian mecca.[3] It is therefore not surprising that Long Beach is also home to the biggest Cambodian New Year celebration in the United States.

Each April, Long Beach's Cambodia Town and El Dorado Park become primary destination points for an estimated twenty thousand celebrants who flock to see mile-long parades, participate in communal religious ceremonies, partake in outdoor community barbecues, and attend live performances.[4] It was against this festive backdrop—during the 2000 Cambodian New Year celebration—that twenty-one-year-old Khmer American rapper praCh (neé Prach Ly) distributed copies of his debut album, *Dalama: The End'n Is Just the Beginnin'*.[5] A self-described "child of the Killing Fields," praCh—the Lys' seventh child—was born on May 5, 1979 in a Democratic Kampuchean labor camp.[6] As the Khmer Rouge struggled to hold power in the face of Vietnamese invasion and seeming liberation, praCh's family (his father, mother, sisters, and brothers) escaped from Veal Srae K'prach (near Battambang) to a Thai refugee camp in the early 1980s.[7] In 1983, after months of bureaucratic red tape, the Lys finally secured U.S. sponsorship and initially settled in Jacksonville, Florida.[8]

Four years later, the family made their way west to El Monte, California, and lived in what praCh describes as "the ghetto of all ghettos." In an interview with Sharon May, praCh elaborates: "It was like a project—apartments on top of apartments—and the school was in the back of the apartments. In the alleyways there were drug deals, and every night we heard helicopters and shoot-outs."[9] Faced with economic uncertainty and impending violence, the Lys relocated to Long Beach in 1989, where praCh spent much of his early teens in an apartment complex on Long Beach Boulevard, just north of the San Diego Freeway (Interstate 405), a few miles outside Compton. Although the complex had a sizeable Khmer/Khmer American population, praCh remembers that once "we went outside, to the stores or the park, no one knew who Cambodians were. We didn't have an identity. They called us Chinese, chinky eyes, gook. I guess that just made me stronger."[10]

Notwithstanding an outwardly hopeful journey from the Killing Fields to the Promised Land, the Lys repeatedly encountered what praCh would lyrically characterize as a de facto "war on the streets," an image that aptly encompasses an amnesiac terrain of systemic racism, limited socioeconomic opportunity, and profound gang violence.[11] In a 2003 *Los Angeles Times* interview with Nancy Wride, praCh explicitly asserts, "Many Cambodian kids, and my friends of other races, can second this opinion, but it's kind of like 'West Side Story' here. Only instead of fights over turf and girls, it's fights over girls and turf and money."[12] According to the California State Department of Justice, California is a home base for approximately five hundred Asian American gangs; Long Beach, with its rapidly growing Asian American population, is the alleged "birthplace of California's Asian gangs."[13] In Los Angeles County alone, an estimated 1,400 different gangs (with 130,000 members) control various city blocks and territories in South Central and southwest LA, Compton, and Long Beach.[14] Even with the *USA Today* claim that Long Beach was, at the start of the new millennium, the nation's "most ethnically diverse city," the municipality was simultaneously infamous for having the tenth highest poverty level in the country.[15] Therefore, while Long Beach may be a home to the largest Cambodian American population in the United States, it is also a socioeconomically unsettled locale.

In light of mass violence, forced relocation, and narrow economic opportunity, Cambodian Americans incontrovertibly fall outside the essentializing parameters of the model minority myth, which problematically privileges a teleological, middle-class reading of racial progress via economic achievement and educational advancement. Indeed, as former Southeast Asian Resource Center (SEARAC) director KaYing Yang reminds, Cambodian Americans (like their Vietnamese and Laotian refugee counterparts) "struggle with formal education due to a variety of factors including limited English language skills, discrimination [and] systematic miscommunication between students, parents, and teachers."[16] These variables, according to Yang, correspondingly engender "widespread feelings of alienation from mainstream schools."[17] Such challenges are statistically evident in the 2000 census, wherein 78.5 percent of Cambodian Americans spoke a "language other than English" and 41.1 percent admitted that they spoke English less than "very well." For those aged twenty-five and older, 38.5 percent had less than a high school diploma and only 11.3 percent completed a bachelor's degree. Socioeconomically, 15.4 percent of Cambodian American families live below the poverty line (compared to 10.5 percent for all U.S. families).[18]

For disaffected, disenfranchised, and disillusioned Cambodian American youth like praCh—the 1.5-generation inheritors of posttraumatic stress and refugee-driven poverty—Southeast Asian American gangs such as the Asian Boyz, Oriental Lazy Boyz, and Tiny Rascals inopportunely afford community, promise protection, and provide employment.[19] While praCh himself never joined a gang, he was a witness to concomitant criminality and violence. In the early 1990s, the future "King of Khmer Rap" was a backseat passenger in a stolen car. For this one-time offense, the fifteen-year-old praCh was arrested, convicted, and sentenced to eighteen months' probation.[20] Soon after, praCh had some heated confrontations with local gang members. As the emcee recalls, "It got to the point where they shot up my house while my parents were in it. . . . I was guilty by association. . . . To save my life [my parents] had to ship me elsewhere."[21] Expressly, praCh's parents, concerned with their present-day livelihood and worried about the future, sent their youngest son back east to live with his older brother in Jacksonville, Florida.

Reminiscent of praCh's previous relocations in the shadow of mass violence (from Democratic Kampuchea) and potential criminal hostility (in El Monte and Long Beach), this third migration nevertheless instantiated a politically motivated, artistically driven Cambodian American consciousness. As praCh relates:

> When I was there [in Jacksonville], he [the brother] was in a singing band. He was like a wedding singer (laughter) though he didn't sing. He was a guitar player, a bass player. Every Saturday he and the other guys in the band would meet up and rehearse. I think it inspired me to think about my own music. I heard the bass, and when I heard the rhythm I just started freestylin' along. . . . Later that night, my brother took me aside and said, "I sense some type of [the] artistic in you but what you're sayin' is in your words but not you. For you to be an artist, you have to project yourself."[22]

This fraternal exchange presages praCh's opening recollection about his brother's past and memories of life under the Khmer Rouge. By stressing who we are and how we got here, praCh's brother issued a creative directive for his younger sibling, who began writing lyrics about the Killing Fields era based on interviews with family members, "band members, nearby elders [Cambodians], and people who visited him." When praCh returned to Long Beach a year later, he had a "notebook of rhymes," the primary source text for *Dalama: The End'n Is Just the Beginnin'*.[23]

Comprised of familial recollections and individual remembrances, with samples from John Pilger's *Year Zero* documentary, excerpts from Roland Joffé's *Killing Fields,* and lyrics about Long Beach gang violence, *Dalama: The End'n Is Just the Beginnin'* is a transnational story of war, relocation, and resettlement. The title *Dalama* emerges from praCh's admission that he "made up [the] word and turned that into the story of his life," making visible a diagnostic reading of refugee personhood.[24] Correspondingly envisioned as a hip-hop memoir, with geopolitical coordinates in Democratic Kampuchea, postconflict Cambodia, and the United States, *Dalama: The End'n Is Just the Beginnin'* reflects praCh's initial artistic desire to marry—by way of title, lyric, sample, and beat—"drama" to "trauma." Syntactically, this union of individual performance and collective grief foregrounds a conspicuous Cambodian American polemic, or "dilemma," composed of historical amnesia, cultural rupture, and unstable identity formation.

This tripartite engagement (between drama, trauma, and dilemma) suggestively concretizes and anticipates the role of memory in the making of praCh's capacious *Dalama* trilogy, which includes the above-mentioned *Dalama: The End'n Is Just the Beginnin'* (1999), *Dalama: The Lost Chapter* (2003), and *Dalama: Memoirs of an Invisible War* (2010).[25] With lyrical allusions to U.S. foreign policy, Khmer Rouge authoritarianism, unreconciled genocide, contemporary Cambodian politics, and present-day Cambodian American deportations, praCh's subsequent references to "lost chapters," "memoirs," and "invisible wars" lay bare the Khmer American rapper's evolving identity politics, multifaceted recovery agenda, and multivalent memory work. As a deeper evaluation of the *Dalama* trilogy underscores, praCh's Cambodian American polemic—or critique—parallels Lisa Lowe's memory-oriented characterization of Asian American cultural production, which accordingly remembers the past "in and through [the] fragmentation, loss, and dispersal that constitutes that past."[26] To that end, praCh's multivolume hip-hop series critically, transnationally, and emblematically remembers a fractured genocidal history, a forgotten postconflict imaginary, and a ruptured Cambodian American selfhood.

Locating Who We Are and Where We Came From: *The End'n Is Just the Beginnin'*

If, as Tricia Rose maintains, East Coast hip-hop "emerges from the deindustrialization meltdown where social alienation, prophetic imagination,

and yearning intersect," then praCh's *Dalama: The End'n Is Just the Beginnin'*
analogously engages a vexed West Coast "retrospective imagination" born
out of refugee alienation, improvisational production, and situational
(be)longing.[27] Indeed, as praCh's track, "Child of the Killing Fields" underscores, integral to the Khmer American rapper's debut album is a re-
flexive remembering of the Cambodian genocide:

> Sometime when I'm alone,
> I sit and stare at the skies.
> My mind starts to wonder,
> about the whats and why,
> are we here and whats
> the meaning of our existences? So I started reading and researching
>   since . . .
> I love my land to death,
> a child of the killing fields.
> now I'm on a quest,
> for the truth to reveal
> cuz' I still feel the pain,
> for all the lost souls,
> from the Khmer Rouge regime,
> that turn Cambodia into a hell hole.

As the above passage reveals, this imagination necessarily begins with
multiple interrogations of refugee subjectivity, replete with whys, whats,
and hows. Concurrently, such geopolitical queries set in motion transnational quests for truth that congruently foreground affective cause/effect
investigations involving Khmer Rouge authoritarianism, state-authorized
mass loss, and refugee displacement.

Notwithstanding the album's global registers, praCh's tactical use of
hip-hop strikes an identifiably domestic chord, establishing the rapper's
simultaneous U.S. location, cultural influences, and racial politics. As the
emcee remembers:

> During that time [in the early 1990s] N.W.A. was huge. . . . They
> had a single, "Fuck the Police," and—with the [Los Angeles]
> riots—it just made sense. . . . [W]hen the breakdancing faded out

[in the mid-1990s], everybody was going to these parks and clubs, where they would freestyle battle. I just got into the mix because I liked poetry. . . . I didn't choose music. I guess music chose me.[28]

Read against a particular locale (Southern California), a distinct temporality (the early 1990s), and a specific aesthetic mode (hip-hop), praCh's artistic coming-of-age is likewise tied to resistive racial politics (against police brutality), West Coast gangsta rap (N.W.A./Niggas wit Attitude), and classed racial uprisings (the 1992 Los Angeles riots).

As the above passage further reveals, the Khmer American artist's initiation into the hip-hop arena was largely shaped by coming up in Long Beach, watching breakdancers, DJs, and rappers move, spin, and battle in local clubs and parks. To be sure, while the SoCal port city remains an indisputable Cambodian mecca, Long Beach is also a verifiable hip-hop hub, the original base of operations for rappers like Snoop Dogg, Nate Dogg, Lil ½ Dead, Daz Dillinger, Twinz, and Warren G. These hip-hop roots extend in a southeasterly direction to Compton, home to Death Row Records CEO Suge Knight and the original members of the aforementioned N.W.A.: Dr. Dre (founder of Death Row Records), Ice Cube (forefather of Da Lench Mob Records), Eazy E (originator of Ruthless Records), MC Ren, and Yella.

Even so, praCh's entrée into the music business—unlike the experiences of his West Coast rap luminaries and influences—was largely a grassroots, low-budget endeavor. In actual fact, *Dalama: The End'n Is Just the Beginnin'* was completed at breakneck speed—within a three-month span—while praCh was working days at a karaoke shop on the corner of Anaheim Street and Martin Luther King Jr. Boulevard. As the Khmer American rapper later recounts, "My friends would come over and we would just sit in the garage and record. . . . [*Dalama*] was [more] about freestylin' . . . more of me and my friends saying, 'I'm going to come into this part, you come into that part.'"[29] With no studio access and little production knowledge, the inexperienced emcee extemporized, making do with a karaoke machine, discarded microphones, and an old tape recorder. The end result was a sixteen-track album marked by intros, punctuated by interludes, and characterized by outros, including songs such as "The YearZero!," "The Letter (Prisoner of War)," "War on the Streetz," and "Ah-Ye (Khmer Rap!)."[30] These titles foreshadow the thematic focus

of *Dalama: The End'n Is Just the Beginnin'* with references to the Khmer
Rouge regime, transnational wars (in Cambodia and the United States),
and hip-hop culture.

Furthermore, in recollecting the Killing Fields era (by way of lyric) and
remembering a fragmented Cambodian American experience (through
rhyme), praCh produces a Cambodian American critique via the social
justice idiom of hip-hop. Even with Tricia Rose's recent critical assertion
that present-day "hip hop is in terrible crisis" due to increased commer-
cialization and mainstream dissemination of "bling" agendas, the form's
historic function as a socially conscious medium—born out of late 1960s
civil rights struggle and antiracist resistance—persists in *Dalama: The
End'n Is Just the Beginnin'*.[31] Indeed, praCh's debut album—which provides a thematic template for the transnational trilogy—draws its affective
power from resistive utterances (proclamations against the Khmer Rouge
regime and shortsighted U.S. foreign policy) and bold declarations (ob-
servations about police corruption and the perils of gang life).

A multiperson enterprise, *Dalama: The End'n Is Just the Beginnin'* features members of Northstar Resurrec (a local hip-hop crew comprised of
Cambodian American rappers sparC da Polar, doZer, and Toeum Tom
Chan), whose beats, rhymes, and raps undergird first-generation survivor accounts of living under the Khmer Rouge. In line with the album's
collected (and collective) imaginary, these narratives uncannily presage
present-day, individualized accounts of gangs, crime, and corruption. As
praCh recalls, "being in Long Beach . . . gave me a lot of resources. . . . I
started talking to people. . . . They are living documents, not something
you put up in a museum or just read about."[32] Although such resources are
"not something you put up in a museum," they are nevertheless integral to
praCh's *Dalama: The End'n Is Just the Beginnin'*, which strategically uses oral
history, deliberately accesses life writing, and dialogically utilizes hip-hop
to tell a transnational story of disruption and violence. Interdisciplinary
and polyvocal, historical and contemporary, *Dalama: The End'n Is Just the
Beginnin'* is a de facto past/present Cambodian American archive, one
that labors—notwithstanding state-sanctioned assaults on history, memory, and protest—to articulate and instantiate an intergenerational story
of survival, displacement, and relocation.

Shifting from theme to distribution, praCh's *Dalama: The End'n Is Just
the Beginnin'* would unquestionably assume a global reach that belied its

humble regional origins. Soon after praCh distributed copies at the 2000 Cambodian New Year celebration, a copy of the album—unbeknownst to the artist—made its way to Cambodia and was played on Phnom Penh radio. Its international sales increased exponentially through bootleg copies, though these pirated versions carried no initial artist attribution. In the face of the album's anti–Democratic Kampuchea lyrics, *Dalama: The End'n Is Just the Beginnin'* was renamed *Khmer Rouge Rap*, confirming (albeit ironically) the work's unconcealed vocal negotiation of the Killing Fields era. Widely circulated yet anonymously ascribed, it took investigative journalism—via Gina Chon, an *AsiaWeek* reporter—to connect rapper to record.[33] As 2000 came to a close, even though praCh had not been back to Cambodia since he was a toddler, the karaoke store employee would nevertheless become the "pioneer of Khmer rap," its "first rap star," and the person responsible for Cambodia's first number one hip-hop album.[34]

Incredibly popular among Khmer youth who connected with *Dalama*'s beats, praCh's bilingual lyrics (in Khmer and English), and the album's intergenerational focus, the Long Beach resident turned international rapper achieved a global success that far surpassed his domestic impact. As Narin Kem (editor of *Serey Pheap News*) explains, the artist's "rap music tells a tale familiar to older refugees. But for young listeners, it chronicles the Khmer Rouge extermination of an estimated one in five Cambodians, a fact well covered in Long Beach schools. In Cambodia, the genocide is not taught [in] school."[35] Situated against this amnesiac context, *Dalama: The Endin' Is Just the Beginnin'* ineludibly—as praCh surmises—"brought attention *back* to the Killing Fields, and kids wanted to know more about their background. . . . They are hearing it from one of their own, and saying, 'Hey, I want to know more'" (emphasis added).[36]

Notwithstanding such affinities, praCh's problematical position—as a Cambodian American refugee born in the Killing Fields and raised in Long Beach—makes unstable a singular nation-state affiliation at work in hip-hop shout-outs about location and personhood. Indeed, the rapper's previous assertion that Khmer youth responded to *Dalama: The End'n Is Just the Beginnin'* because he was "one of their own" underlines a complex transnational orientation that is geopolitically foundational to the Cambodian American experience. Moreover, while praCh's lyrics against Khmer Rouge authoritarianism militate against the forgetful foundations of Democratic Kampuchean selfhood, they analogously engage a Cambodian American critique that actively remembers the impact of cold war policy and the American War in Vietnam. In so doing, *The End'n Is Just the Beginnin'*—which lyrically emphasizes the role of U.S. bombings in the making of both the Khmer Rouge and the Cambodian American refugee—is critically connected to other Southeast Asian American hip-hop producers by way of international locations, forms, forums, and politics.

From Hmong American Taou Saiko Lee's songs about CIA dirty wars to Nam's raps about Vietnamese American refugees, from Geologic's lyrical treatment of the U.S. occupation in the Philippines to Cambodian crew Seasia's cadenced negotiation of neoliberalism and poverty, Southeast Asian American hip-hop remains a contrapuntal site of resistance and a space for social, economic, and political critique. Situated amid a self-deterministic milieu of anti-imperial protest, wherein Southeast Asian American hip-hop artists repeatedly return to the historical (and transnational) circumstances of orchestrated mass loss and state-authorized violence, praCh's *Dalama: The End'n Is Just the Beginnin'* reinscribes a largely ignored Cambodian American agency that incontrovertibly begins and ends with cold war realpolitik, Khmer Rouge authoritarianism, and refugee relocation.

On the whole, as an artist who came of age during the Los Angeles riots, as a dislocated Khmer American intimately cognizant of socioeconomic inequity, and as a frontline spectator to police brutality, praCh's earliest musical influence—Compton-based N.W.A.—attests to a comprehensible hip-hop politics and aesthetic. Correspondingly, praCh's earlier allusion to N.W.A.'s "Fuck the Police" (1988)—which tellingly and subsequently "made sense" in the disastrous afterglow of the riots—foregrounds a political like-mindedness vis-à-vis race, culture, and people of color (non)citizenship. This kinship—born out of fused aesthetics and politicized subjectivities—coheres with a foundational (and hopeful) understanding of hip-hop as a powerful means of expression for the dispossessed, the disenfranchised, and the racially profiled. From N.W.A. to Public Enemy, from Oakland's Tupak to Brooklyn's Jay-Z, from Souls of Mischief to a Tribe Called Quest, what remains a hip-hop constant is a politically conscious message that remembers profound acts of state violence, histories of systemic inequality, biopolitical regulation, and necropolitical socioeconomic oppression.

Between Historical Fact and Historical Truth:
Escapes from the Killing Fields

Insofar as praCh's first *Dalama* commences and concludes with international conflict, civil war, and gang violence, it likewise engages a complex matrix of genocide history and survivor memory. Such a schema—which dialogically attaches individual remembrances to collected experiences—corresponds to what rap pioneer Mos Def argues is hip-hop's central intellectual principle: to reproduce a viable (and visionary) form of knowledge in the fused interstices of historical fact and historical truth.[37] In so doing, Mos Def evokes a relevant past/present reading of the historical that encompasses factual understandings of events and comprehended meanings. Correspondingly, praCh's *Dalama* trilogy, which labors to recollect the facts of failed U.S. policy and Khmer Rouge authoritarianism, concomitantly remembers the Cambodian refugee experience and generates a distinct Cambodian American episteme, or truth.

Such cognition is necessarily referential and citational, joined to an identifiable event (allusions to the Khmer Rouge takeover) and survivor accounts (direct quotes from Cambodian American refugees).[38] This particular correlation, characterized by a legible connection between history and vocalized memory, becomes integral to praCh's multivalent Cambodian American critique, which is further clarified via juxtaposition with an exclusively referential Democratic Kampuchean text: Ice-T's "Escape from the Killing Fields," from the 1991 album *O.G. Original Gangster*. Featuring a total of twenty-four tracks, West Coast rapper Ice-T's *O.G. Original Gangster* was the subject of critical acclaim and the recipient of large-scale commercial success.[39] Avowing that it was "the 1991 equivalent of [Sly and the Family Stone's] *There's a Riot Going On*," *Rolling Stone* critic Mark Coleman wrote that the album was "a bleak, prophetic, and savagely funny dispatch from the front lines of the war at home."[40]

In form and content, *O.G. Original Gangster* undeniably reflects the historical, political, and cultural circumstances that undergird West Coast hip-hop and gangsta rap. Born amid racially antagonistic Reagan-era policies and deindustrialized disillusionment, characterized by urban location, and focused on the lyric, the California-based Ice-T (with the aid of hard, metal-infused beats) forcefully rapped about inner-city violence and Los Angeles decay. As *Entertainment Weekly* reviewer James Bernard observes, a gritty tone infuses "all 24 tracks," and Ice-T "delve[d] into the ugliness that lurks behind headlines on urban blight." Bernard further declares that Ice-T's fourth album "confronts us with the tears of an abused child, the remorseless trigger finger of an urban gangster, and the willingness of the larger society to ignore it all."[41]

Emphasizing the album's function as a "dispatch," reviewers and critics alike consistently accentuated Ice-T's eyewitness role in the violent, war-like narrative of South Central Los Angeles, and the album continues to be ranked as one of the top hip-hop albums ever produced.[42] Considered by many to be the strongest album in Ice-T's oeuvre, *O.G. Original Gangster* would eventually give rise to a 1994 book, *The Ice Opinion: Who Gives a Fuck?*, which selectively drew on the album's track titles as the basis for chapters focused on urban poverty, the hip-hop industry, free speech, and the cultural imaginary of Los Angeles gang life. Released the same year as the Rodney King beating, and a year before Ice-T's most notorious song, "Cop Killer," *O.G. Original Gangster* cemented the rapper's reputation as "that rare gangster rapper who leads with his brain instead of his gun or his crotch."[43]

To be sure, "Escape from the Killing Fields" epitomizes the rapper's turn to interior and communal critiques, a thematic touchstone in *O.G. Original Gangster*. Employing samples from Melvin Bliss's "Synthetic Substitution" and James Brown's "Funky Drummer" (incidentally the most sampled recording in hip-hop), "Escape from the Killing Fields" conceptually diverges from contemporaneous West Coast gangsta artists like N.W.A.'s Ice Cube and solo artist Redman. Combating assertions of South Central Los Angeles 'hood pride, Ice-T potently alleges these notions are held by brainwashed brethren whose mind-sets are chiefly responsible for ongoing oppression. Consequently, Ice-T engenders an alternative reading of the 'hood premised on the impossible task of neighborhood rehabilitation and redemption. Stressing educational limitation, police corruption, and fatal healthcare, Ice-T's "Escape from the Killing Fields" lives up to titular form and portrays South Central Los Angeles as a socioeconomic prison and concomitant extermination site. Circumscribed by systemic racism and faced with a violent governmentality committed to oppression, South Central Los Angeles is—as per Ice-T's characterization—a militarized zone and a maximum-security prison, typified by the presence of high-powered rifles, checkpoints, and watchtowers.

Within the lyrical imaginary of "Escape from the Killing Fields," this defamiliarized environment—despite jus soli citizenship—produces

African American and Latino refugees, who lack a nation-state affiliation and basic human rights. In line with the track's "Killing Fields" theme, these disenfranchised bodies involuntarily take flight in the dead of night, presumably to safer SoCal neighborhoods. This necropoliticized message, which fixes community dystopia to stateless formation, is at the heart of "Escape from the Killing Fields" and persists throughout *O.G. Original Gangster*. Indeed, the connection between local and global is especially evident in the album's final track, "Ya Shoulda Killed Me Last Year," a spoken-word protest piece about the less-than-heroic motivations for the first Gulf War and disastrous overinvestment in the prison-industrial complex.

Ice-T's "Escape from the Killing Fields," replete with lyrical allusions to death, hiding, and escape, purposefully accesses the history of—and dominant associations with—the Cambodian genocide. In particular, Ice-T's reference to hospitals where subjects go to die, coupled with the complementary need to flee in order to stay alive, unintentionally calls forth previously discussed Cambodian American cultural productions that detail life under the Khmer Rouge and narrate harrowing escapes to Thai refugee camps. Moreover, the emcee's condemnations of domestic U.S. modes of racialization, subjugation, and state-sanctioned violence accrete global meaning when set against contemporaneous U.S. foreign policies of excursion, invasion, and imperialism. Accordingly, Ice-T's *O.G. Original Gangster* coheres with Sunaina Maira's astute observation that "domestic histories of race and class relations cannot be isolated from the broader rubric of U.S. empire."[44] As this concise reading makes clear, "Escape from the Killing Fields" implicitly and significantly reminds listeners—through form and content—that hip-hop remains the cultural extension of a past/present civil rights struggle.

These hip-hop matters—corroborated by racially conscious lyrics and civil rights era samples—access the political agendas of the Black Panther Party, the Yellow Power Movement, La Raza, and the American Indian Movement, which pioneered a resistive, racial reading of the personal as political.[45] Such identity politics were, as per late-1960s militant activism, foundational in deconstructing institutionalized modes of racism through neighborhood self-determinism and racially formed critique. By drawing on this established resistance script, "Escape from the Killing Fields" productively highlights a racialized legacy of state-authorized violence comprised of biopolitical regulation (via pointed mentions of police, schools, and hospitals) and necropolitical containment (by way of the prison-industrial complex). At the same time, the West Coast emcee gestures toward a familiar Black Power self-determinism with vigorous renunciations of internalized racism, weighty disavowals of market-driven disenfranchisement, and powerful abjurations of institutionalized oppression.

Notwithstanding undercutting ethnoracial logics, persuasive personal politics, and undeniable activist dynamics, Ice-T's strategic employment of the Killing Fields as both a historical fact and a metaphor for state-authorized violence unconsciously bespeaks the genocide's troubled position as an absent presence within dominant U.S. political and cultural discourses. Explicitly missing from Ice-T's articulation is a reading of the Killing Fields as a specific, Cambodian experience, despite imagistic coherences between the necropolitical imaginary of Democratic Kampuchea and the biopoliticized Los Angeles cityscape. Nor is there an interrogation of racial frameworks beyond a largely black/white binary that could potentially accommodate the aforementioned rise of Southeast Asian (and in particular, Cambodian American) gangs in Los Angeles and nearby Long Beach. Although Ice-T acknowledges Puerto Ricans and Native Americans, the omission of Asian Americans inadvertently accentuates a model minoritized recapitulation that projects (via absence) a superficial characterization of probationary whiteness and obscured reading of U.S. foreign policy.

Hence, in his racially scripted critique of U.S. exceptionalism, Ice-T paradoxically and unconsciously reinscribes mainstream ethnoracial hierarchies within the United States. Unintentionally, Ice-T's "Escape from the Killing Fields" draws upon Cambodian Syndrome amnesiac politics that resemble in form—but not in function—neoconservative and neoliberal co-optations of the catastrophic aftermath of the Khmer Rouge regime. Similarly, the progressive politics embedded in Ice-T's social justice articulation are made less stable by his economic use of the Killing Fields as a fact-oriented—but not truth-centric—signifier of state-authorized violence. Such strategic forgetting fails to link this fact to the historical experience of the Cambodian genocide (and, by proxy, its impact on Cambodian Americans). Set against these amnesiac politics, "Escape from the Killing Fields" obscures Cambodian and Cambodian American history, relegating the genocide to the status of an allusion without explication, a reference without a citation, and an event that is in effect spoken of but not so much spoken about.

Even with problematical registers, Ice-T's "Escape from the Killing

Fields" is undeniably grounded in the hip-hop exploration of racial subjugation and mortal consequences. Correspondingly, the South Central
emcee engenders a formidable template for resistive articulations against
state-sanctioned forms of power. And the song's relevance with regard
to hip-hop form and concomitant political function presages and foregrounds the lyrical moves at work in contemporary Cambodian American
hip-hop, which is analogously engaged in a multivalent project of genocidal remembrance, politicized resistance, and juridical activism. Last, but
certainly not least, Ice-T's position as a West Coast gangsta rapper provides
a divergent model through which to read and deconstruct Cambodian
American hip-hop by way of culturally relevant, unrelenting reportage.

This reportage—or street journalism—makes visible a distinct hip-
hop critique that challenges conservative claims of inherent racial pathology, innate criminality, and intrinsic poverty. As Robin D. G. Kelley provocatively contends,

> When gangsta rappers do write lyrics intended to convey social
> realism, their work loosely resembles a street ethnography of racist
> institutions and social practices, told more often than not in the
> first person. Whether gangsta rappers step into the character of a
> gang banger, hustler, or ordinary working person—that is, prod-
> ucts and residents of the 'hood—they constitute an alternative
> voice to mainstream journalists and social scientists.[46]

By reframing the terms through which hip-hop is intellectually understood—as a mode of "street ethnography" as opposed to strict entertainment commodity—Kelley underscores the form's intellectual agenda and
relevance via socioeconomic critique.

Correspondingly, while Ice-T's "Escape from the Killing Fields" militates (through lyric and sample) against multiculturalist claims of racial
progress, praCh's *Dalama: The End'n Is Just the Beginnin'* combats facile assertions of unimpeded refugee asylum and reconciled Cambodian
American selfhood through transnational dispatches. These frontline
messages, the foundation for Cambodian American memory work, encompass Khmer Rouge killing fields, Thai refugee camps, and Long Beach
streets.

If, as Public Enemy's Chuck D famously remarked, hip-hop functions
as a "Black CNN," then praCh's *Dalama: The End'n Is Just the Beginnin'*

operates as an analogous yet uniquely Cambodian American platform. This program, relevant to Khmer youth and the 1.5 generation, broadcasts stories of genocide, struggle, and socioeconomic oppression. Notwithstanding the power of praCh's intergenerational message, equally significant is the rapper's strategic and ethnographic engagement with Cambodia's musical landscape in subsequent *Dalama* albums. In *Dalama: The Lost Chapter*, this memory work assumes the sampling form of traditional Khmer music. For *Dalama: Memoirs of an Invisible War*, 1960s Cambodian psychedelic pop provides an identifiable and tactically nostalgic audioscape. As heterotopic readings of both *Dalama: The Lost Chapter* and *Dalama: Memoirs of an Invisible War* illuminate, praCh's use of specific samples and critical lyrics evocatively remembers cultural facts and cultural truths that correspondingly facilitate alternative routes to refugee reparation and Cambodian American rehabilitation.

Resampling the Intergenerational Past: *Dalama: The Lost Chapter*

praCh's hip-hop engagement with Cambodian American knowledge production—predicated on a layered contemplation of genocide, civil rights, and human rights—coincides with Michel Foucault's working definition of "heterotopias," or distinct countersites "found within [a] culture." As Foucault asserts, heterotopias from the outset undermine idealized utopic formations via identifiable modes of mimetic subversion. Accordingly, heterotopias embody potentially corrective yet consistently alternative, contradictory spaces. It is precisely within and through heterotopic sites that state-sanctioned discourses are "simultaneously represented, contested, and inverted." Fixed to specific "slices in time," heterotopias are "capable of juxtaposing in a single real place several spaces" and contain "several sites that are in themselves incompatible."[47]

Set adjacent refugee temporalities (before, during, and after the Khmer Rouge era) and multinational spaces (Democratic Kampuchean labor camps and Long Beach streets), a heterotopic reading of *Dalama: The Lost Chapter* brings to light the intergenerational contours of Cambodian American memory work and contemporary contradictions of Cambodian American selfhood. Concomitantly, praCh's multivalent memory work—committed to destabilizing nationalistic narratives via an interdisciplinary soundscape—tirelessly reckons with an overwhelming genocide past.

Indeed, these spectacular registers are contemporaneously evident in the official name given to the current UN/Cambodian War Crimes Tribunal: the *Extraordinary* Chambers in the Courts of Cambodia.[48]

Alternatively, praCh's transnational *Dalama* trilogy—rooted in a problematical refugee history and politicized Cambodian American personhood—must analogously contend with past claims of cold war democratic virtue and assertions of present-day U.S. exceptionalism. Such representations, contestations, and inversions—which continuously collapse historical fact and historical truth—operate as primary bases upon which to investigate, assess, and evaluate a distinct Cambodian American critique. This critical evaluation—by virtue of history, culture, and memory—brings acute, heterotopic attention to past Khmer Rouge authoritarianism, contemporary tribunal machinations, and modern U.S. imperialism. Consequently, praCh's *Dalama: The Lost Chapter*, like *The End'n Is Just the Beginnin'*, necessarily commences with the contradictions of the Democratic Kampuchean era wherein life and human rights are devalued in the aftermath of ostensibly egalitarian revolution.

However, the album's concluding references to 9/11 underline a divergently dislocating narrative marked by abrupt starts, sudden closures, unforeseen ruptures, and traumatic silences. These discordant aural registers are echoed in lyrical articulations of transnational violence that span the war in Vietnam (indirectly responsible for creating Cambodian refugees) and the war on terror (directly culpable for manufacturing Cambodian American deportees). As significantly, this resistive lyricism is joined by a reparative aesthetic comprised of traditional Khmer music, contemporary American R&B, and modern-day hip-hop. Unquestionably, praCh's *Dalama: The Lost Chapter*, through lyric, sample, and backbeat, builds on the initial remembrance labor at work in *The Endin' Is Just the Beginnin'*. In particular, praCh's sequel engages an expanded heterotopic exploration of past, present, and future Cambodian American selfhood.

Bilingual, historical, and transnational, *The Lost Chapter* continues the collected memory program established in the first *Dalama,* and the sequel similarly traverses multiple sociopolitical terrains in Cambodia and the United States. From the outset, these migratory registers and multinational imaginaries are visually signaled in *Dalama: The Lost Chapter*'s front matter. Conceived and drawn by the rapper himself, the album cover depicts Khmer temple *(wat)* architecture, a typical Cambodian domicile (a stilted hut), Southeast Asian flora (a banyan tree), an American cityscape, and a ship. These representations—constitutive of a transnational graphic archive—are analogously fixed to home locations, migration histories, and national citizenship.[49] Less obvious, the inclusion of a smiling face statue within the banyan tree's trunk signifies a direct allusion to Angkor Wat, presaging in the process the album's aural focus on classical Khmer tradition.[50]

Like its *Dalama* predecessor, *The Lost Chapter* is a Khmer-English Mujestic Records production, with a total of twenty-one hard-hitting tracks, including "Power, Territory, and Rice," "Pin Peat's Resurrection," and "Neutral (before the war)."[51] Notwithstanding the album's sequential status as a second *Dalama*, praCh maintains that *The Lost Chapter* is—as the title suggests—a found extension of *The Endin' Is Just the Beginnin'*. As praCh reveals, "I actually didn't intend on having a trilogy. But, after the first album was done, I felt it was short. I felt like I needed to express and explain more."[52] Apropos an intertextual hip-hop imaginary, praCh's *The Lost Chapter* contains cinematic samples (e.g., remixed excerpts from Pilger's *Year Zero* and Joffé's *Killing Fields*), political speeches (namely the opening passage of President George W. Bush's 9/11 address), and oral histories (showcasing praCh's father, Seng Ly, speaking in Khmer).[53] Although praCh is *The Lost Chapter*'s chief emcee, Northstar Resurrec reappear, taking the lyrical lead in four songs. Universal Speakers, a pan–Southeast Asian American, reggae/R&B/hip-hop female trio (composed of vocalists Vice, Versa, and Versatile) make their *Dalama* debut furnishing additional background vocals. Likewise new to praCh's autobiographical project is Cambodian master artist Ho C. Chan, who choreographs and performs the album's distinctively traditional Khmer musical score.[54]

Thematically consistent with *The End'n Is Just the Beginnin'*, the Killing Fields and its legacy figuratively and musically haunt *The Lost Chapter*. Chronologically ordered, *The Lost Chapter*'s tracks bring to light Cambodia's Killing Fields history, the Lys' collected experiences of life under the Khmer Rouge, and the rapper's evolving Cambodian American consciousness. Correspondingly, *The Lost Chapter*'s initial compositions foreground the Khmer Rouge takeover of Phnom Penh (1975); the album's setting then shifts to 1979, the year of praCh's birth. The remaining pieces, which reference the September 11 attacks and the USA PATRIOT Act, are for the most part located in the present.[55] Structurally, *The Lost Chapter* is divided into three primary sections, which (like its predecessor) include an intro (subtitled "invasion"), an intermission ("RULES . . . "), and an outro (aka "p e a C e").

Accordingly, the genocide, which persists as the album's central historical fact, simultaneously serves as the "end'n" of and the "beginnin'" for
the present-day Cambodian American experience. At the same time, *The
Lost Chapter* revises—or rather remixes—this genocide narrative to fit a
more pronounced intergenerational agenda that connects cultural facts
(past Khmer traditions) to cultural truths (reparative meaning). Indeed,
as praCh's "STORIES" (*The Lost Chapter*'s second track) emblematizes,
integral to song and album is a discernible remembrance program that attaches survivor testimony to Cambodian American selfhood. "STORIES"
begins with fellow Khmer American emcee doZer's lyrical account of the
Khmer Rouge takeover. With short, fast rhymes, doZer's rap intro urgently
restages the chaotic start of the Killing Fields era, wherein Cambodians
were forced (as per regime biopower and authoritarian regulation) to
quickly move from city to countryside labor camp.

In turn, these Khmer Rouge biopolitics prefigure a concomitant lyrical
focus on regime necropolitics, typified by undeviating mentions of execution, starvation, and death. Furthermore, as "STORIES" progresses, the
song shifts to a more explicit (and now familiar) familial focus, exemplified by its chorus:

> Stories told by our parents to us
> Before we go to bed about the field revolution
> and two millions that are dead
> Is in our head
> And it's hard to let go
> but instead-a shedding tears
> we're here to let you know
> about the Killing Fields
> not long ago.

Citing the source of traumatic transmission ("our parents"), praCh congruently references the Killing Fields era and its human cost with references to "the field revolution" and the "two millions that are dead." These
parent/child frames—which constitute a distinct memory dyad—are
grammatically confirmed by collective pronouns and possessives (for example, "we" and "our") that foreshadow intergenerational dialogues about
the Khmer Rouge era, ruptured refugee experiences, and legacies of posttraumatic stress.

What is more, the lyrical assertion that the Cambodian genocide did not happen "long ago" makes historically germane survivor memory while militating against teleological readings that troublingly relegate the Khmer Rouge era to the reconciled annals of the distant past. Equally provocative, praCh's lyrics instantiate an active subjectivity built not on "shedding tears" but predicated instead on the intergenerational assertion that "we're here to let you know / about the Killing Fields / not long ago." As "STORIES" makes clear, at stake in *Dalama: The Lost Chapter* is a dialogic transmission of genocide memory between survivors and their 1.5-generation children that instantiates an intergenerational (re)production of knowledge. These multigenerational communications initially assume the lyrical form of admission and testimonial. Nevertheless, such confessions and eyewitness accounts—the basis for a memorial heterotopia—analogously function as citations and referents for a remembered relationship that fixes heroic acts of survivor memory to Cambodian American agency.

The Lost Chapter's intergenerational lyrical emphases set the stage for the album's more expansive audioscape, which (to reiterate) includes traditional Khmer music backbeats, remixed samples, and master musician scores. Whereas *The End'n Is Just the Beginnin'* was—out of economic need and emcee inexperience—largely reliant on prerecorded samples and previously used beats, *The Lost Chapter*'s inventive manipulation of traditional Khmer music forms makes visible the Khmer American emcee's growth as a recording artist. As praCh summarizes,

> I think *Dalama Two* is more—I don't want to say creative, but I gave it its own life. It's not a duplication of the first album. It bears a similarity because it's an autobiography too. But at the same time, it holds its own ground. I mixed Cambodian traditional music with rap; I created a Cambodian hip hop beat. And this time, I was really proud to say, all the beats and instrumentals were ours.[56]

Such compositional differences—which foment a "Cambodian hip hop beat"—substantiate praCh's later assertion that *The Lost Chapter* was more "community-orientated, more 'for the people' type of work."[57]

Indubitably, the heterotopic negotiation of different voices and divergent music forms (multiple artists, parental interviews, hip-hop, and pin peat) in *The Lost Chapter* strikes a differential transnational chord than its predecessor. Indeed, the deliberate incorporation of Khmer music traditions alongside American hip-hop establishes *The Lost Chapter*'s multivalent aural purview, which encompasses both the displaced and relocated. For example, in a track titled "Art of FaCt," the Khmer American rapper avers:

> The trauma of the war
> affect the refugee and foreigner.
> Suffering from deep depression,
> post traumatic stress disorder.
> it's a new world order,
> new threats we're facing
> terrorist and INS deportation. . . .
> There's an epidemic that's killing us surely.
> Over things we don't even own,
> like blocks and territories.
> so call "OG" recruiting young ones.
> jumping them in gangs,
> giving them use guns.
> Not even old enuff to speak,
> already hold'n heat,
> walk'n a dangerous route
> talk'n about "code of the streets."

As the album's lyrics underscore, these transnational bodies must simultaneously negotiate a problematical new world order (replete with new post-9/11 threats and ever-present gang violence) alongside an unreconciled legacy of war, genocide, and relocation.

Even so, *The Lost Chapter* returns to old world frames by way of pin peat, a traditional Khmer music style that includes three singers, two bamboo xylophones, a flute, suspended brass pots, a two-headed drum, a large kettle drum, and a quadruple-reed instrument.[58] A staple of the Khmer royal court, Cambodian pin peat initially drew upon Indian and Javanese traditions and was especially prevalent during the classical Angkor era (ca. 842–ca. 1431 AD). Revived during the twentieth century, pin peat performances were an integral part of Theravada Buddhist religious ceremonies commonly held at the royal palace in Phnom Penh. Considered excessively extravagant and nonrevolutionary, the form (along with classical ballet) was pugnaciously prohibited by the Khmer Rouge, a point made dramatically clear with the execution of an estimated 90 percent of court musicians, dancers, and artists during the Democratic Kampuchean era.

Situated perpendicular to these authoritarian cultural politics, the use of pin peat as a musical foundation in praCh's *The Lost Chapter* signifies a resistive reincorporation of a prerevolutionary Cambodian selfhood that retroactively (and potently) defies past Khmer Rouge directives. As an anonymous *Music Educators Journal* reporter elaborates,

> [during the period of Democratic Kampuchea], the new regime changed the country's name . . . and sought zealously to eradicate all remnants of what they saw as a corrupt, feudal past. In order to murder the old culture they destroyed books, and musical instruments. . . . As a revered symbol of Khmer culture, the musicians and dancers of the Royal Ballet were singled out by the new regime for elimination. They buried some instruments, costumes, and masks, and tried to escape detection by pretending to be workers in the rice fields. A few survived this way; most were put to death.[59]

Accordingly, praCh's use of traditional music forms—a constant throughout the album but most evident in a previously mentioned instrumental track titled "Pin Peat's Resurrection"—memorializes Cambodia's cultural past while monumentalizing a transnational Cambodian American present.[60] Indeed, this resurrectionist track—which features Khmer master musician Ho C. Chan—operates as a forceful reminder of Khmer identity and a prerevolutionary signifier of Cambodian culture. In so doing, "Pin Peat's Resurrection" instantiates a distinct transnational agency rooted in a strategic set of Cambodian American cultural politics.

On the whole, praCh's resurrection of past music traditions attests to an intergenerational capacity (or potential) to reconstruct, rebuild, and reclaim a recognizable Cambodian selfhood in the face of war, relocation, and cultural rupture. Furthermore, the refugee emcee supplements this tactical use of pin peat with another Khmer cultural idiom that makes visible a connection between Cambodian and U.S. aesthetics: the improvisational theatrical form *ayai*, wherein one singer poses a question or rhyme and the other singer responds in kind. The second singer typically answers with the last line sung.[61] As praCh explains,

> Ayai is sort of like rap music, but in a Cambodian way. Ayai is like one poetry master to another poetry master going out on stage

or in front of a village and competing with their wisdom, their knowledge about certain subjects, like their land, but it has to continuously rhyme. So basically—rap. Not all rap is about streets and drugs and partying. There's every variety of rap. With Cambodian ayai, it's sort of like that too.[62]

Traditionally accompanied by musicians, ayai can also be sung a cappella. In *The Lost Chapter,* ayai incontrovertibly resonates with the contours of contemporary rap, which are characterized by a comparable dependence on spoken word, rhymes, and repetition. Whereas traditional Khmer music is at the forefront of "Pin Peat Resurrection," ayai is a genre focus in "refleXion," which features Khmer lyrics. Akin to pin peat with regard to cultural reclamation and memory, ayai is likewise a resurrected marker of Cambodian American selfhood and agency. The combination of such Khmer forms within the album's more expansive Cambodian/Cambodian American imaginary reinforces the transnational nature of *The Lost Chapter,* which charts—through language, beat, and lyric—the trajectory of a Cambodian refugee turned Khmer American rapper.

Within this transnational milieu, praCh creates—by way of traditional Cambodian music, samples from Khmer movies, *The Killing Fields,* and documentaries, and rhymes spoken in English and Khmer—a Cambodian American subjectivity that in the end resists a singular location in one geographic or historical place. Instead, *The Lost Chapter* is invested in an alternate, heterotopic trajectory that maps the contradictory experiences of Cambodian American youth from the Killing Fields of Cambodia to the streets of Long Beach. Paradoxically cast as Khmer Rouge victims in the country of origin, abject refugees in Southeast Asian camps, and vilified perpetrators (gang members) in the country of asylum, Cambodian American masculinity remains a contested site, especially when set against impending post-9/11 deportations. Such characterizations, inclusive of survival success and refugee failure, are undeniably at work in praCh's previously mentioned "Art of FaCt," a composition that in many ways epitomizes the album's vexed engagement with war, relocation, and rupture.

Placed between a track titled "S-21" and a spoken-word outro (which features praCh's previously mentioned father), praCh's "Art of FaCt" concisely encapsulates *The Lost Chapter*'s overriding collected engagement, manifest in samples (artifacts), fused aesthetics (art), and an all-encompassing commitment to historical truth (by way of fact). "Art of FaCt" commences with a digitally manipulated pin peat flute that gives way to a mixed audioscape composed of American R&B marked by an electronic bass line, enhanced pin peat beat, and traditional Khmer reed instrumentation. From the outset, the Khmer American emcee reminds the listener of his refugee past, beginning with the assertion that

> Beyond the killing field,
> a quarter of a century after the genocide.
> after 2 million people murdered,
> the other 5 million survive
> the fabric of the culture,
> beauty drips the texture,
> I find myself in Long Beach,
> the next Cambodian mecca. . . .
> here's a gap in our generation,
> between the adults and kids,
> but since I'm bilingual
> I'm-a use communication as a bridge.

In mentioning the "2 million people murdered" alongside "the other 5 million" who survived, praCh—in "Art of FaCt"—reconfirms the album's undeniable (re)negotiation of the Democratic Kampuchean era. Even so, praCh strategically engages with a geopolitical location "beyond the killing field" by way of "Long Beach," the previously discussed "next Cambodian mecca." Returning to the notion of intergenerational comprehensibility, praCh's "Art of FaCt" acknowledges a "gap in our generation" that nevertheless can be bridged through a committed bilingual cooperation. These linguistic collaborations take on a more resistive register with praCh's subsequent declaration that he is "knock[ing] down the walls / between me and my parents"; indeed, such deconstructions necessarily coincide with a willingness to "listen to their stories on all / without interference."

Notwithstanding the celebratory gestures embedded in "Art of FaCt," the nineteenth track simultaneously engages a series of U.S.-based assessments. In turn, these evaluations foreground a heterotopic Cambodian American critique. Expressly, the utopic tenets of the American dream (manifest in assimilationist rags-to-riches narratives) are countered by lyrics that express the contemporary experiences of Cambodian American youth who face impending "terrorist and INS deportation" due to a U.S. policy of "one strike and you're out" (as per strengthened post-9/11 enforcements of the 1996 immigration reforms). In a more communal vein, praCh takes to task an "epidemic that's killing us surely" (gang violence) by "calling out" and deconstructing shifting family values with lyrics focused on "fixing up marriages" and commodified investments in "fast cars."

Taken together, praCh's *Dalama: The Lost Chapter* concretizes the transnational reaches of praCh's auditory memoir, which strategically accesses and tactically manipulates the interdisciplinary idiom of hip-hop to tell a collected story of Cambodian American survival and conflict. As this evaluation of *The Lost Chapter* brings to light, the Khmer American rapper repeatedly situates the Cambodian American experience within an expanded (and at times contradictory) spectrum of state-authorized loss, systemic racism, and community-sanctioned brutality. To be sure, these critical appraisals—expressed through and against Cambodian American heterotopias—foreground a concluding consideration that involves praCh's third and final installment: *Dalama: Memoirs of an Invisible War.*

Invisible Wars, Folklore, and *Dalama III:*
Remixing Critique and Tradition

Fixed to a distinct Cambodian American history of war, genocide, migration, and adaptation, praCh's *Dalama* trilogy—via articulation, production, and distribution—coheres with Afrika Bambaataa's hopeful observation concerning the genre's global reach. Confessing he "loves that hip hop has become international," the legendary DJ recently averred that, around the world, people are being "educated about some negative and positive things" through rhyme, sample, and lyric.[63] Predicated on an understanding of hip-hop as an established form of global knowledge production, praCh's autobiographical series and Bambaataa's pedagogical statement underscore what S. Craig Watkins notes is "hip hop's widening sphere of influence" by way of history, politics, resistance, and (at times) problematical materialism. Correspondingly situated at the intersection of "mad money," social justice, and cultural action, Watkins evocatively asserts, "Gone are the discussions about *whether* hip hop matters; they have been replaced by the key issues of who and what kinds of values will define *how* hip hop matters."[64]

Building on Watkins's double-sided use of "matter" as subject and verb, indicative of topic and signification, what matters in praCh's oeuvre is a consistent (and often dizzying) transnational negotiation of history, culture, and space via remembrance, reclamation, and revision. Commencing with the Cambodian genocide as unresolved matter of fact in *Dalama: The End'n Is Just the Beginnin'*, praCh continues with the vexed matter of Cambodian American selfhood in *Dalama: The Lost Chapter* through a multifaceted interrogation of cold war realpolitik, racial profiling, and American politics. Befitting such Cambodian American matters, praCh's final *Dalama* is, according to the rapper, his "most explicitly political production" to date, and the Khmer American emcee remixes his transnational critique of past/present U.S. exceptionalism and Cambodian statecraft in *Dalama: Memoirs of an Invisible War.*[65] With twenty-four tracks, *Memoirs of an Invisible War* was originally conceived as a two-album disc (one in Khmer, the other in English) and is currently available only through download.[66]

Unquestionably, as the titular mention of covert conflict foreshadows, praCh's final *Dalama* is very much joined to an exploration of multiple contested imaginaries, evident in tracks such as "Hell's Gate," "i. War," "i deClare War!" and "BahtaWatt! (revolt!)." The repetition of "i" with regard to "war" functions as shorthand for clandestine combat (the American War in Vietnam and the Cambodian Civil War) and hostilities (racial strife and gang violence). Alternatively, the capitalized "C" in consonant titles visually reinforces—as is the case in *The Lost Chapter*'s "Art of FaCt"—praCh's role as primary emcee and storyteller. Thematically, praCh's most recent album marks a slight temporal departure from the previous two *Dalamas*. As praCh asserts, "The last two [albums] were more about the killing fields and my past. This *Dalama* is more about the present and future."[67]

To that end, praCh's *Dalama: Memoirs of an Invisible War* is an incontrovertible contemporary critique of state-sanctioned violence and state-sponsored corruption. As local music critic DemRaw potently characterizes:

> News flash: praCh has just turned in his passport. No more visits to Cambodia to visit the poor, the destitute, and the corrupt. All doors slam shut to words too real for the Killing Field. If this is his last album, then he just slammed the book shut; threw his passport at the face of the Khmer dignitaries and dictators alike. Needless to say, Hun Sen will not be rolling out his Khmer Rouge carpet to welcome the brother back home to the motherland.[68]

Inextricably tied to contemporary Cambodian politics, a connection em-blematized not only by theme but by a greater lyrical reliance on Khmer, *Dalama: Memoirs of an Invisible War* makes visible praCh's growing trans-national consciousness, which is increasingly more concerned with the geopolitical legacies of the Killing Fields era in the motherland, or home-land. If, as Péter Niedermüller asserts, "'Homeland' can be one of the most powerful unifying symbols for mobile and displaced peoples, though the relation to homeland may be very differently constructed in different set-tings,"[69] then praCh artistically engages a country of origin culture war that in part militates against Prime Minister Hun Sen's infamous 1998 directive that his fellow Cambodians "bury the past."[70]

Correspondingly, as a closer examination of praCh's *Dalama: Memoirs of an Invisible War* brings to light, the rapper's third installment remixes, revises, and reinstantiates past/present cultural, social, and political con-cerns involving issues of cultural obliteration, migration, and identity in Cambodia and the United States. With tracks that negotiate refugee dis-enfranchisement (e.g., "Fragile Hope") and songs that lay bare rampant neoliberalism (e.g., "Keep'n it RIEL"), *Dalama: Memoirs of an Invisible War* fuses U.S. critique to global commentary. These transnational con-templations occur alongside local reports of violence and descriptions of life in Long Beach, typified in a resampled version of "War on the Streets" (which differentially appears in *The End'n Is Just the Beginnin'*). Formalistically portentous, praCh's use of traditional Khmer music forms in *Dalama: The Lost Chapter* anticipates a revised recuperation of 1960s Cambodian psychedelic pop. Such samples substantiate an unswerving Cambodian American recovery agenda that in the end engenders a diver-gent reading of praCh's *Dalama* trilogy as a multivolume folkloric project. Indeed, while Robert Georges and Michael Jones define "folklore" as ac-cessing and instantiating "the traditional" via established musical, dance, and storytelling genres, praCh's strategic recuperation of nearly obliter-ated Khmer traditions congruently represents a multidisciplinary, trans-historical archive of and for Cambodian American folklore.[71]

Set against this cultural milieu, hip-hop analogously emerges as a folkloric medium that resistively brings together music, dance, and oral history. Notwithstanding criticisms that such characterizations provoke apolitical, primordial readings of culture, hip-hop from the outset fused centuries-old African griot storytelling and Puerto Rican/Latino dance traditions to contemporary U.S. commentaries about urban life and inner-city decay.[72] These particular folklore traditions—intended to transmit cultural knowledge by way of public performance, interpretation, and critique—intersect with a revolutionary set of identity politics that, in the case of Cambodian American hip-hop, assumes the dimensions of a global human rights movement. As praCh characterizes,

> Hip-hop to me is the voice of the youth. Telling how one really feels about their way of living and how they are living. Their surrounding[s], their environment, or just one's story. . . . It's not just talking into the mic, it's talking to the world. . . . But as an Asian, Cambodian, I had to tell my own story because no one else was going to tell it for me. Once I was able to record my voice I knew what I was going to say. I can only talk about what I know best.[73]

Accordingly, by stressing that hip-hop is "not just talking into the mic, it's talking to the world," praCh reinforces a global reading of the form through folkloric frames. Expressly, the act of articulation—exemplified by the phrase "talking into the mic"—instantly hearkens back to a folkloric tradition of communal, collected storytelling intent on expressing how "one really feels about their way of living and how they are living."

Joined by master Khmer pin peat artists (including Kung Nai, a master *chapei* player known as the "Ray Charles of Cambodia") and armed with samples from sixties Cambodian pop (in particular, Sinn Sisamouth, "The King of Khmer Music," and Ros Sereysothea, "The Golden Voice of Cambodia"), praCh restages in *Dalama: Memoirs of an Invisible War* the story of Cambodia's Killing Fields via a prerevolutionary Cambodian musical tapestry. To be sure, the use of traditional and contemporary Cambodian artists inadvertently (yet effectively) brings to light a Khmer Rouge policing of folklore during the Democratic Kampuchean era. Specifically, whereas the political goal of year zero was to eliminate all royalist influence, prerevolutionary tradition—or classical Cambodian folklore—posed an equally dangerous Democratic Kampuchea memory threat, a reading corroborated by the aforementioned state-authorized execution of traditional Khmer court musicians.[74] Similarly, within the context of a Khmer Rouge directive to eliminate all Western influence, Cambodian pop stars who mixed traditional Khmer music with sixties

R&B and American rock (like Sereysothea, Sisamouth, and Pan Ron) were cast as culturally traitorous enemies of the people.[75] Set within and against a necropolitical Khmer Rouge cultural imaginary, praCh's tactical Cambodian pop samples therefore recover and reclaim an expansive folkloric tradition that includes Royal Court ballads, encompasses traditional Khmer forms, and engages a vibrant pre–Khmer Rouge music scene.

Such resistive cultural politics are typified in "praCh's Bopha" (the album's fourteenth track), wherein the Cambodian American emcee raps in Khmer while accompanied by a recognizable 1960s Cambodian rock backbeat. To be sure, *Dalama: Memoirs of an Invisible War*'s multivalent Cambodian roots are foregrounded in the song's title, which carries a direct allusion to an indigenous Southeast Asian flower *(bopha)*. The song's primary beat is a remixed version of Cambodian pop sensation Sereysothea's cover of "Bopha Angkor," a haunting 1960s rendition of a traditional Khmer ballad. Returning to the title, praCh's deliberate employment of "bopha" speaks to praCh's revisionary project (as the emcee's reimagined version of a canonical Cambodian song) and cultural ownership (manifest in the use of a proper noun possessive). These cultural tactics are matched by the song's Khmer lyrics and samples, rendering visible the rapper's more expansive postgenocide memory work.

Indeed, "praCh's Bopha," as collected Cambodian American artifact, temporarily makes whole a Cambodian/American cultural lineage that includes the time before and the experiences after the Killing Fields era.[76] Consistent with the album's overall resistive utterances, which encapsulate life over here and politics over there, the word "bopha" unintentionally intersects with an antiapartheid etymology that further establishes the song's antiauthoritarian, antiracist agenda. In particular, "bopha," Zulu for "arrest and detain," became a rallying cry among antiapartheid activists targeted by state regulation and containment. In similar protest fashion, "praCh's Bopha" implicitly engages an anti–Khmer Rouge sensibility in its unabashed use of Cambodian tradition.

Whereas "praCh's Bopha" speaks to a politicized mode of recovery, it simultaneously details—in Khmer lyrics focused on homes and homelands—the emcee's particular location as an "Asian, Cambodian" refugee living in the United States. Expressly, insofar as *Dalama: Memoirs of an Invisible War* is rooted in Khmer culture and past/present Cambodian politics, it is equally fixed to a distinctly U.S.-focused alienation that significantly destabilizes the naturalized registers of American citizenship.

This dilemma (or "dalama") of American citizenship is chiefly predicated on an invisible cold war past that brought into being the Khmer Rouge and the Cambodian refugee. In particular, as the album's sixteenth track underscores, correspondingly integral to *Dalama: Memoirs of an Invisible War* is a concomitant uncovering of historical facts and historical truths consistent with praCh's previous *Dalamas*. Specifically, in "Hidden Truth, Open Lies," praCh vehemently asserts:

No lies
Two million murdered, it's Genocide!
I know, I know, it's hard to disguise but it's the truth. And if we don't
     talk about it'll be forgotten
And I'll be damn if I let that happen.
You see its barely even mention,
Barely in school textbooks,
How do you expect the kids to know?

With unforgiving shout-outs to President Richard Nixon and Secretary of State Henry Kissinger, praCh unabashedly critiques U.S. involvement via calls for truth and allegations of forgotten genocide. By emphasizing a problematical relationship between lies, truth, and forgetting, praCh supplements his folkloric recovery project with deconstructive memory work.

This multivalent remembrance labor, predicated on cultural recovery and educational uncovering, thematically reverberates with the rapper's previous *Dalama* installments. Such intertextual engagements are epitomized in "Hidden Truth, Open Lies" and are made most apparent by way of critical lyric and familiar sample. In particular, praCh's "Hidden Truth, Open Lies" once again employs excerpts from John Pilger's documentary, *Year Zero: The Silent Death of Cambodia* (1979). In so doing, praCh accesses a particular tradition within his own oeuvre, bringing to the fore an enduring documentary hip-hop impulse. Concurrently, with overt critiques of U.S. foreign policy via illicit (and invisible) bombings of the Cambodian countryside, the use of Pilger's film in "Hidden Truth, Open Lies" restages a Vietnam War/Cambodian history that, as the rapper avers, is—notwithstanding genocide—"barely even mentioned." Unquestionably concentrated on remembering mass loss, focused on remembering the refugee experience, and transnationally consumed, Cambodian American hip-hop (as characterized by praCh's *Dalama* trilogy) reflects a multinational flow of culture and past/present adaptation that necessarily collides with state-authorized violence, forced migration, and contemporary politics.

In drawing to a close, as praCh's *Dalama* trilogy makes clear, Cambodian American memory work tirelessly marries genocide history, refugee struggle, and—perhaps most important—survivor witnessing. Suggestive of firsthand accounts and first person experiences, praCh's collected witnessing project corroborates a politicized commitment to spinning genocide knowledge and Cambodian American critique. Based on intergenerational exchange, focused on tradition and revision, and forged through vexed locations and identities, praCh's *Dalama* trilogy is, like other Cambodian American cultural productions, improvisational in form and juridically driven in function. With regard to genre, if hip-hop represents a viable and resistive platform, then praCh's production company, Mujestic—which carries the byline, "It's not Just Music, It's a Movement"—makes clear a politicized agenda of resistance that encompasses both the politics of hip-hop and the parameters of Cambodian American memory work.[77] And, while hip-hop is concentrated on the local, then praCh emphasizes the transnational via the multifaceted cultural performance of history, memory, and relocation.

On the whole, through an interdisciplinary negotiation of an identifiably Cambodian American genocide struggle, praCh incontrovertibly uses hip-hop to instantiate a refugee-oriented critique and a social justice–oriented end. These cultural terms correspond to the work of other Cambodian American artists and writers, who (to varying degrees) imagine alternative reparative sites wherein those forgotten can, in fact, be memorialized and remembered in the United States. Concomitantly invested in historical fact and historical truth, praCh's particular message repeatedly returns to the question of refugee subjectivity and post–Killing Fields justice. Illustratively, when asked by an unnamed *Frontline/World* interviewer, "So what are you channeling when you rap? What is it that's possessing you—anger, rage, an insatiable curiosity?" praCh replies:

> It's just justice. That's how I feel. The people have been murdered, they need justice. You can say bury the past . . . but if you bury something, that means it's dead. And if it's dead, if the spirit don't rest in peace, it's going to come back and haunt you. . . . I don't believe in vengeance, I don't believe in killings, but I do believe in justice.[78]

praCh's response lays bare the global migrations, politics, and poetics at work in Cambodian American cultural production. Identifying those who "have been murdered" and observing that the past does indeed "come back and haunt you," praCh directly confronts the still unsettled terrain of genocide remembrance, the vexed nature of international justice, and the resistive potential of Cambodian American selfhood.

Remembering the Forgetting

To articulate the past historically does not mean to
recognize it "the way it really was." It means to seize
hold of a memory as it flashes up at a moment of danger.

—Walter Benjamin, "Theses on the Philosophy of History,"
in *Illuminations: Essays and Reflections*

I often think about our leaving and all we left behind
imagined our lives without this exodus
dreamt of days when I could speak to Loss
to tell her we didn't choose to leave
leaving chose us.

—Anida Yoeu Ali, "Visiting Loss," 2005

I F, AS LISA YONEYAMA MAINTAINS, the "process of remembering . . . necessarily entails the forgetting of the forgetfulness," then Anida Yoeu Ali's "Visiting Loss" (2005) poetically encompasses a contested matrix of disremembered histories, Khmer Rouge politics, refugee memory, and unstable citizenships.[1] A "Cambodian American Muslim transnational," Ali is a Chicago-based 1.5-generation poet/performer/visual artist who left Cambodia soon after the 1979 dissolution of Democratic Kampuchea.[2] An eleven-stanza composition, Ali's "Visiting Loss" details the refugee art-ist's first return to her country of origin after a twenty-five-year absence.[3] Lyrical and autobiographical, epic and elegiac, "Visiting Loss" employs a stream-of-consciousness narration evident in enjambed lines, imagis-tic stanzas, and affective vignettes.[4] While its title foreshadows a mourn-ful journey punctuated by unresolved grief and uneasy reclamation, the poem's subsequent stanzas instantiate—via form, function, and tone— a complicated Cambodian American cartography delimited by state-sanctioned violence, involuntary relocation, and forgetful politics. In so doing, Ali's "Visiting Loss" engages the central aims and agendas of

Cambodian American memory work, a critical mode of cultural labor that brings into dialogue genocide remembrance, collected memory, and juridical activism.

With direct allusions to Khmer Rouge atrocity, free-verse treatments of labor camps, and poignant descriptions of border-crossing refugees, "Visiting Loss" accesses an intergenerational remembrance comprised of parental recollections, childhood accounts, and present-day memory politics. As the poem progresses, "Visiting Loss" becomes an increasingly more intimate contemplation of the historical, judicial, and sociocultural legacies of the Khmer Rouge era. Situated against Cambodia's Killing Fields, which carry with them a particular history of tribunal machinations and belated justice, Ali's epic poem pointedly adheres to the transnational remembrance parameters of Cambodian American memory work. Illustratively, the poem begins with an after-the-fact, familial (and familiar) characterization of Democratic Kampuchea and refugee loss. As Ali asserts,

> GIVEN: 20 million refugees
> GIVEN: individuals who return home are not the same people they
>   were when they left
> GIVEN: nearly every single family in Cambodia suffered losses during
>   the time of the Khmer Rouge
> PROVE: the journey never ends for the refugee
> PROVE: survivors must learn to live with the absence of 2 million
> PROVE: it is absence that propels the living to remember.[5]

Set within a contemporary imaginary of human rights and international law, Ali's mention of "givens" and "proves" assumes an immediate evidentiary (and prosecutorial) register. Indeed, it is through this schema that Ali codifies Khmer Rouge crimes by way of numbers, familial experiences, and "the absence of 2 million."

At the same time, Ali's opening statement of "20 million refugees" concisely characterizes displaced subjectivities in the aftermath of the American War in Vietnam, cold war realpolitik, and forced relocation. These quantifiable losses and impacts—concomitantly situated along a before, during, and after Khmer Rouge temporality and axis—collide with qualitative, less discernible legacies made plain in unending, largely unreconciled refugee journeys. Structurally, these same givens and proves

foreground a vexed Cambodian American selfhood metaphorically configured by (and initially comprehended through) geometry. Greek for
"earth measurement," geometry as a distinct disciplinary mode intersects
with a cartographical agenda composed of transnational locations and refugee histories. Whereas Euclidian geometry systemizes the relationship
between lines and points, it analogously encompasses the evaluation of
surfaces, shapes, and angles. Befitting this geometric matrix, Ali's "Visiting
Loss" connects "20 million refugees" to a "journey [that] never ends,"
links individual survivors to "the absence of 2 million," and fixes "losses
during the time of the Khmer Rouge" to an "absence that propels the living to remember."

Furthermore, the tactical placement of givens and proves prefigures a
set of specific circumstances that quickly give way to less tangible experiences of survivor loss. Such melancholic frames—which render palpable
senses of constant mourning and unresolved loss—are apparent in the
haunted memories of displaced refugees, relocated citizens, and "every
single family in Cambodia." In turn, these historical and experiential facts
prefigure a poetic impulse to confirm, corroborate, and substantiate the
affective consequences of war, genocide, and authoritarianism. As a closer
reading makes clear, "Visiting Loss" refuses to adhere to a strict linear evaluation of the time before, during, and after the Democratic Kampuchean
era. Instead, Ali's composition eschews this structure in favor of a radial
engagement with history, memory, and trauma that reinforces the artist's
epigraphical desire to "speak to Loss" and attendant assertion that she
(and other Cambodian refugees) "didn't choose to leave." Emblematically,
the poem's title gestures toward an initially unfixed location in its use of
a nonfinite gerund ("visiting") modified by an ill-defined noun ("loss").

Such grammatical strategies foreground Ali's recurring interrogative
construction, which (from the beginning) is mediated through what the
poet anticipates she will encounter upon her return to Cambodia. For example, in the second stanza, Ali writes:

I will return to a country I have never known
that burns a hole inside my heart the size of home
when I arrive,
will I recognize Loss if she came to greet me at the airport
will she help me with my bags
usher me through customs

will she take me to my birth village
point me to the graves of ancestors
will she share silence with me
will she embrace me
will I ask these same questions
or will I be asked to prove my belonging[6]

Despite Ali's assertion that she "will return to a country [she has] never known," what follows is a decidedly less stable "will I" construction about what the poet will encounter upon her return to Cambodia: "will I recognize," "will I ask these same questions," and "will I be asked to prove my belonging." Notwithstanding this unsettled language, Ali's "Visiting Loss" does have an identifiable destination—modern-day Cambodia—and a legible (albeit incomplete) setting: post–Democratic Kampuchea.

With regard to Ali's initial statement that she "will return to a country I have never known," the use of a future declarative alternatively makes visible a refugee unfamiliarity born out of Ali's abrupt departure as a young child. Concurrently, Ali highlights an emotional relationship to Cambodia, one that characteristically "burns a hole inside my heart the size of home."[7] This embodied metaphor of "home"—focused on the heart as sentimental emblem—determines an interrogative structure that affectively attaches the Cambodian refugee protagonist to the personified "Loss." As a transnational returnee, no family members meet the artist/poet at the airport, reemphasizing the devastating and ongoing impact of Cambodia's genocidal past. In its place is the feminized Loss who, like Cambodia, is uncannily unrecognizable and who, like Ali, is born out of familial separation, cultural depravation, and state-authorized ruination. Ali substantiates this spatial reading with later mentions of "birth villages," ancestor graves, and "silences," which concretizes wholesale wartime costs and postconflict collateral damage by way of sites and nonspeech acts.

In the process, Ali cartographically reproduces—vis-à-vis preliminary allusion and subsequent negotiation—a legible set of refugee coordinates that identifies distinct points of U.S. foreign policy, modern Cambodian history, and contemporary Cambodian American survivor memory. This forced out-of-country journey brings with it a profound unspeakability salient in Ali's assertion that she must—while in-country—"pul[l] out remnants of [her] broken tongue." These "remnants"—a bifurcated testament to fragmented language ("tongue") and fractured cultural practices—are joined to uncontrolled memories that are, according to Ali, "the only proof of our surviving."[8] Concentrated on survival, which calls forth assessments of subsistence, perseverance, and persistence, these memory flashes resemble third-person snapshots that interrupt the poem's first-person narrative.

Undeniably, such remembrances continually rupture the poem's setting, collapsing the space between past and present through speech act and memory work. For example, in the fifth stanza, Ali writes:

> will I be at a loss for words
> or will I speak to Loss with what few memories I have kept secret
> stowed away in a glass jar like inescapable fireflies
> these memories flicker randomly
> a dirty-face girl whimpers
> one hand desperately balances a dripping wooden bowl
> as her other scrapes her spilt ration off the floor,
> then wipes her tears, runny nose, and a trail of porridge off her face.[9]

The passage begins with two questions that hinge on a previously established (in)ability to "speak" about the past. At a "loss for words," Ali's unspeakability is rooted in a Killing Fields history that correspondingly remains integral to her present-day status as a Cambodian American returnee. Even so, though Ali is at a loss for words, she is not at a loss for memories, which she has voluntarily "kept secret."

Incontrovertibly, in the face of Ali's vocal intention, these memories still "flicker randomly," calling forth a frenzied, unrestrained sensation typified by the sporadic movement of "inescapable fireflies." What follows is an emotionally charged image of disenfranchised desperation, unfathomable sorrow, and unimaginable want. A "dirty-face girl [who] whimpers," the child version of Ali, "desperately balances a dripping bowl" and "scrapes her spilt ration off the floor." The performance of desperate balance, the equally hopeless act of scraping, and the mention of spilled ration illustrate by way of imagistic brevity the regimented, restricted, and despairing existence consistent with life under the Khmer Rouge. A de facto portrait of the artist as a young girl, this snapshot of labor camp life contrasts with a remembrance of escape, which consumes the sixth stanza.

Accordingly, Ali recalls, "a child's throat slices dry on piggyback rides / her tiny fingers slip, / grip the back of her father's wet neck."[10] Concurrent with the previous image, the second self-portrait assumes the shape of an inescapable flickering memory that details a narrative of escape via active, present-tense verbs. These memories of surviving the Khmer Rouge regime are literally contained in "this same child's body [that] still remembers / the tangling of flesh against jungle leaves, / clothes against barbed wires." Amid mentions of "remnants" and "barbed wires," Ali utilizes a visual archive of ruination that makes poetically tangible year zero destruction, involuntary imprisonment, and state-sanctioned, Democratic Kampuchean violence. This connection to the Cambodian genocide is plain in the ninth stanza, wherein Ali asserts,

> yet, I never chose to leave
> but there were those who understood things that I could not
>   yet fathom
> like the smell of a pogrom disguised as knuckles knocking at the door
> faces of death angels sporting shoes made from old worn tires
> maniacal laughter of gunfire mocking the unsuspecting
> sound emptiness makes inside a newborn's belly
> color of red pulled slowly to close off the sky[11]

Opening with a qualified statement of forced departure ("yet, I never chose to leave"), Ali fuses visual signifiers to other sensory markers ("smell of a pogrom," "maniacal laughter of gunfire," and the "unsuspecting sound emptiness makes inside a newborn's belly").[12] In the process, Ali draws on and fleshes out collected memories of the Khmer Rouge, who, as "death angels sporting shoes made from old worn tires," are the principal culprits behind a profound, multifaceted loss.

It is this multivalent contemplation (or visiting) of loss, embedded in a discernible Cambodian American critique, that—to revise Lisa Lowe's characterization of Asian American cultural production—unavoidably reckons with U.S. cold war policy, the Cambodian genocide, and the Cambodian American refugee present.[13] Analogously, Ali (like Cambodian American writers and artists Loung Ung, Chanrithy Him, Socheata Poeuv, and Prach Ly) memorializes the passing of family members, homelands, and childhoods to instantiate juridical claims of profound communal injury in need of recognition and justice. As important, Ali's memory work simultaneously monumentalizes survivor remembrance and recuperates refugee selfhood, gesturing toward a largely underexamined survivor agency. In line with the poem's geometrical structure and this juridically driven narrative arc, Ali charts a set of transnational refugee coordinates that in the end extend—like lines in geometry—infinitely in both directions (the United States and Cambodia). Indeed, Ali's mapping of great distances, profound timelessness, and absence-driven memories—manifest in the poem's future present setting, its repetition of "loss," and multiple allusions to arrivals and departures—forms an unfixed diasporic cartography that grammatically and syntactically dominates Ali's elegy to home, family, and nation.

Set against this unbounded milieu, the personification of Loss—and Ali's relationship to her—poetically reifies the transnational curves and unstable citizenships that exemplify the Cambodian American experience. Divergently, while Ali's "Visiting Loss" (focused on survivors and an "absence that propels the living to remember") is emblematic of contemporary Cambodian American cultural production about the Killing Fields era, it also dialectically engages Walter Benjamin's opening assertion about memory politics and ruptures in "Theses on the Philosophy of History" (1940).[14] Written during a profound international crisis (the strengthened presence of fascism in Europe and on the world stage), Benjamin's consideration of history militates against allegedly progressive and complicit uses of the past. To that end, individual memory and collected remembrance, as Benjamin avers, combat "politicians' stubborn faith in progress, their confidence in their 'mass basis,' and . . . their servile integration in an uncontrollable apparatus." Such "mass basis," or conformism, relies on a reading of history as a "progression through homogeneous empty time" that fails to address the primacy of the present in the production of state narratives.[15]

As compelling, this "homogeneous empty time"—inclusive of static, vacant frames—underscores (and undermines) teleological assertions of inevitability and foregrounds exclusionary, disastrous readings of progress foundational to Adolph Hitler's Final Solution and presciently apt for Pol Pot's Wheel of History. Through strategic verbalization, unadulterated expression, historic recognition, and collected remembrance, Benjamin's history thesis makes possible contradistinguished, non-state-sanctioned routes to the past. These uncharted historical transits, the consequence of catastrophic authoritarian crises, are marked by dangerous moments and eruptive memory flashes that carry the potential to destabilize national narratives of cohesion and amnesiac uniformity. Tellingly and productively, Benjamin rejects teleology and supplements the primacy of concrete historical facts (dates, leaders, and battles) with intangible but by no means less valid modes of seized remembrance. These distinct seizures—consistent with force, indicative of rupture, and prone to containment—become opportunities of recovery that evocatively collapse the boundaries between history and memory.

Benjamin's cacophonous, disruptive reading of conformist historicity naturalizes individual and collected memory by means of inclusion, assimilating such remembrances to fit a more expansive articulation of the past. What is more, Benjamin codifies the chief parameters through which to construct a contrapuntal archive that challenges strategic, nationalistic amnesias. Arguing that a "redeemed mankind has its past become citable in all its moments," the German Jewish philosopher elaborates, "For every image of the past that is not recognized by the present as one of its own concerns threatens to disappear irretrievably."[16] This historical labor—which speaks to a syncretic understanding of the past and present—accretes political significance when placed perpendicular to dominant narratives of the past like amnesiac readings of the Khmer Rouge era. Such antithetical placement further revises an official vector that indubitably privileges exclusive stories of progress and state-authorized tales of singularity and exceptionalism. Similarly, Benjamin's historical reading reinscribes the primacy of the oppressed in the production of a new historical archive.

Correspondingly, as Benjamin persuasively notes, "the tradition of the oppressed teaches us that the 'state of emergency' in which we live is not the exception but the rule. We must attain to a conception of history that is in keeping with this insight."[17] By forging a political connection between the way it really was and the way it was remembered, Benjamin undermines nation-state claims and political arguments of teleological uniqueness, engendering a heterogeneous historicity constitutive of counterhegemonic, remembrance-oriented resistance. In sum, "Theses on the Philosophy of History" positions, locates, and instantiates the oppressed as resistive agents of memory. In turn, these agents have the potential to produce a citable archive constructed according to episodic yet nonetheless significant memory moments. Lastly, the collection and production of this archive makes possible an alternative to state-sanctioned memories employed to exclude, disenfranchise, and forget. Apropos Lisa Yoneyama's previous assertion, such an archive recalls the past while it potently and subversively remembers the forgetting.

Pertaining to contemporary Cambodian American cultural production, Benjamin's history thesis—which fuses resistance to memory,
agency, and archive and necessitates a remembering of the forgetting—
highlights what is theoretically and thematically at stake in Anida Yoeu
Ali's "Visiting Loss," a text that on multiple levels fits and emblematizes the
complex contours of Cambodian American memory work and critique.
Like other Cambodian American writers and artists, Ali, via individual
and familial narratives of survival and loss, at once memorializes the period of the Killing Fields. In related fashion, Ali also articulates—through
the revelation and negotiation of trauma—calls for justice and negotiates
the complicated question of postconflict, post–Democratic Kampuchean
reconciliation. As *War, Genocide, and Justice: Cambodian American Memory
Work* contends, Ali and Cambodian American cultural producers such as
Poeuv, Ung, Him, and Ly actively engage a form of archival labor that revisits—through multiple idioms and encounters—state-authorized loss
and state-sanctioned forgetting. Situated adjacent these forgetful frames,
such production indefatigably militates against Khmer Rouge year zero
frames, recuperates prerevolutionary traditions, and archives survivor
testimonials.

This transnational cartography, punctuated by multinational coordinates, evidentiary agendas, and unreconciled remembrances, is in the
end at the forefront of "Visiting Loss," a melancholic evaluation of the
Cambodian American experience that dialogically engages Anne Anlin
Cheng's reading of "racial melancholia." Cheng's evocative psychoanalytic
reading of race, gender, and nation commences with the following question: "How does an individual go from being a subject of grief to being
a subject of grievance?"[18] Cast as a specific "transformation," Cheng observes that such melancholic movement "from grief to grievance, from
suffering injury to speaking out against that injury, has always provoked
profound questions about the meaning of hurt and its impact."[19]

Correspondingly, Ali's "Visiting Lost" thematically and imagistically
addresses this melancholic trajectory, for it is a poem that plots the political movement and personal journey of Cambodian refugees (and
Cambodian Americans) from grief to grievance via U.S. foreign policy,
Khmer Rouge authoritarianism, and postconflict Cambodia. Hence, if
Cambodian American critique ruptures dominant histories and national
narratives (à la Benjamin), it also negotiates a loss-oriented journey
from "grief to grievance" that begins and ends with absent presences that

politically, juridically, and culturally persist in the more than three decades
that have passed since the dissolution of Democratic Kampuchea. Such
absent presences are the foundation for Ali's "Palimpsest for Generation
1.5," which, as textual coda for this book, fittingly encapsulates a final facet
of Cambodian American critique: as *embodied* memory work.

On December 11, 2009, "Palimpsest for Generation 1.5" premiered
at Chicago's Betty Rymer Gallery. A stark installation, "Palimpsest for
Generation 1.5" features Ali, dressed in an unadorned white dress, with her
face turned to a wall. The artist's hair is pinned upward, and her back is
bare and exposed.

The placement of the hair and the whiteness of Ali's dress call to mind
an old edifice that is home to hanging vines, evoking in its staging a profound passage of time. To be sure, "Palimpsest for Generation 1.5" inten-
tionally assumes the registers of a built memorial, wherein Ali's body—as
a wall—functions as a commemorative site. According to Ali, "Palimpsest
for Generation 1.5" was initially "inspired by a scene in Maxine Hong
Kingston's *The Woman Warrior*."[20] As the poet/artist concisely describes:

> [The installation] includes inscriptions written onto my back
> along with the gesture of washing them away. Text pulled from my
> family's memories and histories related to Cambodia are inscribed
> in ink on my back. As a result of the act, ink and water drip onto

*Anida Yoeu Ali, "Palimpsest for Generation 1.5." Inscription on reverse: "I WITNESS
HER LAST BREATH."*

my back and stain the dress. When the gestures end and the body leaves the installation, detached roots, a disembodied dress, and faint traces of a performed history remain.[21]

Suggestive of a tablet upon which earlier writing has been erased, a palimpsest likewise underscores a beneath-the-surface layering of the past that remains—notwithstanding close proximity—covered. Accessing Kingston's "White Tigers" revision of the Fa Mu Lan myth, in which the would-be heroine's back becomes a foundation upon which kinship grievances are written, Ali similarly engages a contested familial history marked by the above-mentioned U.S. bombings, Khmer Rouge authoritarianism, refugee camps, and posttraumatic stress.

Like Kingston's Fa Mu Lan protagonist, Ali's back—which faces the gallery audience—becomes a canvas upon which intergenerational grievances are inscribed and summarily erased. Another woman, also dressed in white, performs this writing/erasing ritual, which occurs at timed intervals.[22] Over the course of the installation, the following inscriptions appear:

"Father School Teacher"
"Nixon Orders Bombings"
"Khmer Rouge Regime"
"90% Artists Killed"
"Family Trip: Refugee Camps"
"Family Trip: Chicago"
"Family Trip: First Home"
"Family Trip: Malaysia"
"Family Trip: Niagara Falls"
"Family Trip: Distant Cousins"
"Family Trip: Hawaii"
"From Somewhere Else"
"Father PTSD Panic Attacks"
"Return After 15 Years"
"Return After 25 Years"
"Return After 30 Years"
"Never Returned"
"Site of Tourism and Atrocities"
"Sugar Palm Trees"
"Graceland Chapel"
"I WITNESS HER LAST BREATH"

As these captions reveal, central to Ali's performance is the articulation of an absent presence intertextually and thematically linked to the memory politics at work in "Visiting Loss." Dialogically integral to Ali's bodily installation is an intergenerational reading of 1.5-generation Cambodian American selfhood, a subjectivity formed by way of connection to and alienation from parental histories, experiences, and memories.

À la the individual refugee journey that dominates Ali's "Visiting Loss," "Palimpsest for Generation 1.5" collectively investigates how children of the Killing Fields struggle to comprehend an overwhelming set of geographic and temporal coordinates foundational to the Cambodian refugee experience. As a self-identified member of this stateless 1.5 generation, Ali must imagine and remember a series of events and locations that, hearkening back to Prach Ly's previous interrogation of identity and location, answer the vexed question of who one is, how one left, and how one got here. In the face of such indeterminacies, Ali's "Palimpsest for Generation 1.5" does in fact enunciate (by way of performance) a sense of Cambodian American selfhood. As the artist surmises, "when the gestures end and the body leaves the installation, detached roots, a disembodied dress, and faint traces of a performed history remain." Alternatively, despite Ali's original allusion—to Kingston's *Woman Warrior*—the image of the disembodied dress, coupled with the mention of faint traces and performed histories, makes visible an inadvertent connection to another memory-oriented text, Toni Morrison's critically acclaimed novel *Beloved* (1987).

Explicitly, the spectral form of Ali's dress at once visually brings to mind the white garment worn by Beloved, who (as the novel eventually makes clear) is Sethe's long-dead daughter. Alongside this visual coherence, Ali and Morrison concentrate their storytelling attention on the faint traces of history and memory. As Sethe tells her still-living daughter Denver:

> I was talking about time. It's so hard for me to believe in it. Some things go. Pass on. Some things just stay. I used to think it was my rememory. You know. Some things you forget. Other things you never do. But it's not. Places, places are still there. If a house burns down, it's gone, but the place—the picture of it—stays, and not just in my rememory, but out there, in the world. . . . Someday you be walking down the road and you hear something or see something going on. So clear. And you think it's you thinking it up. A thought picture. But no. It's when you bump into a rememory that belongs to somebody else.[23]

Sethe's characterization of "rememory"—simultaneously located within and divorced from concrete temporality and spatiality—relies on what Brenda Marshall persuasively argues is a "present absence, a remembered absence, not a void."[24] Maintaining that a house remains despite its lack of physicality, Sethe suggests a permanent dimension to memory that defies erasure.

Consequently, the individual ownership of memories necessarily gives way to a collected articulation. According to Marshall, "rememory" as a process "not only calls upon a history, a past that is known to a particular people, it also contains an acknowledgment of its own imaginative role in re-reading, remembering (or putting back together) the collective memory."[25] Critical to these moments of remembering is how such acts exist within and alongside traumas that have yet to be reconciled. For Cambodian American cultural producers like Ali, Poeuv, Ung, Him, and Ly, their engagements with the past involve a distinct remembering of the forgetting. Militating against what Yoneyama terms "amnes(t)ic" narratives that undergird exceptionalist readings of national trauma, Cambodian American memory work attempts to remember a history of U.S. imperialism, Khmer Rouge authoritarianism, and involuntary refugee dispersal.[26]

Congruently, "rememory" as a practice actively resists the amnesiac effects of trauma. In *Beloved,* the legacy of slavery as an exploitative, inhumane, and state-supported system persists despite the Civil War, abolition, and Reconstruction. Set against this multivalent legacy, Sethe's reconsideration of the past operates as an individual act of memorialization unquestionably fixed to marginalized and largely silenced communal histories. Most significantly, Morrison's deployment of "rememory" motions toward alternative routes of negotiating unreconciled trauma in the absence of state-sanctioned justice. To be sure, Morrison revises the nineteenth-century genre of the American slave narrative in a manner that speaks to its function as a form of antebellum testimonial that remains relevant, more than a century after the passage of the thirteenth amendment.

Qualifying Elie Wiesel's claim ten years prior to the publication of *Beloved* that genocide in the twentieth century gave rise to "a new literature, that of testimony," Morrison compellingly reminds readers through her collected revision that testimonial responses to mass violence were fundamental to narratives told by former slaves about their lives under the "peculiar institution."[27] This conflation of the literary and the juridical, at the heart of Morrison's novel, echoes a similar discursive relationship in nineteenth-century slave narratives. Denied the right to testify in courts of law and without state-authorized citizenship, former slaves could ostensibly appeal to the court of public opinion through the publication of narratives focused on firsthand accounts of abuse, loss, and cruelty committed, facilitated, and embodied by slave owners, mistresses, and those sympathetic to slavery. The published text, constitutive of testimonials against slavery, therefore served as a mode of memory work that fomented complementary debates over abolition and selfhood.

Accordingly, Morrison's memory project in many ways speaks to the work of Cambodian American artists and writers who take on the responsibility of reassembling—or re-collecting—communal memory without the luxury of justice at the level of the nation-state. Engaged in multivalent processes of "rememory," wherein individual experiences of mass violence yield to collective negotiations of genocide-induced trauma, Cambodian American cultural production is principally invested in rearticulating modes of selfhood that, after the Khmer Rouge takeover of Phnom Penh in 1975, ceased to exist. Cambodian American cultural producers, via geographic locations in the United States and political categorizations as refugees, must traverse temporal-spatial distance and competing post–Democratic Kampuchean senses of selfhood. In so doing, Cambodian American artists and writers negotiate an at times unimaginable spatiality and seemingly unspeakable temporality vis-à-vis state-authorized mass violence, or genocide. Taken together, what characterizes and categorizes Cambodian American memory work is a generational impulse to constantly remember the forgetting as an alternative means to justice, reclamation, and reparation.

Acknowledgments

UNDENIABLY, *War, Genocide, and Justice: Cambodian American Memory Work* owes an enormous debt to the Cambodian American artists, writers, and activists whose commitment to human rights, genocide remembrance, and social justice—notwithstanding the passage of more than three decades after the 1979 dissolution of the Khmer Rouge regime—served as this book's primary impetus. In many ways a labor of love, born out of my own complicated location as an adopted biracial Cambodian American, this project benefited greatly and sincerely from the kindheartedness of those within diaspora. From Long Beach, California, to Lowell, Massachusetts, from Seattle to Chicago, and from Philadelphia to Phnom Penh, Cambodian American writers, directors, rappers, breakdancers, and performance artists generously agreed, often sight unseen, to interviews; shared their family histories; and gave me unfettered access (in the form of permissions and articles) to their work. Socheata Poeuv, Prach Ly, and Anida Yoeu Ali never hesitated to answer any request, large or small, and exhibited a generosity of spirit that serves as the foundation for a lasting, respectful friendship. Sambath Hy, Leng Phe, "Boomer" from Tiny Toones Cambodia, and Youk Chhang (director of the Documentation Center of Cambodia) munificently offered advice, answered questions, and supported this project from inception to completion.

I am likewise indebted to Richard Morrison at the University of Minnesota Press, who from the outset saw a potential in this project that I must admit went beyond my original purview for it. Richard consistently supported this book and did so with incredible patience. His thoughtful guidance at critical moments pushed me to complicate its arguments, as did the anonymous readers who graciously gave judicious feedback that shifted the book in dramatically productive ways. Erin Warholm genially offered answers to what may have seemed an endless number of questions. I am honored by the willingness of the

University of Minnesota Press to undertake this project, and I am particularly obliged to the faculty review board and the marketing department.

Many scholars, colleagues, and friends in Southeast Asian American studies, Asian American studies, and American studies willingly served as readers and mentors for this project: Mariam Lam, Mimi Nguyen, Fiona Ngô, Nerissa Balce, Joseph Ponce, Jonathan H. X. Lee, Mark Padoongpatt, Lan Dong, Martin Manalansan, Asha Nadkarni, Khatharya Um, Linda Vo, K. Scott Wong, Louisa Schein, Nitasha Sharma, Jeffrey Santa Ana, Sharon Delmendo, Floyd Cheung, Min Hyoung Song, Daniel Kim, Evelyn Hu-DeHart, Michael Liu, Jack Tchen, Paul Watanabe, Madeline Hsu, Josephine Lee, Sylvia Chong, Quan Tran, James Kim, James Lee, Cynthia Enloe, Wendy Hesford, Glenn Hendler, Gordon Hutner, Nina Ha, Martin Manalansan, Kent Ono, Jennifer Ho, Rudy Guevarra, Laura Kina, Anne-Marie Lee-Loy, Robin Berenstein, Wing-Kai To, Tim August, and Mitch Ogden.

Kate Douglas and Gillian Whitlock, who edited a special issue of *Life Writing* focused on trauma in the twenty-first century, helped me develop my arguments about Cambodian American memory work. I am grateful for the opportunity to present this work at Drew University, Creighton University, the University of North Carolina–Chapel Hill, SUNY Stony Brook, Rutgers University, San Francisco State University, Miami University, Oberlin College, and Fordham University. The questions asked by students and faculty at each of these locations incontrovertibly raised the stakes and quality of this project.

This book owes a great debt to James Young, Kandice Chuh, Lisa Lowe, Viet Nguyen, Lisa Yoneyama, and Marita Sturken, whose respective projects on memory and resistance foreground a larger conversation about Cambodian genocide remembrance. Allan Isaac proved a key interlocutor and was instrumental as I moved to this project's completion. Anita Mannur remains a beloved friend, a fantastic reader, and a remarkable scholar in her own right.

I have been fortunate to receive the utmost support from administrators and my colleagues at the University of Connecticut, including Dean Jeremy Teitelbaum and Associate Dean Jeffrey Ogbar in the College of Liberal Arts and Sciences. The English department kindly granted a semester research leave and allowed me to workshop chapters at various stages, as did the Human Rights Institute, the Asian American Studies Institute, the Humanities Institute, the Women's Studies Program, and the Asian American Cultural Center. The UConn Research Foundation granted significant monies to fund research in Cambodia, as did New York University's A/P/A program. I owe much to Leakhena Nou and Theodora Yoshikami, whose work with Cambodian survivors in the Applied Social Research Institute of Cambodia (ASRIC) is exemplary. Richard Wilson, director of the Human Rights Institute, made a very important introduction to Michael Karnavas and rightly pushed me on tribunal politics.

I would like to personally acknowledge Wayne Franklin, Margaret Breen, Eleni Coundouriotis, Veronica Makowsky, Dwight Codr, Sarah Winter, Margaret Higonnet, Guillermo Irizarry, Kathy Knapp, Anna Mae Duane, Alexis Dudden, Shirley Roe, Mark Overmeyer-Velasquez, Kerry Bystrom, Jason Oliver Chang, Roger Buckley, Jennifer Terni, Tom Recchio, Maxine Smestad-Haines, Fe Delos-Santos, Angela Rola, Sheila Kucko, Doreen Bell, Manisha Desai, Nancy Naples, Penelope Pelizzon, Marysol Asencio, Diana Rios, and Robin Worley for their tireless advice and counsel. Martha Cutter, Sherry Harris, and Kate Capshaw-Smith are close friends and wonderful allies; Shawn Salvant, Kathleen Tonry, Clare King'oo, Lynn Bloom, and Hap Fairbanks continue to be ideal colleagues. Greg Semenza and Charles Mahoney are likewise invaluable. With an exceptional mix of wit and kindness, Robert Hasenfratz has on more than one occasion pushed me to continue, and did so with true generosity of spirit. Margo Machida has been a constant source of strength and mentoring. Jerry Phillips and Mary Gallucci provided much needed input over dinners and drinks. Heather Turcotte has proven an invaluable writing partner, and I value her unmatched sense of humor. Michelle Maloney-Mangold, Samantha Buzzelli, and Gordon Fraser deserve commendation for their help in the final stages of the manuscript.

Finally, like the Cambodian American artists and writers whose work instantiates this examination of memory, politics, and activism, I am indebted to my immediate family: my mother Ginko, my father Charles, my twin brother (also Charles). My parents embody an openness I have rarely encountered and perpetually treasure. Indeed, my work is greatly influenced by their respective life stories, and I am proud to be their daughter. My brother Charles has always been my anchor and my compass, and I cherish him more than I can express. In an extended vein, Peter and Judy Vials delightfully concretize the adage that one does gain a parent through marriage. Last but certainly not least, I am beholden to my husband, Christopher Reichert Vials, a model scholar and an eternal advocate who never failed to remind me why such memory work matters.

Notes

Introduction

1. As narrated by John Pilger in the film *Year Zero*.

2. Both the Nixon administration and the Ford administration supported (financially and politically) the Lon Nol government, which was vociferously anticommunist. This support was part of a more expansive Vietnam War strategy that sought—at all costs—to eliminate communist influence in the region. Between 1969 and 1973, the United States orchestrated covert bombings of the Cambodian countryside under the largely unproven assumption that Viet Cong were headquartered in the area. According to Ben Kiernan, by 1973, "half a million tons of U.S. bombs had killed over 100,000 peasants and devastated the countryside" ("Recovering History and Justice in Cambodia," 78). The amount of munitions tonnage was the equivalent of five Hiroshima bombings.

3. The term, "enemies of the people," comes from a speech delivered by Pol Pot that aired in 1977 warning his fellow Democratic Kampucheans that there were potential traitors in their midst. This is also the title of the recently released documentary film directed by Rob Lemkin and Sambath Thet (2010). It should be noted that Cambodia was officially renamed Democratic Kampuchea as per the adoption of a Khmer Rouge constitution on January 5, 1976.

4. The term "genocide" is contested vis-à-vis the Khmer Rouge. Some have argued that what happened in Cambodia constituted an "autogenocide" because—unlike other genocides—no one group was targeted. Ben Kiernan and others have argued against this reading, pointing to the Cham and the Khmer Khrom. Given that Cambodian American cultural producers by and large refer to this era as a period of genocide, I have followed suit with terminology.

5. Kiernan, "Recovering History and Justice in Cambodia," 80.

6. Ibid.

7. Pilger in *Year Zero*.

8. Locard, *Pol Pot's Little Red Book*, 269. Also, Pol Pot was the nom de guerre for Saloth Sar.

9. Kiernan, "Recovering History and Justice in Cambodia," 80.

10. Pilger in *Year Zero*.

11. Leitner Center for International Law and Justice, "Removing Refugees:

U.S. Deportation Policy and the Cambodian-American Community," Southeast Asian Resource Center, Spring 2010, http://www.searac.org/sites/default/files/2010%20Cambodia%20Report_FINAL.pdf.

12 Ibid.

13. Ibid.

14. Young, *Texture of Memory.*

15. Chuh, *Imagine Otherwise*, 62.

16. Madra, "Cambodians Mark 30 Years Since Fall of Pol Pot." According to another Associated Press article, an estimated forty thousand Cambodians were present; Sopheng Cheang, "Cambodia Marks Khmer Rouge Fall," Irrawaddy, January 7, 2009, http://irrawaddy.org/article.php?art_id=14882.

17. Osborne, *Phnom Penh*, 33. During the Khmer Rouge era, the stadium was also used as a cabbage field.

18. Sokheng, "CPP Celebrates Victory over KR."

19. Madra, "Cambodians Mark 30 Years Since Fall of Pol Pot."

20. Edkins, *Trauma and the Memory of Politics*, 117.

21. *Washington Times*, "3 Decades Later, Khmer Rouge Leaders to be Tried for Atrocities." Klein, "National Holiday – Wednesday, 7.1.2009." Sim's thirtieth anniversary speech, in its praise of the Vietnamese in a liberation narrative, echoes in form and content a twenty-fifth-anniversary address the politician gave on January 7, 2004. Interestingly, this particular speech directly mentioned the UN/Cambodian War Crimes Tribunal, which had recently been formed (in 2003). Sim stated, "In the future, we will be in a position to close once [and] for all this dark page through the successful enforcement of the Law on the Creation of the Extraordinary Chamber in the existing Cambodian court system to prosecute crimes committed during the Democratic Kampuchea with the cooperation from the United Nations." BBC, "Chea Sim's Speech at the Cambodian Victory Day Celebration."

22. Quoted in Hinton, "A Head for an Eye," 271.

23. Hughes, "Memory and Sovereignty in Post-1979 Cambodia," 285.

24. "Cambodia: Gambling Fuels Poverty," UN Office for the Coordination of Humanitarian Affairs, September 2, 2008, http://www.irinnews.org.

25. Khamboly Dy, "Teaching Genocide in Cambodia: Challenges, Analyses, and Recommendations," Documentation Center of Cambodia (DC-Cam), accessed January 14, 2009, http://www.dccam.org/Projects/Genocide/Boly_Teaching_Genocide_in_Cambodia1.pdf.

26. "Convention on the Punishment and Prevention of the Crime of Genocide."

27. Following the deposal of the Khmer Rouge by the Vietnamese military, a series of trials was staged in Cambodia (then the People's Republic of Kampuchea, or PRK), which did in fact find Pol Pot guilty of crimes against humanity,

though the Khmer Rouge leader was not present at the trial. Additionally, 995 pages of testimony was gathered during the PRK era that recounted abuses and human rights violations during the Khmer Rouge era. Nevertheless, the UN Commission on Human Rights refused to consider these documents because of their political connection to the Vietnamese government.

28. MacKinnon, "Khmer Rouge Leader in Dock as Cambodian Trial Starts." It was not until March 2003 that the United Nations reached a draft agreement with the Cambodian government for the formation of an international criminal tribunal to try former Khmer Rouge leaders. Such an effort occurred after five years of negotiation and twenty-four years after the Khmer Rouge were driven out of power. I refer to the tribunal as the UN/Cambodian War Crimes Tribunal, yet it should be noted that the tribunal is also referred to as the ECCC (Extraordinary Chambers in the Courts of Cambodia) and the KRT (Khmer Rouge Tribunal). To date, the tribunal has not been completed, and though indictments have been made, trials are still ongoing and no clear verdict has been reached.

29. Daniel Ten Kate, "Cambodian Court Fights Time in Trying Aging Khmer Rouge Leaders," KI-Media, August 6, 2008, http://ki-media.blogspot .com/2008/08/cambodian-court-fights-time-in-trying.html. According to Kate, DC-Cam has collected "more than 650,000 papers and 6,000 photographs from 1975 to 1979."

30. Kerry, "Still Awaiting Justice."

31. Fundamental to Khmer Rouge ideologies was the paradoxical absence and presence of memory. In the interest of turning the nation back to year zero, the Khmer Rouge enacted a multifronted assault on public, private, and familial institutions, foregrounding the common Khmer Rouge saying, "To dig up the grass, one must dig up the roots." Individuals and families were divided according to past affiliations, rural versus urban subjectivities, and degrees of Western and pre–Democratic Kampuchean influence. The attempted obliteration of pre–Democratic Kampuchean practices has dramatically impacted the formation of the tribunal. As historian David Chandler potently observes, only nine judges survived the Democratic Kampuchean regime, uncovering another impediment to the tribunal while simultaneously highlighting the extent to which the Cambodian judicial system was obliterated during the reign of the Khmer Rouge. Such obliteration, as Ben Kiernan and other Cambodian scholars maintain, included the forced dissolution of familial affiliations and the outlawing of religious practices.

32. Mydans, "Cambodian Leader Resists Punishing Top Khmer Rouge."

33. "Cambodia: Political Pressure Undermining Tribunal," Human Rights Watch, July 22, 2009, http://www.hrw.org/en/news/2009/07/22 /cambodia-political-pressure-undermining-tribunal.

34. Madra, "Cambodians Mark 30 Years Since Fall of Pol Pot."

35. Ibid. Given Sim's position within the CPP, which arose during and was

affiliated with the Vietnamese occupation, the absence of an alternative, nonliberation narrative is not surprising. Nonetheless, the lack of acknowledgment highlights the contested narratives of history in contemporary Cambodia.

36. Hillary Rodham Clinton, "Town Hall with Cambodian Youth," November 1, 2010, http://www.state.gov/secretary/rm/2010/11/150230.htm.

37. *New York Times*, "Transcript of President Bush's Speech at the Veterans of Foreign Wars Convention."

38. PBS, "Cambodia: Pol Pot's Shadow." As many scholars within the field of Cambodian studies have observed, more bombs were dropped on Cambodia during this time than the amount used against Japan in the Second World War. According to David Chandler, "In the first half of 1973 the United States brutally postponed a Communist victory by conducting a bombing campaign of Cambodia that, in its intensity, was as far-reaching as any during World War II. Over a hundred thousand tons of bombs fell on the Cambodian countryside before the U.S. Congress prohibited further bombing." Chandler, *A History of Cambodia*, 3rd ed., 252.

39. In a piece titled, "The Cambodian Genocide and Imperial Culture," which appeared in *90 Years of Denial*, a special publication of *Aztag Daily* (Beirut) and the *Armenian Weekly* (Boston) in April 2005 to commemorate the ninetieth anniversary of the 1915 genocide of Armenians, Ben Kiernan documents the "economic rehabilitation of the defeated Khmer Rouge" from 1975 to the present (20–21). Kiernan cites Linda Mason and Roger Brown's *Rice, Rivalry and Politics* with regard to U.S.-backed relief for the Khmer Rouge during the ten-year Vietnamese occupation. Kiernan also notes the lack of media coverage with regard to U.S. support and the consistent failure of Congress to fund war crime tribunals against Khmer Rouge officials. George Chigas, associate director of the Yale Genocide Project, has also highlighted the extent of U.S. culpability in the rise of and continued support of the Khmer Rouge between 1975 and the present.

40. The lack of a nationally sanctioned memorial in Cambodia is reflected by the absence of justice for victims of the Killing Fields on the world stage.

41. The establishment of this office helped facilitate the formation of DC-Cam. A not-for-profit organization affiliated with Yale University's Cambodian Genocide Program, DC-Cam's mission is twofold. DC-Cam is dedicated to "record[ing] and preserv[ing] the history of the Khmer Rouge regime for future generations" and "compil[ing] and organiz[ing] information that can serve as potential evidence in a legal accounting for the crimes of the Khmer Rouge." Fundamental to the organization's educational and online aims is the promotion of both "memory and justice . . . which are critical foundations for the rule of law and genuine national reconciliation in Cambodia" (see the DC-Cam Web site at http://www.dccam.org/#/our_mission/purpose). The Foreign Operations Appropriations Act of 2005 declared, "None of the funds appropriated or other-

wise made available by the Act may be used to provide assistance to any tribunal established by the Government of Cambodia." The absence of any mention of Cambodia in the 2006 version of the act finally enabled funding of the tribunal through congressional appropriations. See Cohen, "For Cambodia's Dead, Farce Heaped on Insult."

42. In February 2008, Scot Marciel, the U.S. State Department's deputy assistant secretary for East Asian and Pacific affairs, pushed Cambodia to sign an agreement to reconcile a $339 million debt to the United States, which was accumulated during the U.S.-backed Lon Nol regime. In response, Cambodian government spokesperson Khieu Kanharith stated that the United States "has not compensated the Cambodian people for its bombing of Cambodia during the Vietnam war either" and connected contemporary difficulties in Cambodia to U.S. cold war policy, which "are also partly the result of the American bombing." Ker Munthit, "Cambodia Rebuffs US Call to Repay Millions Dollars in Debt," Irrawaddy, February 15, 2008, http://www.irrawaddy.org/cartoon.php?art_id=10412.

43. Myers, "Justice Past Due in Cambodia."

44. According to an August 25, 2008 Associated Foreign Press report, the United States "will give its first donation to Cambodia's cash-strapped Khmer Rouge genocide trial as soon as the UN-backed court resolves corruption allegations" as per the U.S. ambassador to Cambodia. Associated Foreign Press, "US Plans to Pledge Funds for KRouge Court," August 25, 2008, http://ecccreparations.blogspot.com/2008_08_01_archive.html.

45. Shawcross, *Sideshow.*

46. Renan, "What Is a Nation?"

47. On August 18, 2008, Republican presidential nominee John McCain echoed President Bush's justification for a continued U.S. presence in Iraq at the Veterans of Foreign Wars national convention in Orlando, Florida.

48. Such aggravated felonies could take the form of writing bad checks or committing murder. Notwithstanding the ambiguity with regard to definition, the 1996 Immigration Reform Acts disallowed judges from making individualized rulings; instead, judges were—when faced with nonresidents who had committed such felonies—left only with the decision to deport.

49. The USA PATRIOT (Uniting and Strengthening America by Providing Appropriate Tools Required to Intercept and Obstruct Terrorism) Act of 2001 was passed following the September 11, 2001, attacks. A 342-page document, the act was linked to national, state, and local antiterrorist initiatives. Much more can certainly be written with regard to the act's impact on civil liberties and law enforcement, but what is most relevant is that the act reconfigured the authority of the Immigration and Naturalization Service (INS) and was used to facilitate the deportation of individuals who had committed aggravated felonies. As of

2005, 127 Cambodians and Cambodian Americans had been deported. Nonetheless, more than 1,200 Cambodians and Cambodian Americans are still awaiting deportation.

50. Shay, "In Cambodia, a Deportee Breakdances to Success."

51. According to Lisa Yoneyama, "The U.S. government's claims to power and authority with which it has defined and administered justice for the rest of the world . . . is by no means a new phenomenon. 'Americanization of world justice' was constitutive of the Cold War strategy that posited the North Americans as the supreme defender of the 'free world'. . . . [I]t has been inseparably tied to prevailing American war memories in which the U.S. war against Japan is remembered as a 'good war.' According to this dominant way of remembering, the U.S. war against Japan (1941–45) not only liberated Asians, including Japanese themselves, from Japan's military fanaticism, but also rehabilitated them into free and prosperous citizens of the democratic world. Put differently, dominant American war memories are tied to what might be called an imperialist myth of 'liberation and rehabilitation,' in which violence and recovery are enunciated simultaneously. According to this myth, the enemy population's liberation from the barbaric and the backward and its successful rehabilitation into an assimilated ally are both anticipated and explained as an outcome of the U.S. military interventions." Yoneyama, "Traveling Memories, Contagious Justice," 57–58.

52. Sturken, *Tangled Memories,* 122. Though Sturken focuses attention on remembrance in the United States, I draw on her work because it examines the function of cold war logics, which are of great relevance to past and contemporary examinations of Cambodian politics and genocidal remembrance.

53. Caruth, *Unclaimed Experience,* 91.

54. Edkins, *Trauma and the Memory of Politics,* 178.

55. Michael Karnavas, e-mail message to author, February 15, 2010.

56. Edkins, *Trauma and the Memory of Politics,* 178.

57. Um, "Exiled Memory."

58. Laub, "Truth and Testimony," 74.

59. Kerry, "Youk Chhang."

60. "'Long-overdue' Justice Necessary in Cambodia, Says Secretary-General Ban," April 15, 2008, http://www.un.org/apps/news/story.asp?NewsID=26330&Cr=cambodia&Cr1=khmer&Kw1=Justice+Necessary+in+Cambodia&Kw2=&Kw3=.

61. Independently, Ruth Hsu and Stephen Hong Sohn have evocatively theorized Asian American literature vis-à-vis frames of refraction. See Sohn, Lim, Gamber, and Valentino, *Transnational Asian American Literature,* and Hsu's essay in the same volume, "The Cartography of Justice and Truthful Refractions."

62. Foucault, *Order of Things,* xix.

63. Foucault, "Dits et écrits 1984," 46.

64. Ibid., 48.

65. Lowe, *Immigrant Acts*, 28–30.

66. Sam Hy, e-mail message to author, February 6, 2011.

67. praCh, "Resurrec," on *Dalama: The End'n Is Just the Beginnin'*.

68. Um, "Exiled Memory."

1. Atrocity Tourism

1. This observation is based on a visit to Phnom Penh in July 2010 and grounded in discussions had with Cambodians who lived in the surrounding area. According to those residents closest to Tuol Sleng Genocide Museum, the overt presentation of bone violates Therevada Buddhist practice, which dictates that a proper burial takes the form of cremation. Consequently, such a site—like Choeung Ek—is considered haunted.

2. Paul Williams makes a significant contribution via his consideration of the efficacy of Tuol Sleng and Choeung Ek as memorials and argues that the politics are, when situated within the context of culturally sensitive remembrance, at best paradoxical. Notwithstanding Williams's argument, I situate my reading of both sites within the larger context of diasporic memory work. See Williams, "Witnessing Genocide." Carla Rose Shapiro has also done work on genocide exhibits in Cambodia, and she connects the curatorial work of both sites to Auschwitz, where Mai Lam (the curator for Tuol Sleng Genocide Museum and the Choeung Ek Center for Genocide Crimes) visited. See Shapiro, "Exhibiting the Cambodian Genocide: The Pasts and Present of the Tuol Sleng Genocide Museum and Choeung Ek Genocidal Center" (abstract), http://webapp.mcis.utoronto.ca/ai/pdfdoc/Shapiro_camb_1.pdf.

3. Youk Chhang, "The Poisonous Hill That Is Tuol Sleng," Documentation Center of Cambodia, accessed May 4, 2010, http://www.dccam.org/Tuol_Sleng_Prison.htm.

4. Chandler, *Voices from S-21*, 2.

5. Chhang, "The Poisonous Hill That Is Tuol Sleng."

6. Ibid.

7. Chandler, *Voices of S-21*, 6.

8. Hinton, "A Head for an Eye," 273.

9. Quoted in Maguire, *Facing Death in Cambodia*, 26–27.

10. Hughes, "Abject Artifacts of Memory," 25.

11. Bell, "Comrade Duch 'Smashed' Thousands in His Notorious Jail."

12. The term "killing machine" is taken from Rithy Panh's 2002 documentary film, *S-21: The Khmer Rouge Killing Machine*.

13. BBC, "Khmer Rouge Survivor Testifies."

14. See the Web site of the Choeung Ek Center for Genocide Crimes, accessed January 12, 2009, http://www.cekillingfield.com (site no longer exists).

15. Chandler, *Voices of S-21*, 6.

16. Dunlop, *The Lost Executioner*. Also see Dacil Keo, "Fact Sheet on 'S-21' Tuol Sleng Prison," DC-Cam, last modified December 6, 1010, http://www.dccam .org/Archives/Documents/Confessions/pdf/Fact_Sheet_on_S-21_Tuol_Sleng _Prison.pdf.

17. "Kaing Guek Eav Convicted of Crimes Against Humanity and Grave Breaches of the Geneva Conventions of 1949," Extraordinary Chambers in the Courts of Cambodia, July 26, 2010, http://www.eccc.gov.kh/en/articles /kaing-guek-eav-convicted-crimes-against-humanity-and-grave-breaches-geneva -conventions-1949.

18. Choeung Ek Online, accessed January 12, 2009, http://choeungek.com (site no longer exists).

19. Maguire, *Facing Death in Cambodia*, 67.

20. Ibid.

21. The number three million was from the outset contested. Those who opposed the Vietnamese occupation within the international community claimed that the number was exaggerated for political purposes. To date, the accepted number of those who perished is 1.7 million, which is based on the mapping and cataloguing of mass graves.

22. Maguire, *Facing Death in Cambodia*, 66.

23. In *Enemies of the People*, Khmer Rouge perpetrators confess to eating victims' gall bladders as per orders from cadres.

24. Maguire, *Facing Death in Cambodia*, 67.

25. Ibid., 70.

26. Hughes, "Abject Artifacts of Memory," 26.

27. Chhang, "The Poisonous Hill That Is Tuol Sleng."

28. Ibid.

29. Hughes, "Memory and Sovereignty in Post-1979 Cambodia," 272.

30. Judy Ledgerwood persuasively argues that the rehabilitation of such sites coincided with a particular "metanarrative" of Vietnamese liberation. I draw from this reading but maintain that the emphasis on perpetrators foreshadows a twenty-first-century preoccupation with atrocity tourism. See Ledgerwood, "Cambodian Tuol Sleng Museum of Genocidal Crimes."

31. Quoted in Hughes, "Abject Artifacts of Memory," 24. Taken from Tuol Sleng Genocide Museum brochure.

32. The notion of a screen and its connection to a built memorial is drawn from Marita Sturken's work on the Vietnam War Memorial. See Sturken, *Tangled Memories*.

33. Sontag, *Regarding the Pain of Others*. Rachel Hughes's work on these images is especially instructive, for she places the S-21 photographs in a larger conversation about the mass circulation of Cambodia's genocide memory. See Hughes, "Abject Artifacts of Memory."

34. Transcribed from a photograph taken by the author on January 6, 2010 at Tuol Sleng Genocide Museum.

35. Chhang, "The Poisonous Hill That Is Tuol Sleng."

36. Transcribed from a photograph taken by the author on January 6, 2010 at Tuol Sleng Genocide Museum.

37. Hughes, "Abject Artifacts of Memory," 24.

38. Maguire, *Facing Death in Cambodia*, 67.

39. In like fashion, Sarah Jones Dickens (of the DC-Cam) notes that the museum provides "very little historical overview and context" to visitors, a point raised in surveys wherein "most respondents have stressed that there is scant information about the reasons behind the Khmer Rouge and life under the Khmer Rouge." Dickens, "Stilled Lives, Victims, or Perpetrators?"

40. Transcribed from a placard at the Choeung Ek Center for Genocide Crimes, Phnom Penh, Cambodia, January 8, 2010 visit.

41. Quoted in Ledgerwood, "Cambodian Tuol Sleng Museum of Genocidal Crimes," 89.

42. Hughes, "Memory and Sovereignty in Post-1979 Cambodia," 270.

43. Ibid., 276.

44. Ibid., 275–76.

45. Wynne Cougill, "Buddhist Cremation Traditions for the Dead and the Need to Preserve Forensic Evidence in Cambodia," DC-Cam, http://www.d.dccam.org/Projects/Maps/Buddhist_Cremation_Traditions.htm.

46. Hughes, "Memory and Sovereignty in Post-1979 Cambodia," 276.

47. Ibid.

48. Ledgerwood, "Cambodian Tuol Sleng Museum of Genocidal Crimes," 84.

49. *New York Times*, "Around the World."

50. Hinton, "A Head for an Eye."

51. Ibid.

52. See Williams, "Witnessing Genocide" and Williams, "The Atrocity Exhibition."

53. "Multilateral Agreement on a Comprehensive Political Settlement of the Cambodian Conflict," United Nations, accessed December 29, 2010, http://untreaty.un.org/unts/120001_144071/2/2/00000971.pdf.

54. "United Nations Transitional Authority in Cambodia," United Nations, accessed December 29, 2010, http://www.un.org/en/peacekeeping/missions/past/untac.htm.

55. Widyono, *Dancing in Shadows*.

56. *CNN*, "Hun Sen Claims No Coup in Cambodia."

57. Ieng Sary had defected to Phnom Penh in 1996 and had received a royal pardon that was confirmed again in 1998.

58. Mydans, "Cambodian Leader Resists Punishing Top Khmer Rouge."

59. Yoneyama, *Hiroshima Traces*, 32–33.

60. Sturken, *Tangled Memories*, 43.

61. Cougill, "Buddhist Cremation Traditions for the Dead and the Need to Preserve Forensic Evidence in Cambodia."

62. *Los Angeles Times*, "Skull Exhibit Must Go, Sihanouk Says."

63. Quoted in Cougill, "Buddhist Cremation Traditions for the Dead and the Need to Preserve Forensic Evidence in Cambodia."

64. *Independent*, "Cambodian Referendum Over Khmer Rouge Victims' Remains."

65. Cougill, "Buddhist Cremation Traditions for the Dead and the Need to Preserve Forensic Evidence in Cambodia."

66. Ibid.

67. Ibid.

68. Despite the fact that the defendant confessed to his involvement and to various crimes, the court had no provision in place to consider a guilty plea and was thus forced to review the entire case. See Saliba and Nims, "Duch Sentenced to 35 Years in Prison; Will Serve Only 19."

69. "Closing Arguments in Duch Case before ECCC," Hague Justice Portal, November 27, 2009, http://www.haguejusticeportal.net/index.php?id=11254.

70. Mydans, "Khmer Rouge Defendant Apologizes for Atrocities."

71. Munthit, "Khmer Rouge Official Revisits Atrocities."

72. Based on the author's attendance at the July 26, 2010 reading of Kaing Guek Eav's verdict at the ECCC courthouse.

73. Because of the hybrid nature of the court, the charges that were considered in Case 001 included Geneva Conventions and violations of the 1956 Cambodian Penal Code.

74. Based on the author's attendance at the July 26, 2010 reading of Kaing Guek Eav's verdict at the ECCC courthouse.

75. Notwithstanding the long list of crimes, the UN/Cambodian War Crimes Tribunal ultimately concluded that the defendant was part of a joint criminal enterprise, which gestured toward Case 002 involving higher-level Khmer Rouge leaders (the previously mentioned Chea, Samphan, Thirith, and Sary). In asserting a particularly horrific "chain of command," the court established a precedent upon which to try surviving leaders of the regime by way of hierarchy and superior-driven genocidal policy. Even though the court established—by way of ruling—that Kaing Guek Eav was part of a "joint criminal exercise," it nevertheless did not recognize the "following orders" defense put forth by Kaing Guek

Eav's legal team. Such a defense is not recognized in international cases involving defendants facing charges of crimes against humanity and war crimes.

76. "Victims Support Unit," Extraordinary Chambers in the Courts of Cambodia, accessed January 10, 2011, http://www.eccc.gov.kh/en/victims-support.

77. Based on the author's attendance at the July 26, 2010 reading of Kaing Guek Eav's verdict at the ECCC courthouse.

78. Ibid.

79. Ibid.

80. Interestingly, days before the scheduled reading of the verdict, Kaing Guek Eav dismissed his international counsel (Francois Roux), leading many to speculate that he was planning an appeal. In March 2011, Kaing Guek Eav filed an appeal; on February 3, 2012, his appeal was denied and his sentence increased to life imprisonment.

81. "Theary Seng's Comment on Duch's Verdict," KI-Media, July 28, 2010, http://ki-media.blogspot.com/2010/07/theary-sengs-comment-on-duchs-verdict.html.

82. Cambodian Human Rights Action Committee, "Conference on Reparations for Victims of the Khmer Rouge Regime."

83. Gross, "Constitution of History and Memory."

84. It should be noted that the DC-Cam (under Youk Chhang's directorship) is currently planning a permanent center in Phnom Penh that will include a museum, a research facility, and a genocide education center (Youk Chhang, personal correspondence with author, July 28, 2010).

85. Huyssen, "Monument and Memory in a Postmodern Age," 12.

86. *USA Today,* "Genocide Site in Cambodia Draws Tourists."

87. Principally focused on artifacts from the classical Khmer empire (twelfth and thirteenth centuries), the National Museum was initially under the curatorial administration of French historian George Groslier. The museum opened in August 1917, and its first Cambodian director, Chea Thay Seng, was appointed in 1966. The museum remained in operation until the Khmer Rouge takeover of the city in April 1975. The museum was closed during the Democratic Kampuchean era and was reopened soon after the dissolution of the Khmer Rouge regime in 1979. See "Museum History," National Museum of Cambodia, last updated 2010, http://www.cambodiamuseum.info/museum_history.html.

88. Chandler, *A History of Cambodia,* 4th ed., 11.

89. During the period of French colonization, Angkor Wat was rediscovered in 1860 by French naturalist Henri Mouhot. Early in 2003, Suvanant Kongying (a Thai soap opera actress) was rumored to have stated that Angkor Wat belonged to Thailand, not Cambodia. Though unsubstantiated, the claim prompted a series of riots in Cambodia. The Thai embassy was vandalized and burned, Thai businesses were targeted, and Kongying's life was threatened by angry protestors. See Paddock, "Rumor of Thai Actress' Words Salted a Wound."

90. Chandler, *A History of Cambodia,* 4th ed., 11.

91. "Angkor Wat Dreams: Jacqueline Kennedy's 1967 visit to Cambodia," Devata.org, January 6, 2010, http://www.devata.org/2010/01/angkor-wat-dreams-jacqueline-kennedys-1967-visit-to-cambodia/.

92. Burmon, "Dark Tourism."

93. "Invasion of Angkor Wat," Heritage Watch International, August 21, 2010, http://www.heritagewatchinternational.org/invasion-of-angkor-wat.html.

94. The Cambodian Land Mine Museum was founded and is directed by Aki Ra, a former child soldier who was forcibly conscripted by the Khmer Rouge. Aki Ra has spent his adult life advocating for land mine victims and clearing land mines from the Cambodian countryside. He currently leads the Cambodian Self Help Demining Group, which has cleared fifty thousand mines. The Cambodian Land Mine Museum faced some controversy due to the fact it exhibited still-active munitions and was—for a brief period—shut down. Aki Ra was recently named a "CNN hero" in 2010: CNN, "Aki Ra: Community Crusader."

95. Istvan, "'Killing Fields' Lure Tourists in Cambodia."

96. A third dimension of Cambodia's tourist industry involves its underground sex industry. Cambodia is a Southeast Asian hub for trafficking and sex work as per a 2003 U.S. State Department report. According to UNICEF and Save the Children, an estimated fifty thousand to one hundred thousand women and children are involved in the industry. What is more, approximately 30 percent of sex workers in Phnom Penh (Cambodia's capital) are under eighteen. Not only is the sex industry a problem in Cambodia; it is also a dilemma funded by Americans. As per a recent report issued by ECPAT (End Child Prostitution, Child Pornography, and the Trafficking of Children for Sexual Purposes) highlights, Americans constitute almost 25 percent of all sex tourists (including 38 percent of such tourists in Cambodia and 80 percent of those in Costa Rica). See Rivers, "Girl, 6, Embodies Cambodia's Sex Industry," and Susan Song, "Global Child Sex Tourism: Children as Tourist Attractions," Youth Advocate Program International, http://www.yapi.org/rpchildsextourism.pdf.

97. "Mapping Project: 1995–Present," DC-Cam, accessed November 19, 2010, http://www.dccam.org/Projects/Maps/Mapping.htm.

98. Stone and Sharpley, "Consuming Dark Tourism," 574.

99. Wiesel, "The Perils of Indifference."

100. Foley and Lennon, "JFK and Dark Tourism." Also Lennon and Foley, *Dark Tourism.*

101. See Stone and Sharpley, "Consuming Dark Tourism."

102. Auschwitz-Birkenau Memorial and Museum, "Numbers of People Visiting Yearly the Auschwitz Memorial," http://en.auschwitz.org/z/index.php?option=com_content&task=view&id=56&Itemid=24 (accessed January 11, 2011).

103. Doyle, "Revenue Fields."

104. See International Justice Tribune, "'Genotourism' at Choeung Ek."

105. Ibid.

106. Doyle, "Revenue Fields." Notwithstanding his potent critique, Say does directly profit from Choeung Ek tourism—he runs a small on-site business just outside the memorial's gates.

107. Brady, "Postcard: Anlong Veng," 9.

108. This was not the first time the controversial S-21 photographer attempted to cash in on Khmer Rouge memorabilia. Notwithstanding En's public critique of a 2007 eBay sale involving a 1973 Mercedes limousine that allegedly belonged to the Khmer Rouge leader, En was unsuccessful in his 2009 attempt to auction Pol Pot's sandals for $500,000. The only bid En received was a commitment of $790,000 in "ghost" money. Such ghost money refers to paper that is burned at funerals as per a Cambodian memorial tradition.

109. Burmon, "Dark Tourism."

110. Ibid.

111. As Andrew Buncombe, reporter for the *Independent,* reconfirms, the planned development of Khmer Rouge sites "underlines the increasing allure of the country's genocidal history and importance of tourists to Cambodia's coffers." Buncombe, "Cambodia Puts the Cremation Site of Pol Pot on 'Historic' Tourist Trail."

112. Brady, "Postcard: Anlong Veng," 9.

113. Doyle, "Revenue Fields."

114. Simmons, "Commentary: 'Atrocity Tourism' Overkill?"

115. Amanpour, "Survivor Recalls Horrors of Cambodia Genocide."

116. According to Raymond Williams, "structures of feeling" refer to "meanings and values as they are actively lived and felt" and represent "characteristic elements of impulse, restraint, and tone; specifically affective elements of consciousness and relationships." Such "structures" are comprised of "specific internal relations, at once interlocking and in tension." See Williams, *Marxism and Literature,* 132.

117. From a speech given by Ferstman at a 2009 symposium hosted by the Cambodian Human Rights Action Committee.

118. See the Web site of the Cambodian Association of Illinois, http://cai .maaillinois.org/ (accessed January 17, 2011).

119. Ibid.

120. Cambodian Association of Illinois, "Killing Fields Memorial," http://cai .maaillinois.org/news/submit-names-wall-remembrance (accessed December 12, 2010).

121. Deanna Isaacs, "A New Collection in Chicago Shows There's More to Cambodian Culture than the Killing Fields," *Chicago Reader,* http:// www.chicagoreader.com/chicago/khmer-here/Content?oid=926121.

122. Chuh, *Imagine Otherwise,* 3.

2. Screening Apology

1. Schanberg was the recipient of the Pulitzer Prize for International Reporting in 1976.

2. Schanberg, "The Death and Life of Dith Pran," in *Beyond the Killing Fields*, 66.

3. "The Death and Life of Dith Pran" was published in book form by Penguin in 1985, following the release of *The Killing Fields* film.

4. In John 11:25, Jesus, replying to Lazarus's sister Martha, proclaims, "I am the Resurrection and the Life. He who believes in Me shall live, even if he dies. And everyone who lives and believes in Me shall never die in eternity." Schanberg's assertion that he and Pran were reunited almost four and a half years after they were separated at the French embassy recalls an allusion to Lazarus, who was resurrected after four days, and matches the almost four-year reign of the Khmer Rouge.

5. Schanberg, "The Death and Life of Dith Pran," 63.

6. Ibid., 64.

7. Ibid., 64–65.

8. Ibid., 94.

9. Yen Le Espiritu makes this observation in "The 'We-Win-Even-When-We-Lose' Syndrome," as do Marita Sturken, *Tangled Memories*; Viet Nguyen, *Race and Resistance*; and Susan Jeffords, *Remasculinization of America*.

10. Nguyen, *Race and Resistance*, 109.

11. Espiritu, "The 'We-Win-Even-When-We-Lose' Syndrome," 329. See also Sturken, "The Wall, the Screen, and the Image," 121.

12. Espiritu, "The 'We-Win-Even-When-We-Lose' Syndrome," 329.

13. In an address delivered to the Veterans of Foreign Wars in Chicago on August 18, 1980, the Republican candidate Reagan averred, "Peace must be such that freedom can flourish and justice prevail. Tens of thousands of boat people have shown us there is no freedom in the so-called peace in Vietnam. The hill people of Laos know poison gas, not justice, and in Cambodia there is only the peace of the grave for at least one-third of the population slaughtered by the Communists. For too long, we have lived with the 'Vietnam Syndrome.' Much of that syndrome has been created by the North Vietnamese aggressors who now threaten the peaceful people of Thailand. Over and over they told us for nearly 10 years that we were the aggressors bent on imperialistic conquests. They had a plan. It was to win in the field of propaganda here in America what they could not win on the field of battle in Vietnam." Ronald Reagan, "Address to the Veterans of Foreign Wars Convention in Chicago," American Presidency Project, August 18, 1980, http://www.presidency.ucsb.edu/ws/index.php?pid=85202.

14. Bush, "Quotation of the Day."

15. Pelaud, *This Is All I Choose to Tell*, 15.

16. Wiesel, "Letters to the Editor."

17. Navarro, "Letters to the Editor."

18. *New York Times,* "Transcript of President Bush's Speech at the Veterans of Foreign Wars Convention."

19. Schanberg, "The Death and Life of Dith Pran," 84.

20. Ibid., 63.

21. The "three million" Schanberg attests as the number who perished during the Killing Fields era coheres with the estimates put forth by the Vietnamese-occupied People's Republic of Kampuchea.

22. Barkan, "Truth and Reconciliation in History," 8.

23. Freedman, "In 'The Killing Fields,' a Cambodian Actor Relives His Nation's Ordeal."

24. Historically, Cambodia and Thailand have shared a contentious political history, redolent in frequent debates over the ownership of various temple sites. Moreover, the forced closure of border refugee camps, which prompted the involuntary return of hundreds of thousands of Cambodian refugees, makes the choice to cast Thais even more complex.

25. Freedman, "In 'The Killing Fields,' a Cambodian Actor Relives His Nation's Ordeal."

26. Ibid.

27. Ibid.

28. Ibid.

29. On February 25, 1996, Ngor was the victim of a gang shooting and died in front of his downtown Los Angeles home. Notwithstanding the three gang members charged and tried for his murder, Ngor's outspoken criticism of the Cambodian government led many to speculate whether this was a politically motivated shooting.

30. This is drawn from Samuel Freedman's title, which includes the phrase "a Cambodian Actor Relives His Nation's Ordeal."

31. Freedman, "In 'The Killing Fields,' a Cambodian Actor Relives His Nation's Ordeal."

32. Ibid.

33. Schickel, "Cinema: Ordeal of a Heroic Survivor."

34. *Variety,* "The Killing Fields."

35. In addition to Ngor's nomination (and win) for Best Supporting Actor, the film was nominated for six other Academy Awards: Best Picture, Best Director, Best Actor (Sam Waterston), Best Adapted Screenplay (win), Best Film Editing, and Best Cinematography (win). Ngor won the award against fellow *Killing Fields* cast member John Malkovich (for *Places in the Heart*) and Asian American Pat Morita (for *The Karate Kid*).

36. "Haing S. Ngor, Acceptance speech at the 57th Academy Awards," Academy of Motion Picture Arts and Sciences, March 25, 1985, http://aaspeechesdb .oscars.org/ics-wpd/exec/icswppro.dll?AC=qbe_query&TN=AAtrans&RF= WebReportOscars&MF=oscarsmsg.ini&NP=255&BU=http://aaspeechesdb .oscars.org/index.asp&QY=find+acceptorlink+%3d057-2.

37. Freedman, "In 'The Killing Fields,' a Cambodian Actor Relives His Nation's Ordeal."

38. Ibid.

39. This is a deliberate allusion to William L. Shirer's famous history, *The Rise and Fall of the Third Reich*.

40. Sturken, "The Wall, the Screen, and the Image," 118.

41. Ibid.

42. Ebert, *Roger Ebert's Four Star Reviews*, 388.

43. Ikui, "Reprogramming Memories," 45–47.

44. Lee, *Orientals*, 190.

45. There are two notable exceptions to the characterization of Khmer Rouge. The first is a young Khmer Rouge soldier Pran befriends prior to the Khmer Rouge takeover. In a later scene, Pran is held by cadres following an accusation of theft. The same soldier is at the scene and convinces the others to let Pran live. The second involves a Khmer Rouge cadre Pran encounters near the end of the film. The cadre, who is about to be executed, entrusts Pran with the care of his son on the condition that he leave Cambodia.

46. This particular incident is covered in Schanberg's "Death and Life of Dith Pran."

47. See "Burrows, Larry," 187.

48. See *Life*, "Behind Enemy Lines."

49. Sontag, *Regarding the Pain of Others*, 59–60.

50. See *Denver Post*, "Captured."

51. Lennon, *Imagine*.

52. Hirsch, "Past Lives," 662.

53. Socheata Poeuv, "Khmer Legacies: The Desire to be Heard," Huffington Post, May 12, 2008, http://www.huffingtonpost.com/socheata-poeuv/khmer -legacies-the-desire_b_101377.html.

54. Foucault, *Security, Territory, Population*, 2.

55. Mbembe, "Necropolitics," 12.

56. Ibid., 17.

57. See Hong, *Ruptures of American Capital*. Hong compellingly maps the analytical interplay between biopower, social death, and necropolitics.

58. In a special feature that appears on the *New Year Baby* DVD, composer Gil Talmi relates that he was invested in a transnational musical composition that spoke to Poeuv's own location in the "East and West."

59. See Maguire, *Facing Death in Cambodia.*

60. Socheata Poeuv, e-mail message to author, March 18, 2011. The largest number of Cambodians living outside Southeast Asia can be found in Paris, France.

61. Socheata Poeuv, interview with the author, June 12, 2009. According to Poeuv, "Without memory, there can be no justice."

62. Sandra Fierlinger is a coanimator (with her husband) in *New Year Baby.*

63. See "Paul Fierlinger," Zanimation, accessed March 24, 2011, http://www.zanimation.tv/index.php?option=com_hwdvideoshare&task=viewcategory&cat_id=24&Itemid=30.

64. See "Paul Fierlinger (Co-director, animator, writer)," *My Dog Tulip,* accessed March 24, 2011, http://speakery.com/mydogtulipfilm/paul-fierlinger -co-director-animator-writer/, and "Drawn from Memory," http://history .sundance.org/films/112.

65. See "Animator: Paul Fierlinger," on *New Year Baby* DVD.

66. Ibid.

67. Ibid.

68. Socheata Poeuv, interview with the author, June 12, 2009.

69. Socheata Poeuv, interview with the author, June 12, 2009.

70. Even though Poeuv refers to herself as a "second-generation" subject, her place of birth (in Thailand) makes possible a 1.5-generation subjectivity.

71. Fein, "Holocaust as a Cartoonist's Way of Getting to Know His Father."

72. Smith, "From Mickey to Maus."

73. Barkan and Karn, "Introduction," 7.

74. Socheata Poeuv, interview with the author, June 12, 2009.

75. Lowe, "The International within the National," 77.

76. Ibid.

77. I want to thank Mariam Lam for her reading of "reckoning" vis-à-vis memory work.

78. Kim, *Ends of Empire,* 10 (emphasis in original).

79. Hong, *Ruptures of American Capital.*

3. Growing Up under the Khmer Rouge

1. Shenk, "Memories of Genocide."

2. Yamada, "Cambodian American Autobiography," 147.

3. Schaffer and Smith, "Conjunctions," 7.

4. Shenk, "Memories of Genocide."

5. Ibid.

6. Pran, "Compiler's Note," x.

7. I want to thank Allan Isaac for his thoughts with regard to memoir and Cambodian American cultural production.

8. Gordon, *Ghostly Matters*, 8.

9. Him, *When Broken Glass Floats*, 19. Him's allusion to 1990 reminds readers of the period following the departure of the Vietnamese and the dissolution of the People's Republic of Kampuchea.

10. Ung, *First They Killed My Father*, 235.

11. Caruth, *Unclaimed Experience*, 3.

12. Ibid., 4.

13. Yathay, *Stay Alive My Son*, 237. Incidentally, Yathay's memoir was reissued the same year that Him's and Ung's memoirs were published. Yathay's memoir originally appeared in essay form under the title "L'Utopie Meurtriere" (Murderous Utopia) in 1979. Of relevance to this chapter is Yathay's dedication, which is consistent with other Cambodian/Cambodian American memoirs: "This is a true story. I dedicate it to the memory of my children, my wife, my parents, and other members of my family, as well as to the memory of millions of my compatriots."

14. Lee, *Urban Triage*, xxvi.

15. Bernstein, "Books of the Times."

16. Ung, "A Birthday Wrapped in Cambodian History."

17. Slaughter, *Human Rights, Inc.*, 123.

18. Minow, *Between Vengeance and Forgiveness*, 138.

19. Him, "Please Give Us Voice," in *When Broken Glass Floats*, front matter.

20. Ung, *First They Killed My Father*, author's note.

21. As Teri Shaffer Yamada notes, Cambodian American memoir in particular "'signifies' a painful testimony of culture genocide and dislocation, as it recenters the ideological discourse of American autobiography from a national debate on the perimeters of American identity to an international application of American values in the form of global human rights. . . . [Its] form and content act synergistically to frame an ideological perspective reflective of a hybrid Cambodian American identity, unique to the Cambodian American experience." Yamada, "Cambodian American Autobiography," 144.

22. Schaffer and Smith, "Conjunctions," 4.

23. This is the title Him ascribes to these targets, which are named as such on the Cambodian map included in the text.

24. Him, *When Broken Glass Floats*, 54.

25. Ibid., 30.

26. Ibid.

27. Ibid., 33.

28. According to Him, on "April 20, 1970—in an attempt to incapacitate the Viet Cong troops operating in the border sanctuaries of Cambodia—forces from the United States and South Vietnam launched a massive drive into Cambodia, making Cambodia a stage for war. Early on, U.S. leaders denied involvement, until finally the American public demanded the truth. This Vietnamese conflict

violated Cambodia's borders, disregarding the precarious neutrality Cambodian Prince Norodom Sihanouk had sought to preserve for years. On March 18, 1970, Prince Sihanouk was ousted by his premier, Lon Nol, and his cousin, Prince Sisowath Serik Matak, in a bloodless coup backed by the United States. China welcomed Sihanouk with open arms, eager to help save Cambodia from 'American imperialists.' Later, Chinese leaders encouraged him to form a government in exile consisting primarily of his enemies, the Khmer Rouge, a band of guerillas who had exploited the upheaval of the Vietnamese conflict. Thus, another invisible tail of the comet emerged. This one pointed to China, which had helped create the Khmer Rouge—a lethal virus that would years later destroy most of its former host, Cambodia, and so many of its own people" (*When Broken Glass Floats*, 33).

29. Ung, *First They Killed My Father*, 40. This concession is interesting given the position Ung's father holds at the beginning of the narrative. Ung's father was formerly employed with the Cambodian Royal Secret Service (under Prince Norodom Sihanouk). Following the rise of the Lon Nol government in 1970, Ung's father was forcibly conscripted as a soldier in the new regime. According to Ung, "Pa said he did not want to join but had to, or he would risk being persecuted, branded a traitor, and perhaps even killed" (ibid., 12).

30. Nixon, "Speech on Cambodia."

31. Him, "Dedication," in *When Broken Glass Floats*. "Pa" and "Mak" refer to Him's father and mother, respectively. Basaba is a younger brother born soon after the U.S. bombings began. Map is Him's younger brother and Chea was Him's oldest sister. Ra, Ry, and Avy are sisters, whereas Tha and Than are older brothers. Vin is Him's younger brother. Cheng is a friend made in a labor camp. Map, Ra, Ry, and Than are not included in the dedication.

32. Him, "Author's Note," in *When Broken Glass Floats*.

33. Ung, "Dedication," in *First They Killed My Father*.

34. Kiernan, "Introduction," xiv.

35. Him, *When Broken Glass Floats*, 14.

36. Chan, *Survivors*, 25.

37. Ung, *First They Killed My Father*, 60.

38. Him, *When Broken Glass Floats*, 100.

39. Ibid., 110.

40. Ibid., 120–21.

41. Ung's assertion that she is a daughter of Cambodia is transformed through the course of the narrative. At the beginning of *First They Killed My Father*, Ung presents herself as a child who is inquisitive and respects her father's commands. However, her role in the family shifts as a result of their experiences living under the Khmer Rouge. For example, in one scene Ung steals food from the family, which in view of the circumstances and the threat of famine has greater consequences than it might otherwise have. This act of childish selfishness becomes a

severe crime against the family and the source an intense amount of guilt for the protagonist (90).

42. Ben Kiernan also notes that part of the political strategy that undergirded the Khmer Rouge's rise to power was based on the destruction of both the family and Buddhism. Temples were destroyed, monks executed, and religious practice outlawed during this time. The title of Him's memoir, *When Broken Glass Floats*, refers to a Buddhist narrative about good and evil. According to this narrative, shards of broken glass represent evil, and good is represented by a squash. Although glass will float, it will eventually sink, and the squash will rise to take its place. The narrative reflects a focus on Buddhist notions of balance. With regard to the text, the broken glass represents the Khmer Rouge regime. The use of Buddhist thought in the title and throughout the text is therefore significant given that the Khmer Rouge during the period of Democratic Kampuchea forcefully outlawed mentions to and practices of Buddhism, the major religion in Cambodia.

43. Ung, *First They Killed My Father*, 15.

44. Him, *When Broken Glass Floats*, 29. The setting for this description occurs in the wealthy Cambodian province of Takeo. The bombing of the region prompts a relocation to Phnom Penh.

45. Lee, *The Americas of Asian American Literature*, 54.

46. Within Democratic Kampuchea, those who lived in the cities were labeled "New People" or "April 17th People." This label contrasted with the Khmer Rouge classification of "Base People," who lived in rural Cambodia and/or were supporters of the Khmer Rouge prior to the 1975 takeover.

47. Edkins, *Trauma and the Memory of Politics*, 178.

48. Hirsch, *Family Frames*, 22.

49. Ibid., 251.

50. See Barthes, *Camera Lucida*, 5. Barthes observes, "A specific photograph, in effect, is never distinguished from its referent (from what it represents), or at least it is not *immediately* or *generally* distinguished from its referent."

51. Lee, *Orientals*, 7.

52. As discussed in chapter 1, the images from S-21 of prisoners about to face execution and torture, released after the demise of the Khmer Rouge, visually speak to life during the Democratic Kampuchean regime. Similarly, photographs of labor camps—often used to further Khmer Rouge propagandistic claims of revolutionary success—provide a euphemistic view of life under the Khmer Rouge.

53. Him, *When Broken Glass Floats*, 330.

54. Ung, *First They Killed My Father*, 237.

55. Ibid., 238.

56. Ibid.

57. Gwartney, "Broken Promises."

58. Ibid.

59. See Jacklet, "Cambodian Collaborations."

60. See Gwartney, "Broken Promises."

61. Unintentionally, Schanberg's role in the controversy speaks to his unique authenticating position in the production of Killing Fields narratives. As discussed in the previous chapter, Schanberg's prominence in the production of Killing Fields narratives has given rise to a particular master narrative that necessarily locates the U.S. subject in an at times problematic recuperative role.

62. Interestingly, Dith Pran, the subject of Schanberg's most famous article, did not publicly respond to the controversy. To reiterate, Schanberg's position as a foundational figure in Cambodian American genocidal remembrance is of primary importance in chapter 2.

63. Ung, *First They Killed My Father*, 2–4.

64. The Khmer Institute put forth the following proclamation against Loung Ung: "We are not engaged in a crusade against the author; our crusade, if it can be described as such, is to expose the truth so that people may know what the Killing Fields really meant for Cambodians who lived through it." Review of *First They Killed My Father*, by Loung Ung, Khmer Institute, accessed December 1, 2004, http://www.khmerinstitute.org/ung.html. Ung's status as a marginalized minority subject in her country of origin echoes earlier accounts of Chinese immigration in the dissertation. Her status as a stranger is also reminiscent of the Jewish diasporic experience, in which one's claim of nation-state affiliation is discounted in favor of native-born citizenships.

65. Ung, *First They Killed My Father*, 62.

66. For a detailed critique of *First They Killed My Father*, please refer to Soneath Hor, Sody Lay, and Grantham Quinn, "First They Killed Her Sister: A Definitive Analysis," Khmer Institute, last modified 2001, http://www.khmerinstitute.org/articles/arto4.html." This article provides an in-depth analysis of Ung's text and raises issues of authenticity and veracity.

67. Ung, *First They Killed My Father*, 54.

68. Another controversial issue embedded in Ung's text is her father's aforementioned position with the Royal Cambodian Secret Police and the Lon Nol regime. Critics claim that Ung's father was most likely involved in state-authorized violence against Cambodians, though Ung counters this with the assertion that her father was forced to join the Lon Nol regime through conscription.

69. See Review of *First They Killed My Father*, by Loung Ung, Khmer Institute.

70. See Zaleski and Abbott, "Forecasts: Nonfiction." See also Bernstein, "Books of the Times."

71. See Lay, "The Cambodian Tragedy." Lay was the former director for the Khmer Institute.

72. Reminiscent of Cambodian American daughterly frames and situated

within a pre–2007 UN Declaration on the Rights of Indigenous Peoples milieu, Menchú's memoir is composed of political and politicized remembrances focused on the protagonist's father (Vincente Menchú Perez), mother (Juana Tum Cotoja), and eight siblings. Expressly, *I, Rigoberta Menchú,* by way of *testimonio,* tactically unearthed an indigenous leftist struggle against state-authorized exploitation and state-sanctioned discrimination. Recounting human rights violations vis-à-vis familial losses (wherein parents and siblings were disappeared and murdered), the memoir was a runaway best seller, and quickly became a curricular staple in classrooms across the United States and around the globe. Not surprising given the memoir's success, Menchú would emerge as a key spokesperson in a more global indigenous rights movement.

73. See Rohter, "Tarnished Laureate."

74. Responding to requests to revoke Menchú's Nobel Peace Prize, Geir Lundestad (director of the Norwegian Nobel Institute and permanent secretary of the Norwegian Nobel Committee) refused, stating that "all autobiographies embellish to a greater or lesser extent" and that the award "was not based exclusively or primarily on the autobiography." Lundestad further asserted that, while "the details of the family history are not without relevance, they are not particularly important, so this will lead to no reconsideration on our part." See Rohter, "Tarnished Laureate."

75. Gilmore, "Jurisdictions," 696.

76. Ibid.

4. Lost Chapters and Invisible Wars

1. The downtown section was officially named Cambodia Town in 2007, following a series of debates between Cambodian American leaders and Long Beach city politicians. See Krasnowsky, "'Cambodia Town' Controversy."

2. Cambodian consulates in the United States exist in two other places: Seattle, Washington, and Lowell, Massachusetts.

3. To reiterate, following the dissolution of Democratic Kampuchea in 1979, Cambodian refugees began to come en masse to the United States, which remains—along with France and Australia—one of the primary coordinates for a post–Democratic Kampuchean diaspora. Undeniably, the 1980 passage of the Refugee Act made possible a cold war transpacific transit from Thai and Philippine refugee camps to the United States. Between 1975 and 1979, an estimated 13,300 Cambodians sought asylum in the United States; from 1980 to 1990, this exodus grew, encompassing approximately 117,000 Cambodian refugees who successfully gained entrance into the United States. Such displaced subjects—by way of sponsorship—resettled across the nation, from San Francisco to Philadelphia, from Seattle to Washington, D.C., and from Portland, Oregon, to Chicago,

Illinois. Even so, the majority of Cambodians and Cambodian Americans (who most recently number 236,000) live in two distinct bicoastal locales: Long Beach, California, and Lowell, Massachusetts, which is home to twenty-five thousand Cambodians and Cambodian Americans.

4. See the Cambodia Town official Web site at http://www.cambodiatown.org/.

5. For the remainder of this chapter, I will be using the rapper's stage name, praCh.

6. praCh, e-mail message to author, April 1, 2011.

7. See May, "Art of faCt," 73. Srae K'prach was also the source of praCh's name (which designated where he was born).

8. praCh, personal correspondence with author, April 3, 2011.

9. May, "Art of faCt."

10. Ibid.

11. "War on the Streets" is a track that appears on both *Dalama: The End'n Is Just the Beginnin'* and *Dalama: Memoirs of an Invisible War*.

12. Wride, "Soundtrack of Violent Streets."

13. Moore, "Ruthless Asian Gangs Blaze Trail of Violence."

14. See Willwerth, "From Killing Fields to Mean Streets."

15. Geis, "Long Beach Awaits Hate Crime Verdict."

16. Yang, "Southeast Asian American Children," 128.

17. See SEARAC's "Southeast Asian Americans at a Glance: Statistics on Southeast Asians adapted from the American Community Survey," last updated January 19, 2011, http://www.searac.org/sites/default/files/SEAAs_At_A_Glance_Jan_2011.pdf.

18. Ibid.

19. Ironically, Haing S. Ngor of *Killing Fields* fame was gunned down in his driveway by members of the Oriental Lazy Boyz gang.

20. Wride, "Soundtrack of Violent Streets."

21. Schlund-Vials, "Hip Hop Memoirs."

22. Ibid.

23. Ibid.

24. Ibid.

25. praCh's *Dalama: Memoirs of the Invisible War* is at this date only available for download.

26. Lowe, *Immigrant Acts*, 29.

27. Rose, *Black Noise*, 21.

28. Schlund-Vials, "Hip Hop Memoirs."

29. Ibid.

30. The complete track listing is [1] "Intro: The Temple of Peace—Takeover"; [2] "The Letter (Prisoner of War)"; [3] "Skit: Start anew, nuth'n has gone before";

[4] "The YearZero!" [5] "Interlude: Peak of Light"; [6] "Welcome"; [7] "Interlude: New Hope"; [8] "Out-tro: The Burden of Power—The Countdown 3, 2, 1..."; [9] "NorthSide (We High)" (featuring Toeum); [10] "Walk-a-Block" (with hip-hop trio Northstar Resurrec); [11] "War on the Streetz"; [12] "Knowledge, Nix-Mo"; [13] "Ah-Ye (Khmer Rap!)"; [14] "Child of the Killing Fields"; [15] "Zip (Da N Nite)"(showcasing fellow emcees doZer and Pinner; [16] "Take Your Time"; and [17] "Make Money Take Money."

31. Rose, *Hip Hop Wars*.

32. Schlund-Vials, "Hip Hop Memoirs," 165.

33. Ibid., 162.

34. Ibid.

35. See Wride, "Soundtrack of Violent Streets."

36. Schlund-Vials, "Hip Hop Memoirs."

37. Hip-hop, as an interdisciplinary form of resistance, has not escaped scholarly attention within the United States. Jeff Chang and Nitasha Sharma have written extensively and provocatively about hip-hop as a form in which to examine racial and ethnic construction. Chang's *Can't Stop, Won't Stop* (2005) is a useful introduction to the history of the form from the 1970s to the present. Sharma's work examines hip-hop through a comparative ethnoracial frame that brings together African American and South Asian American cultural producers. S. Craig Watkins's text *Hip Hop Matters* (2005) highlights the contradictory nature of hip-hop as a terrain of commodification and a significant site of resistance. Other useful examinations of the form include Tricia Rose's *Black Noise* (1994); *Droppin' Science* (1995), edited by William Eric Perkins; Russell A. Potter's *Spectacular Vernaculars* (1995); and *The 'Hood Comes First* (2002), edited by Murray Forman.

38. I am indebted to Patrick Lawrence's reading of "references" and "citations" in a conversation about this project.

39. Other tracks on the album are "Home of the Bodybag," "First Impression," "Ziplock," "Mic Contract," "Mind over Matter," "New Jack Hustler," "Ed," "Bitches 2," "Straight up Nigga," "O.G. Original Gangster," "The House," "Evil E-What About Sex," "Fly By," "Midnight," "Fried Chicken," "M.V.P.S.," "Lifestyles of the Rich and Infamous," "Body Count," "Prepared to Die," "Street Killer," "Pulse of the Rhyme," "The Tower," and "Ya Shoulda Killed Me Last Year." Ice-T is the pseudonym of Tracy Marrow.

40. Coleman, "*O.G. Original Gangster* and *New Jack City* Review."

41. Bernard, "Music Review: Ice-T's *O.G. Original Gangster*."

42. *The Source*, "Top 100 Hip-Hop Albums of All Time," January 1998, http://www.listsofbests.com/list/49397. *O.G. Original Gangster* is ranked forty-fifth on the *Source* list.

43. Greg Knot (*Chicago Tribune*) quoted in NPR, "'Original Gangster': Rapper and Actor Ice-T."

44. Maira, "Flexible Citizenship/Flexible Empire." Though Maira's primary consideration involves South Asian Muslim youth, her consideration of resistance and U.S. exceptionalism productively connects to Ice-T's and, by extension, praCh's and Seasia's hip-hop projects.

45. The mention of "hip-hop matters" draws on Watson's *Hip Hop Matters*.

46. Kelley, "Kickin' Reality, Kickin' Ballistics," 121.

47. Foucault, *Order of Things*, xix.

48. See Lowe, *Immigrant Acts*.

49. These specific representations—which access a distinct Cambodian flora (the banyan tree) and a particular Khmer architecture (the thatched domestic structure)—accrete further meaning when considered alongside the physical location of praCh's birth. According to praCh, in 1979 "my mom was pregnant with me. She had me in a hut. Later, my parents went back to Cambodia and videotaped the tree I was born under, but the hut's no longer there." May, "Art of faCt," 73.

50. praCh's *Dalama: The End'n Is Just the Beginnin'* also features an album cover drawn by the artist.

51. The track listing for *Dalama: The Lost Chapter* is as follows: [1] intro ("invasion"); [2] "STORIES" (featuring doZer); [3] skits, "the YearZero and One" (Pilger documentary sample); [4] "Power, Territory, and Rice"; [5] skits, "the aftermath" (Pilger documentary sample); [6] "The Great Escape!"; [7] "Pin Peat's Resurrection" (featuring Khmer traditional musician Ho C. Chan); [8] "I Just Want You to Understand!"; [9] "D'eBreeZZe" (featuring sparC da Polar); [10] "Min-Tom-Ie-Da"; [11] "Sox-Si-Bie"; [12] intermission ("RULES ..."); [13] "refleXion"; [14] "Wisc's That"; [15] "Neutral (before the war)"; [16] "Tues"; [17] "s.i.c."; [18] "S-21" (Tuol Sleng); [19] "Art of FaCt"; [20] "out-tro" and [21] "p e a C e."

52. Schlund-Vials, "Hip Hop Memoirs."

53. See praCh, *Dalama: The Lost Chapter*.

54. According to the Mujestic Records Web site, the Universal Speakers, who include Cambodian American, Laotian American, and Thai American female singers, combine reggae, hip-hop, and R&B in their music. See praCh, "It's Not Just Muzix, It's a Movement," May 12, 2007, http://www.mujestic.com/p_r_a_c_h.

55. To reiterate, sixteen hundred Cambodians/Cambodian Americans living in the United States were threatened with deportation, and this story is mentioned in May, "Art of faCt." See U.S. Congress, Uniting and Strengthening America by Providing Appropriate Tools Required to Intercept and Obstruct Terrorism (USA PATRIOT) Act of 2001.

56. May, "Art of faCt," 80.

57. Schlund-Vials, "Hip Hop Memoirs."

58. The Khmer names for the instruments enumerated are as follows: *reneat* (bamboo xylophones), *gong vong* (brass pots), *kloy* (flute), *sampho* (two-headed drum), *skorthom* (a large kettle drum), and *srlai* (the oboe-like instrument).

59. See "America Provides Refuge for an Imperiled Art," 37–38.

60. The track's title admittedly carries an intertextual register when set against praCh's "Resurrec," from his debut album, which is discussed in the introduction.

61. In *Dalama: The End'n Is Just the Beginnin'*, praCh's "Ah-Ye (Khmer Rap!)" likewise alludes to this traditional Khmer form.

62. May, "Art of faCt," 80–81.

63. Nelson, "Hip-Hop's Founding Fathers Speak the Truth," 54.

64. Watkins, *Hip Hop Matters*, 6.

65. May, "Art of faCt," 81.

66. The twenty-four tracks on *Dalama: Memoirs of an Invisible War* are [1] "Hell's Gate"; [2] "Fragile Hope"; [3] "This land . . ."; [4] "War on the Streets"; [5] "Shall not be Moved!"; [6] "i.War"; [7] "The Rose's Thorn"; [8] "A.A. / The Flirtation of Death"; [9] "Through the Night / 2 O'Clock"; [10] "R.O.D. Drift"; [11] "Simplistic"; [12] "Keep'n it RIEL"; [13] "BahtaWatt! (revolt!)"; [14] "praCh's Bopha"; [15] "King praCh"; [16] "Hidden Truth, Open Lies"; [17] "Silent Cry (Clear and Present Danger)"; [18] "Corruption!"; [19] "I deClare War!"; [20] "eXile"; [21] "Therapeutic"; [22] "New Day Tomorrow"; [23] "Homage"; and [24] "Song Kun (the Kun Song)."

67. Mellen, "For Cambodian Rapper, 'Words Are Weapons.'"

68. "Dalama 3 Reviews." Mujestic, accessed April 12, 2011, http://mujestic.com/dalama_3_reviews.

69. Niedermüller, "Ethnicity, Nationality, and the Myth of Cultural Heritage," 248.

70. Mydans, "Cambodian Leader Resists Punishing Top Khmer Rouge."

71. Georges and Jones, *Folkloristics*.

72. Flores, *From Bomba to Hip Hop*, 135–37.

73. praCh, interview with the author, November 24, 2006.

74. Rashaan Meneses, "The Near Extinction of Cambodian Classical Dance," UCLA International Institute, May 7, 2004, http://www.international.ucla.edu/article.asp?parentid=10982.

75. It should be noted that the band Dengue Fever is in part responsible for a revived interest in Cambodian psychedelic pop.

76. This engagement with Khmer tradition is apparent at the level of artistry. In addition to praCh, the album features compositions by Cambodian American poet U Sam Oeur (who now translates Walt Whitman's work into Khmer), Kung Nai (master *chapei* musician), and artists from Cambodia Living Arts (Sovey,

Sinat, and Sophea). These traditional artists are joined by rapper Silong Chhun and members of the aforementioned Universal Speakers.

77. praCh emblematizes street entrepreneur realism, producing not only his own albums but those of other Southeast Asian American artists (e.g., the previously mentioned female hip-hop/R&B group Universal Speakers and Cambodian American rap crew 2nd Language).

78. PBS, "Prach Ly: The Rapper."

Epilogue

1. Yoneyama, *Hiroshima Traces*, 32.

2. Anida Yoeu Ali, e-mail to author, June 23, 2010.

3. Ibid.

4. I want to thank Gordon Fraser for his observation about genre and the epic. In particular, Fraser observes that an epic is fixed to a distinctly national agenda. Such nationalistic frames are revised in Ali's poem, which maps a transnational agenda by way of an identifiable epic form.

5. Anida Yoeu Ali, "Visiting Loss," 2005, http://atomicshogun.com/writing _visitingloss.htm.

6. Ibid.

7. Ibid.

8. Ibid.

9. Ibid.

10. Ibid.

11. Ibid.

12. The use of "pogram" speaks to the forced relocation and persecution of European Jews at the turn of the twentieth century.

13. Lowe, *Immigrant Acts*.

14. See Benjamin, *Illuminations*, 255. In the original quote, Benjamin cites Leopold von Ranke, a prominent German historian who rejected Hegel's notion of historical materialism in favor of a source-based historicism. Lisa Lowe, in *Immigrant Acts*, also draws on this particular quote (97), as does Lisa Yoneyama in the introduction to *Hiroshima Traces*. Lowe uses Benjamin's compression of time and space to examine Asian American cultural production via "decolonization, displacement, and disidentification." Each work is instructive with regard to applications of Benjamin's work within spaces of trauma and subjugation. I diverge from Lowe and Yoneyama by using Benjamin's work as a foundation upon which to examine the types of labor enacted by remembrance (memory work).

15. Benjamin, *Illuminations*, 258.

16. Ibid., 255.

17. Ibid., 257. Benjamin's use of "state of exception" brings to mind Giorgio

Agamben's later examination of states of exception via *homo sacer*. Interestingly, Agamben and Benjamin explicitly respond to German political philosopher Carl Schmitt, who in his 1921 essay "Die Diktatur" justified dictatorship during states of emergency.

18. Cheng, *Melancholy of Race,* 3.

19. Ibid.

20. Anida Yoeu Ali, "Palimpsest for Generation 1.5," unpublished performance script (2009).

21. Ibid.

22. The headdress worn by the "washer woman" figure is reminiscent of the dress worn by the Cham (Cambodian Muslims). This allusion underscores Ali's own location as a Cambodian American Muslim.

23. Morrison, *Beloved,* 35–36.

24. Marshall, *Teaching the Postmodern,* 191.

25. Ibid.

26. Yoneyama, *Hiroshima Traces,* 32.

27. Wiesel, *Dimensions of the Holocaust,* 9.

Bibliography

Amanpour, Christiane. "Survivor Recalls Horrors of Cambodia Genocide." *CNN*. April 7, 2008. http://www.cnn.com/2008/WORLD/asiapcf/04/07/amanpour.pol.pot/index.html?eref=rss_topstories.

"America Provides Refuge for an Imperiled Art." *Music Educators Journal* 69 (May 1983): 37–38.

Barkan, Elazar. "Truth and Reconciliation in History." *American Historical Review* 114, no. 4 (2009): 899–913.

Barkan, Elazar, and Alexander Karn. "Introduction." In *Taking Wrongs Seriously: Apologies and Reconciliations,* ed. Elazar Barkan and Alexander Karn. Palo Alto, Calif.: Stanford University Press, 2006.

Barthes, Roland. *Camera Lucida: Reflections on Photography.* Trans. Richard Howard. New York: Hill and Wang, 1981.

BBC. "Chea Sim's Speech at the Cambodian Victory Day Celebration." BBC Monitoring International Reports. January 8, 2004. http://www.accessmylibrary.com/coms2/summary_0286-19930942_ITM.

———. "Khmer Rouge Survivor Testifies." *BBC News.* June 29, 2009. http://news.bbc.co.uk/2/hi/world/asia-pacific/8123541.stm.

Bell, Thomas. "Comrade Duch 'Smashed' Thousands in His Notorious Jail." *Telegraph.* February 17, 2009. http://www.telegraph.co.uk/news/worldnews/asia/cambodia/4681267/Comrade-Duch-smashed-thousands-in-his-notorious-jail.html.

Benjamin, Walter. *Illuminations: Essays and Reflections.* Ed. Hannah Arendt. London: Schoken, 1969.

Bernard, James. "Music Review: Ice-T's *O.G. Original Gangster* Review." *Entertainment Weekly.* May 24, 1991. http://www.ew.com/ew/article/0,,314429,00.html.

Bernstein, Richard. "Books of the Times: Chilling First-Person Tales from Cambodia." *New York Times.* April 19, 2000. http://partners.nytimes.com/library/books/041900ung-book-review.html.

Brady, Brendan. "Postcard: Anlong Veng." *Time Magazine,* August 23, 2010.

Buncombe, Andrew. "Cambodia Puts the Cremation Site of Pol Pot on 'Historic' Tourist Trail." *Independent,* March 11, 2010.

Burmon, Andrew. "Dark Tourism: Cambodia Tries to Turn Its Bloody History into a Sightseeing Boom." *Atlantic.* November 2010. http://www.theatlantic.com/magazine/print/2010/11/dark-tourism/8250.

"Burrows, Larry." In *Encyclopedia of 20th-Century Photography,* ed. Lynn Warren, vol. 1, A–F. New York: Routledge, 2006.

Bush, George H. W. "Quotation of the Day." *New York Times*. March 2, 1991. http://
    www.nytimes.com/1991/03/02/nyregion/quotation-of-the-day-256291.html?src=pm.
Cambodian Human Rights Action Committee. "Conference on Reparations for Victims of
    the Khmer Rouge Regime" (summary). July 30, 2009. In-house publication.
Caruth, Cathy. *Unclaimed Experience: Trauma, Narrative, and Theory*. Baltimore: Johns
    Hopkins University Press, 1996.
Chan, Sucheng. *Survivors: Cambodian Refugees in the United States*. Urbana: University of
    Illinois Press, 2004.
Chandler, David. *A History of Cambodia*. 3rd ed. Boulder, Colo.: Westview Press, 2000.
———. *A History of Cambodia*. 4th ed. Boulder, Colo.: Westview Press, 2008.
———. *Voices from S-21: Terror and History in Pol Pot's Secret Prison*. Berkeley: University
    of California Press, 1999.
Chang, Jeff. *Can't Stop, Won't Stop: A History of the Hip Hop Generation*. New York:
    St. Martin's, 2005.
Cheng, Anne Anlin. *The Melancholy of Race: Psychoanalysis, Assimilation, and Hidden Grief*.
    London: Oxford University Press, 2001.
Chuh, Kandice. *Imagine Otherwise: On Asian American Critique*. Durham, N.C.: Duke
    University Press, 2003.
CNN. "Aki Ra: Community Crusade." Accessed December 31, 2010. http://edition.cnn
    .com/SPECIALS/cnn.heroes/archive10/aki.ra.html.
———. "Hun Sen Claims No Coup in Cambodia." July 10, 1997. http://articles.cnn.com
    /1997-07-10/world/9707_10_cambodia_1_ranariddh-loyalists-hun-sen-first-prime
    -minister-prince?_s=PM:WORLD.
Cohen, Roger. "For Cambodia's Dead, Farce Heaped on Insult." *International Tri-
    bune*. April 2, 2005. http://www.globalpolicy.org/intljustice/tribunals/cambodia
    /2005/0402farce.htm.
Coleman, Mark. "*O.G. Original Gangster* and *New Jack City* Review." *Rolling Stone*.
    June 13, 1991. http://www.rollingstone.com/reviews/album/233609/review/5944014
    /ogoriginalgangster.
"Convention on the Punishment and Prevention of the Crime of Genocide." Last updated
    December 12, 1998. http://www.ess.uwe.ac.uk/documents/gncnvntn.htm.
Denver Post, "Captured: A Look Back at the Vietnam War on the 35th Anniversary of
    the Fall of Saigon." April 30, 2010. http://blogs.denverpost.com/captured/2010/04
    /30/captured-a-look-back-at-the-vietnam-war-on-the-35th-anniversary-of-the-fall-of
    -saigon/1781.
Dickens, Sarah Jones. "Stilled Lives, Victims, or Perpetrators?" In *REFLECTIONS: Democratic
    Kampuchea and Beyond*, exhibition catalog, Documentation Center of Cambodia, 2008, 3.
Doyle, Kevin. "The Revenue Fields." *Time Magazine*. April 11, 2005. http://www.time.com
    /time/printout/0,8816,1047552,00.html.
Dunlop, Nic. *The Lost Executioner: A Journey into the Heart of the Killing Fields*. New York:
    Walker & Company, 2005.
Ebert, Roger. *Roger Ebert's Four Star Reviews: 1967–2007*. Kansas City, Mo.: Andrews
    McMeel Publishing, 2007.
Edkins, Jenny. *Trauma and the Memory of Politics*. Cambridge: Cambridge University Press, 2003.

Emmrich, Stuart. "Next Stop: In Phnom Penh, Hopefulness Replaces Despair." *New York Times.* February 11, 2007. http://travel.nytimes.com/2007/02/11/travel/11next.html.

Espiritu, Yen Le. "The 'We-Win-Even-When-We-Lose' Syndrome: U.S. Press Coverage of the Twenty-fifth Anniversary of the 'Fall of Saigon.'" *American Quarterly* 58, no. 2 (2006): 329–52.

Fein, Esther B. "Holocaust as a Cartoonist's Way of Getting to Know His Father." *New York Times,* December 10, 1991.

Flores, Juan. *From Bomba to Hip Hop: Puerto Rican Culture and Latino Identity.* New York: Columbia University Press, 2000.

Foley, Malcolm, and John J. Lennon. "JFK and Dark Tourism: A Fascination with Assassination." *International Journal of Heritage Studies* 2, no. 4 (1996): 198–211.

Forman, Murray. *The 'Hood Comes First: Race, Space, and Place in Rap and Hip-Hop.* Middletown, Conn.: Wesleyan University Press, 2002.

Foucault, Michel. "Dits et écrits 1984." In "Des espaces autres: Conférence au Cercle d'études architecturales, 14 mars 1967," special issue, *Architecture, Mouvement, Continuité,* no. 5 (October 1984): 46–49.

———. *The Order of Things.* 1966; repr. London: Routledge, 2002.

———. *Security, Territory, Population (Lectures at the College de France).* New York: Palgrave-Macmillian, 2007.

Freedman, Samuel. "In 'The Killing Fields,' a Cambodian Actor Relives His Nation's Ordeal." *New York Times.* October 28, 1984. http://www.nytimes.com/1984/10/28/movies/in-the-killing-fields-a-cambodian-actor-relives-his-nation-s-ordeal.html.

Geis, Sonya. "Long Beach Awaits Hate Crime Verdict." *Washington Post.* January 23, 2007. http://www.washingtonpost.com/wpdyn/content/article/2007/01/22/AR2007012201143.html.

Georges, Robert A., and Michael Owen Jones. *Folkloristics: An Introduction.* Bloomington: Indiana University Press, 1995.

Gilmore, Leigh. "Jurisdictions: I, Rigoberta Menchú, The Kiss, and Scandalous Self-Representation in the Age of Memoir and Trauma." *Signs* 28, no. 2 (2002): 695–718.

Gordon, Avery. *Ghostly Matters: Haunting and the Sociological Imagination.* 1997; repr., Minneapolis: University of Minnesota Press, 2008.

Gross, Ariela. "The Constitution of History and Memory." In *Companion to Law and the Humanities,* ed. Austin Sarat. London: Cambridge University Press, 2009.

Gwartney, Debra. "Broken Promises." *Willamette Week.* June 14, 2000. http://wweek.com/html/urbanpulse061400.html.

Him, Chanrithy. *When Broken Glass Floats: Growing Up under the Khmer Rouge.* New York: Norton, 2000.

Hinton, Alexander Laban. "A Head for an Eye: Revenge in the Cambodian Genocide." In *Genocide: An Anthropological Reader,* ed. Alexander Laban Hinton, 254–85. Malden, Mass.: Blackwell, 2002.

Hirsch, Marianne. *Family Frames: Photography, Narrative, and Postmemory.* Cambridge, Mass.: Harvard University Press, 1997.

———. "Past Lives: Postmemories in Exile." *Poetics Today* 17, no. 4 (Winter 1996): 659–86.

Hong, Grace. *The Ruptures of American Capital: Women of Color Feminism and the Culture of Immigrant Labor.* Minneapolis: University of Minnesota Press, 2006.

Hsu, Ruth Y. "The Cartography of Justice and Truthful Refractions in Karen Tei Yamashi-
ta's Tropic of Orange." In *Transnational Asian American Literature: Sites and Transits*,
ed. Stephen Hong Sohn, Shirley Lim, John Gamber, and Gina Valentino. Philadelphia:
Temple University Press, 2006.

Hughes, Rachel. "The Abject Artifacts of Memory: Photographs from Cambodia's Genocide." *Media, Culture, and Society* 25, no. 1 (2003): 23–44. http://mcs.sagepub.com
/content/25/1.toc.

———. "Memory and Sovereignty in Post-1979 Cambodia: Choeung Ek and Local Genocide Memorials." *Macmillan Center Genocide Studies* 26 (2004): 269–92. http://opus
.macmillan.yale.edu/workpaper/pdfs/GS26.pdf.

Huyssen, Andreas. "Monument and Memory in a Postmodern Age." In *The Art of Memory:
Holocaust Memorials in History*. Munich: Prestel-Verlag, 1994.

Ikui, Eikoh. "Reprogramming Memories: The Historicization of the Vietnam War from the
1970s through the 1990s." *Japanese Journal of American Studies* 12 (2001): 41–63.

Independent. "Cambodian Referendum over Khmer Rouge Victims' Remains." April 25,
2001.   http://www.independent.co.uk/news/world/asia/cambodian-referendum
-over-khmer-rouge-victims-remains-753716.html.

International Justice Tribune. "'Genotourism' at Choeung Ek." *Radio Netherlands
Worldwide*.   April   21,   2008.   http://www.rnw.nl/international-justice/article
/genotourism-choeung-ek.

Istvan, Zoltan. "'Killing Fields' Lure Tourists in Cambodia." *National Geographic Today*.
January 10, 2003. http://news.nationalgeographic.com/news/2003/01/0110_030110
_tvcambodia.html.

Jacklet, Ben. "Cambodian Collaborations." *Willamette Week*. July 19, 2000. http://wweek
.com/html/urbanpulse061400.html.

Jeffords, Susan. *The Remasculinization of America: Gender and the Vietnam War*. Bloomington, Ind.: Indiana University Press, 1989.

Kelley, Robin D.G. "Kickin' Reality, Kickin' Ballistics: Gangsta Rap and Postindustrial
Los Angeles." In *Droppin' Science: Critical Essays on Rap Music and Hip Hop Culture*, ed.
William Eric Perkins. Philadelphia: Temple University Press, 1995.

Kerry, John. "Still Awaiting Justice." *Lowell Sun*, May 22, 2008.

———. "Youk Chhang." *Time Magazine*. May 3, 2007. http://www.time.com/time/specials
/2007/article/0,28804,1595326_1615754_1615879,00.html.

Kiernan, Ben. "The Cambodian Genocide and Imperial Culture." In "90 Years of Denial," special publication of *Aztag Daily* (Beirut) and the *Armenian Weekly* (Boston), April 2005.

———. "Introduction: A World Turned Upside Down." In *Children of Cambodia's Killing
Fields*, ed. Kim Depaul and Dith Pran, xi–xvii. New Haven: Yale University Press, 1999.

———. "Recovering History and Justice in Cambodia." *Comparativ* 14 (2004): 76–85.

Kim, Jodi. *The Ends of Empire: Asian American Critique and the Cold War*. Minneapolis:
University of Minnesota Press, 2010.

Klein, Norbert. "National Holiday – Wednesday, 7.1.2009." *The Mirror*. January 8, 2009. http:
//cambodiamirror.wordpress.com/2009/01/08/national-holiday-wednesday-712009.

Krasnowsky, Matt. "'Cambodia Town' Controversy." *San Diego Union Tribune*. March 11,
2007. http://www.signonsandiego.com/uniontrib/20070311/news_1n11cambodia.html.

LA Times. "Skull Exhibit Must Go, Sihanouk Says." November 22, 1991. http://articles .latimes.com/1991-11-22/news/mn-108_1_skull-exhibit.

Laub, Dori. "Truth and Testimony: The Process and the Struggle." In *Trauma: Explorations in Memory,* ed. Cathy Caruth, 61–75. Baltimore: Johns Hopkins Press, 1995.

Lay, Sody. "The Cambodian Tragedy: Its Writers and Representations." *Amerasia Journal* 27, no. 2 (2001): 171–82.

Ledgerwood, Judy. "The Cambodian Tuol Sleng Museum of Genocidal Crimes: National Narrative." *Museum Anthropology* 21, no. 1 (1997): 82–98.

Lee, James Kyung-Jin. *Urban Triage: Race and the Fictions of Multiculturalism.* Minneapolis: University of Minnesota Press, 2004.

Lee, Jonathan H. X., and Kathleen M. Nadeau. "Introduction: Asian American Folklore and Folklore." In *Encyclopedia of Asian American Folklore and Folklife,* ed. Jonathan H. X. Lee and Kathleen Nadeau. Westport, Conn.: Greenwood Press, 2010.

Lee, Rachel C. *The Americas of Asian American Literature: Gendered Fictions of Nation and Transnation.* Princeton, N.J.: Princeton University Press, 1999.

Lee, Robert G. *Orientals: Asian Americans in Popular Culture.* Philadelphia: Temple University Press, 1999.

Lennon, John, and Malcolm Foley. *Dark Tourism: The Attraction of Death and Disaster.* London: Continuum, 2000.

Life. "Behind Enemy Lines: 'Reaching Out,' 1966." Accessed February 3, 2010. http:// www.life.com/gallery/26812/image/53368350/in-combat-lifes-great-war-photos.

Locard, Henri. *Pol Pot's Little Red Book: The Sayings of Angkar.* Chiang Mai: Silkworm Books, 2004.

Lowe, Lisa. *Immigrant Acts: On Asian American Cultural Politics.* Durham, N.C.: Duke University Press, 1996.

———. "The International within the National: American Studies and Asian American Critique." *Cultural Critique* 40 (Autumn 1998): 29–47.

MacKinnon, Ian. "Khmer Rouge Leader in Dock as Cambodian Trial Starts." *Guardian.* February 17, 2009. http://www.guardian.co.uk/world/2009/feb/17/war -crimes-tribunal-cambodia.

Madra, Ek. "Cambodians Mark 30 Years Since Fall of Pol Pot." *Reuters.* January 7, 2009. http:// www.reuters.com/article/2009/01/07/us-cambodia-rouge-idUSTRE50612920090107.

Maguire, Peter. *Facing Death in Cambodia.* New York: Columbia University Press, 2005.

Maira, Sunaina. "Flexible Citizenship/Flexible Empire: South Asian Muslim Youth in Post-9/11 America." In "Nation and Migration, Past and Future," ed. David G. Guitierrez and Pierrette Hondagneu-Sotelo, special issue, *American Quarterly* 60, no. 3 (2008): 697–720.

Marshall, Brenda. *Teaching the Postmodern: Fiction and Theory.* London: Routledge, 1992.

May, Sharon. "Art of faCt: An Interview with praCh." *Manoa* 16, no. 1 (2004): 73–82.

Mbembe, Achille. "Necropolitics." *Public Culture* 15, no. 1 (2003): 11–40.

Mellen, Greg. "For Cambodian Rapper, 'Words Are Weapons.'" *Press Telegram.* April 9, 2010. http://www.presstelegram.com/news/ci_14853709.

Menchú, Rigoberta. *I, Rigoberta Menchú: An Indian Woman in Guatemala.* Ed. Elisabeth Burgos-Debray. Trans. Anne Wright. New York: Verso, 1984.

Minow, Martha. *Between Vengeance and Forgiveness: Facing History after Genocide and Mass Violence.* Boston: Beacon Press, 1998.

Moore, Derek J. "Ruthless Asian Gangs Blaze Trail of Violence." *Press Democrat.* March 15, 2008. http://www.pressdemocrat.com/article/20080315/NEWS/803150313?p=3&tc=pg.

Morrison, Toni. *Beloved.* New York: Alfred A. Knopf, 1986.

Munthit, Ker. "Khmer Rouge Official Revisits Atrocities." *USA Today.* February 27, 2008. http://www.usatoday.com/news/world/2008-02-27-1013612312_x.htm.

Mydans, Seth. "Cambodian Leader Resists Punishing Top Khmer Rouge." *New York Times.* December 29, 1998. http://query.nytimes.com/gst/fullpage.html?res= 9E0DE2DE153FF93AA15751C1A96E958260.

———. "Khmer Rouge Defendant Apologizes for Atrocities." *New York Times.* March 31, 2009. http://www.nytimes.com/2009/04/01/world/asia/01cambo.html.

Myers, Nathaniel. "Justice Past Due in Cambodia." *Washington Post,* December 24, 2005.

Navarro, Nelson A. "Letters to the Editor." *New York Times,* February 24, 1980.

Nelson, George. "Hip-Hop's Founding Fathers Speak the Truth." In *That's the Joint: The Hip-Hop Studies Reader,* 2nd ed. London: Routledge, 2012.

New York Times. "Around the World: Cambodian Day of Hate Marks Pol Pot's Victims." May 21, 1984. http://www.nytimes.com/1984/05/21/world/around-the-world -cambodian-day-of-hate-marks-pol-pot-s-victims.html.

———. "Transcript of President Bush's Speech at the Veterans of Foreign Wars Convention." August 22, 2007. http://www.nytimes.com/2007/08/22/washington /w23policytext.html.

Nguyen, Viet. *Race and Resistance: Literature and Politics in Asian America.* New York: Oxford University Press, 2002.

Niedermüller, Péter. "Ethnicity, Nationality, and the Myth of Cultural Heritage: A European View." *Journal of Folklore Research* 36, nos. 2/3 (1999): 243–53.

Nixon, Richard. "Speech on Cambodia, April 30, 1970." *Public Papers of the Presidents of the United States: Richard Nixon,* 1970, 405–9.

NPR. "'Original Gangster': Rapper and Actor Ice-T." *Fresh Air.* August 31, 2005. http:// www.npr.org/templates/story/story.php?storyId=4824690.

Osborne, Milton E. *Phnom Penh: A Cultural History.* London: Oxford University Press, 2008.

Paddock, Richard C. "Rumor of Thai Actress' Words Salted a Wound." *LA Times.* February 3, 2003. http://articles.latimes.com/2003/feb/03/world/fg-cambo3.

Parmar, P. J. *101 Countries: Discovering the World through Fast Travel.* College Station, Tex.: Virtual Bookworm, 2003.

PBS. "Cambodia: Pol Pot's Shadow." *Frontline/World.* Last modified October 2002. http:// www.pbs.org/frontlineworld/stories/cambodia/tl02.html.

———. "Prach Ly: The Rapper." In "Cambodia: Pol Pot's Shadow." *Frontline/World.* Last modified October 2002. http://www.pbs.org/frontlineworld/stories/cambodia/ly _interview.html.

Pelaud, Isabelle. *This Is All I Choose to Tell: History and Hybridity in Vietnamese American Literature.* Philadelphia: Temple University Press, 2010.

Perkins, William Eric. *Droppin' Science: Critical Essays on Rap Music and Hip Hop Culture.* Philadelphia: Temple University Press, 1995.

Poeuv, Socheata. "Memory, Justice, and Pardon: What Does it Take to Heal?" *Justice Initiatives,* Open Society Initiative, Spring 2006.

Potter, Russell A. *Spectacular Vernaculars: Hip Hop and the Politics of Postmodernism.* Albany, N.Y.: State University of New York Press, 1995.

Pran, Dith. "Compiler's Note." In *Children of Cambodia's Killing Fields,* ed. Kim Depaul and Dith Pran, ix–x. New Haven: Yale University Press, 1999.

Reagan, Ronald. Ronald Reagan to Ty Him Hel and Eng Sun Hel, August 27, 1982. In *Reagan: A Life in Letters,* ed. Kiron K. Skinner, Annelise Anderson, and Martin Anderson. New York: Free Press, 2003.

Renan, Ernest. "What Is a Nation?" In *Becoming National: A Reader,* ed. Geoff Eley and Ronald Grigor Suny, 41–55. New York: Oxford University Press, 1996.

Rivers, Dan. "Girl, 6, Embodies Cambodia's Sex Industry." *CNN.* January 23, 2007. http:// www.cnn.com/2007/WORLD/asiapcf/01/23/sex.workers/index.html.

Rohter, Larry. "Tarnished Laureate: Nobel Winner Finds Her Story Challenged." *New York Times,* December 15, 1998.

Rose, Tricia. *The Hip Hop Wars: What We Talk About When We Talk About Hip Hop—and Why It Matters.* New York: Basic Books, 2009.

———. *Black Noise: Rap Music and Black Culture in Contemporary America.* Middleton, Conn.: Wesleyan University Press, 1994.

Saliba, Michael, and Tyler Nims. "Duch Sentenced to 35 Years in Prison; Will Serve Only 19." *Cambodia Tribunal Monitor.* July 26, 2010. http://www.cambodiatribunal.org/sites /default/files/ctm_blog_7-26-2010.pdf.

Schaffer, Kay, and Sidonie Smith. "Conjunctions: Life Narratives in the Field of Human Rights." *Biography* 27, no. 1 (Winter 2004): 1–24.

Schanberg, Sydney. *Beyond the Killing Fields: War Writings.* Dulles, Va.: Potomac Books, 2010.

———. "The Death and Life of Dith Pran." *New York Times Magazine,* January 20, 1980.

Schickel, Richard. "Cinema: Ordeal of a Heroic Survivor." *Time Magazine.* November 5, 1984. http://www.time.com/time/magazine/article/0,9171,954486-1,00.html #ixzz1Drp5AoFV.

Schlund-Vials, Cathy. "Hip Hop Memoirs: An Interview with Khmer American Rapper praCh." *MELUS* 34, no. 6 (Winter 2011).

———. "A Transnational Hip Hop Nation: Cambodian American Rap and Memorialization." *Life Writing* 5, no. 1 (2008): 11–27; repr. in *Trauma Texts,* ed. Kate Douglas and Gillian Whitlock. New York: Routledge, 2009.

Sharma, Nitasha Tamar. *Hip Hop Desis: South Asian Americans, Blackness, and Global Race Consciousness.* Durham, N.C.: Duke University Press, 2010.

Shawcross, William. *Sideshow: Kissinger, Nixon, and the Destruction of Cambodia.* 1979; repr. Lanham, Md.: Cooper Square Press, 2002.

Shay, Christopher. "In Cambodia, a Deportee Breakdances to Success." *Time Magazine.* September 19, 2009. http://www.time.com/time/world/article/0,8599,1924835 ,00.html.

Shenk, Joshua Wolf. "Memories of Genocide." Review of *First They Killed My Father: A Daughter of Cambodia Remembers,* by Loung Ung and *When Broken Glass Floats: Growing Up Under the Khmer Rouge,* by Chanrithy Him. *New York Times,* June 11, 2000.

Simmons, David. "Commentary: 'Atrocity Tourism' Overkill?" *AsiaTimes Online*. October 10, 2002. http://www.atimes.com/atimes/Southeast_Asia/DJ10Ae03.html.

Slaughter, Joseph R. *Human Rights, Inc.: The World Novel, Narrative Form, and International Law*. New York: Fordham University Press, 2007.

Smith, Graham. "From Mickey to Maus: Recalling the Genocide through Cartoon." *Oral History Journal* 15, no. 1 (Spring 1987): 26–34.

Sohn, Stephen Hong, Shirley Lim, John Gamber, and Gina Valentino, eds. *Transnational Asian American Literature: Sites and Transits*. Philadelphia: Temple University Press, 2006.

Sokheng, Vong. "CPP Celebrates Victory over KR." *Phnom Penh Post,* January 8, 2009.

Sontag, Susan. *Regarding the Pain of Others*. New York: Picador, 2003.

Stoll, David. *Rigoberta Menchú and the Story of All Poor Guatemalans*. Boulder, Colo.: Westview Press, 1998.

Stone, Philip, and Richard Sharpley. "Consuming Dark Tourism: A Thanatological Perspective." *Annals of Tourism Research* 35, no. 2 (2008): 574–95.

Sturken, Marita. *Tangled Memories: The Vietnam War, the AIDS Epidemic, and the Politics of Remembering*. Berkeley: University of California Press, 1997.

———. "The Wall, the Screen, and the Image: The Vietnam Veterans Memorial." *Representations* 35 (Summer 1991): 118–42.

Um, Khatharya. "Exiled Memory: History, Identity and Remembering in the Southeast Asian Diaspora." Conference presentation, Southeast Asians in the Diaspora conference, University of Illinois, Urbana-Champaign, April 16, 2008.

Ung, Loung. "A Birthday Wrapped in Cambodian History." *New York Times,* April 17, 2005.

———. *First They Killed My Father: A Daughter of Cambodia Remembers*. New York: Harpers Collins, 2000.

USA Today. "Genocide Site in Cambodia Draws Tourists." August 14, 2006. http://www.usatoday.com/travel/destinations/2006-08-14-cambodia-genocide-tourism_x.htm.

U.S. Congress. Uniting and Strengthening America by Providing Appropriate Tools Required to Intercept and Obstruct Terrorism (USA PATRIOT) Act of 2001. Pub. L. No. 107–56.

Variety. "The Killing Fields." December 31, 1983. http://www.variety.com/review/VE1117792303?refcatid=31.

Washington Times. "3 Decades Later, Khmer Rouge Leaders to be Tried for Atrocities." January 9, 2009.

Watkins, S. Craig. *Hip Hop Matters: Politics, Pop Culture, and the Struggle for the Soul of a Movement*. Boston: Beacon Press, 2005.

Widyono, Benny. *Dancing in Shadows: Sihanouk, the Khmer Rouge, and the United Nations in Cambodia*. New York: Rowman & Littlefield, 2007.

Wiesel, Elie. *Dimensions of the Holocaust*. Evanston, Ill.: Northwestern University Press, 1977.

———. "Letters to the Editor." *New York Times,* February 24, 1980.

———. "The Perils of Indifference: Seventh Whitehouse Millennium Meeting 12 April 1999." In *Speeches that Changed the World,* ed. Simon Sebag Montefiore, 214–19. London: Quercus Publishing, 2005.

Williams, Paul. "The Atrocity Exhibition: Touring Cambodian Genocide Memorials." In

On Display: New Essays in Cultural Studies, ed. Anna Smith and Lydia Wevers. New Zealand: Victoria University Press, 2005.

———. "Witnessing Genocide: Vigilance and Remembrance at Tuol Sleng and Choeung Ek." *Holocaust and Genocide Studies* 18, no. 2 (2004): 234–54.

Williams, Raymond. *Marxism and Literature.* London: Oxford University Press, 1978.

Willwerth, James. "From Killing Fields to Mean Streets." *Time Magazine.* June 24, 2001. http://www.time.com/time/magazine/article/0,9171,1101911118-155910,00.html.

Wride, Nancy. "Soundtrack of Violent Streets." *Los Angeles Times.* December 17, 2003. http://articles.latimes.com/print/2003/dec/17/local/me-rapper17.

Yamada, Teri Shaffer. "Cambodian American Autobiography." In *Form and Transformation in Asian American Literature,* ed. Zhou Xiaojing and Samina Najimi. Seattle: University of Washington Press, 2005.

Yang, KaYing. "Southeast Asian American Children: Not the Model Minority." *Children of Immigrant Families* 14, no. 2 (Summer 2004).

Yathay, Pin. *Stay Alive My Son.* 1988; repr., Ithaca, N.Y.: Cornell University Press, 2000.

Yoneyama, Lisa. *Hiroshima Traces: Time, Space, and the Dialectics of Memory.* Berkeley: University of California Press, 1999.

———. "Traveling Memories, Contagious Justice: Americanization of Japanese War Crimes at the End of the Post-Cold War." *Journal of Asian American Studies* 6, no. 1 (2003): 57–93.

Young, James. *The Texture of Memory: Holocaust Memorials and Their Meaning.* New Haven: Yale University Press, 1993.

Zaleski, Jeff, and Charlotte Abbott. *"Forecasts: Nonfiction."* Publishers Weekly, January 17, 2000.

Discography

Lennon, John. *Imagine.* Apple Records, 1971, compact disc.

praCh. *Dalama: The End'n Is Just the Beginnin'.* Mujestic Records, 2000, compact disc.

———. *Dalama: The Lost Chapter.* Mujestic Records, 2003, compact disc.

———. *Dalama: Memoirs of an Invisible War.* Mujestic Records, 2010.

Filmography

Enemies of the People. Direct. Lemkin and Thet Sambath. 2010. Bicester: Old Street Films, 2011. DVD.

The Killing Fields. Dir. Roland Joffé. 1984. Burbank, Calif.: Warner Home Video, 2001. DVD.

New Year Baby. Dir. Socheata Poeuv. 2006. New York: Broken English Productions, 2009. DVD.

S-21: The Khmer Rouge Killing Machine. Dir. Rithy Panh. 2002. New York: First Run Features, 2003. DVD.

Year Zero: The Silent Death of Cambodia. Dir. David I. Munro. 1979. London: ATV Network Limited, 1979. DVD.

Index

CATHY J. SCHLUND-VIALS is associate professor of English and Asian American studies and director of the Asian American Studies Institute at the University of Connecticut. She is author of *Modeling Citizenship: Jewish and Asian American Writing.*

CPSIA information can be obtained
at www.ICGtesting.com
Printed in the USA
BVHW081626041218
534638BV00014BA/1273/P